Joy Comes With Dawn:
Reflections on Scripture and Life

by Abbot Joseph Homick

ISBN-10: 1-4243-2178-6
ISBN-13: 978-1-4243-2178-0

Cover photos: Abbot Joseph
Cover design and graphics: Clare Mulderink
Illustration: Rebecca Romanchuk

Printed by
Fidlar Doubleday, Inc.
4570 Commercial Ave. Suite A
Portage, MI 49002

Dedicated to
God the Holy Spirit,
without whom this book would not be possible,
without whom I would not be possible.

Thanks and Praise

I'll try to keep this to the essential, since nobody reads acknowledgment pages anyway. But at least it's here in black and white.

I would first like to thank God the Father, who created me, and his Son, Jesus Christ, who saved me from my sins, and the Blessed Mother, who has put up with a lot, and is still with me.

For labors of love on this book I want to thank Carol O'Reilly, for proofreading and cheerleading; Kathryn Mulderink, for formatting and publishing expertise, and patiently answering a million questions while having to do a million other things; Clare Mulderink for gracious graphic arts; Laura Grossman, for prayer, support, and a listening ear; Rebecca Romanchuk, for tireless and thankless intercession and the final illumination of the manuscript, and anyone else who may have sent a prayer my way as I labored to complete this project, for nothing succeeds without prayer.

May the blessing of the Lord be upon all, through his grace and love for mankind.

~ Contents ~

Introduction

"At night there are tears, but joy comes with dawn" (Psalm 30:6). In a sense, this psalm verse captures the essence of our earthly pilgrimage to the Kingdom of Heaven. We experience darkness and light, sorrow and joy, but we are convinced by the promises of God that joy and light will have the last word. It is encouraging to know, if we find ourselves still in the long and tearful night, not only that it won't last forever, but that even while walking in the valley of the shadow of death, we need have no fear, for the Lord is at our side (see Psalm 23). We can expect the eventual coming of joy as surely as we expect each new morning.

The night of tears and the dawn of joy can also be metaphors for the mysteries of Christ's death and resurrection, the grace of which forms the spiritual "milieu" in which we live our lives. The first Good Friday was the darkest and most tearful night in the history of mankind, and the first Easter Sunday was the most glorious and joyful dawn. Henceforth our days are marked in various ways with this paschal mystery: "always carrying about in the body the dying of Jesus, so that the life of Jesus may also be manifested in our body" (2Cor. 4:10).

Life in the crucified and risen Christ is not easy, but it is rewarding. Life is not easy, period, but to follow Jesus is to have your vision sharpened by faith, your heart purified for love, and your mind focused on truth. Thus we are prepared to meet life's challenges and to engage in a life-giving relationship with the all-demanding, all-loving Savior of our souls. He is the Alpha and the Omega, the origin and the destiny, of the universe as well as of our own lives.

Excess baggage must be left behind on the journey to Paradise, for "the world with its seductions is passing away" (1John 2:17). Even so, many people seem to be content to live on the surface of life, following its trends and trivia as if these had some substantial or lasting value. But if, as the Apostle says, "to live is Christ" (Phil. 1:21), our lives must go deeply into his mystery if we are to discover the richness and meaning of life—for we are men and women created in the image of God. So we need to reflect on the many shining facets of life in the Spirit of Christ.

This book is a collection of short meditations on Scripture and the spiritual life, most of which were previously published on my internet web-log (usually referred to as a "blog") called Word

Incarnate. If I'm still alive and posting by the time you read this, you may find some new meditations at http://wordincarnate.blogspot.com. (If you happen to be an archaeologist, however, and have found this book under the ruins of American civilization, then you can be reasonably certain that the address is no longer valid.)

I almost hesitate to say that these reflections are mere blog-posts, since "blog" is a kind of "four-letter word" among literary people, and such evanescent entities (the blogs, not the people) are mostly not taken too seriously, and often with good reason. But I have not maintained the Word Incarnate site for the sake of news or chatting or superficial, self-serving, stream-of-consciousness rambling. Instead, I am trying to preach the Gospel of Jesus to those who have ears to hear, through a medium that has potential to reach thousands. As you read this book you may conclude that I do it in a way that is perhaps neither standard blog-style nor standard book-style. You may find some passages to be rather humorous, and others to be dead serious, even a little stern (by today's mushy standards, anyway). My intention, however, is to write neither comedy nor tragedy, but simply to offer you a slice of real life—and life, as you know, has tearful nights and joyful dawns, and much in between. Real life must mean life in Christ, who is the Way, the Truth, and the Life. Therefore, when I reflect on "real life" it is not on digital culture or sports or fashions, but on the word of God and on living in such a way as to establish "a good foundation for the future, so as to take hold of the life which is life indeed" (1Tim. 6:19).

Since this is a collection of meditations written over a period of a year, they could only be rather loosely organized under topical chapter headings. The disadvantage to this is a certain lack of clear and coherent structure and development of thought, but the advantage is that you can open the book almost anywhere and start reading without missing the "plot." There is, however, a general and intended progression from the night to the dawn. The early chapters focus on some of the more difficult struggles of life, like repentance, spiritual warfare, and suffering. Toward the end things get brighter, as if we can at least intimate the approach of dawn, so you'll find more on gratitude, joy, and praise. But all of it is in some way a perspective on one or another aspect of the mystery of God, and of the Incarnate Son of God present in our lives through the love and grace of the Holy Spirit.

There are a couple other practical notes. Since I am a Catholic of the Byzantine tradition, there are some references to the Byzantine liturgical calendar (with which you may not be familiar) and other aspects of this particular tradition. I'm hoping that this will be an enrichment and not a source of head-scratching for you, but in any case it will at least be a little different than what you are used to reading! Also, a note on the psalms: there are two systems for numbering the psalms, which are not quite the same. One is used in the Greek version of the Psalter (the Septuagint) and in the Latin Vulgate. The other is used in the Hebrew version, which is found in just about all modern English Bibles. I'm accustomed to using the former, but since you are probably accustomed to using the latter, I've given citations to the psalms according to the Hebrew numbering. In case I made a mistake, however, in getting all the right numbers, in general it goes this way: after Psalm 8 and before Psalm 148, the Greek numbering is in most cases one less than the Hebrew. I say all this in the (somewhat faint) hope that you'll actually look up the Scripture references in this book and bring them into your meditation.

So, read on. My prayers are with all who will read, and hopefully benefit from, this book. In our tradition we face east when we worship, as did the early Christians, because it is the place of light, of the rising sun, and hence symbolically of the return of our Savior. Despite the surrounding darkness, turn toward the Light. Christianity has little meaning if it is not a religion of hope—for healing, enlightenment, and resurrection unto eternal life. "Besides this, you know what hour it is, how it is full time now for you to wake from sleep. For salvation is nearer to us now than when we first believed; the night is far gone, the day is at hand..." (Romans 13: 11-12).

September 14, 2006
Feast of the Exaltation of the Holy Cross

❧ Chapter One:
The State of Affairs ❧

We live in a fallen world, yet it is redeemed. We are unworthy, because of our sins, of God's call to eternal happiness, yet He loves us and calls us still. We are sick, blind, and more or less clueless, but the Lord comes to heal, enlighten, and guide us. So we live in a milieu of paradoxes, but Grace always has the final word.

Still Hope

There are a lot of things going on in the world that can become a cause of discouragement, and for some even of despair. Wars, earthquakes, hurricanes, abortions, the savaging of moral traditions, the crises in the Church, all weigh heavily on hearts that are seeking the face of God and struggling to endure. God sometimes seems silent, and in our worst moments we might even think He is unwilling or unable to stem the crushing tide of suffering, evil, and chance disasters. But there is still hope.

Some years ago—when I was able to spare some time to tend the retreat house rose garden—I was thinking about similar issues. I had just cut a lovely rose and I was taking it to set before Our Lady. I remember thinking to myself, as I examined its delicate and intricate beauty and breathed its exquisite perfume: if God goes on creating such beauty, then there is still hope for the world. (Sometimes I see a tiny wildflower growing out of bare rock, and I receive a similar message.) Perhaps not everyone would make the connection between the silent splendor of a rose and hope for the eradication of the world's intractable evils. But at that moment it seemed clear: signs of the profound truths about God and the world can be found in hidden and unexpected places. God goes on revealing beauty, as if to say that horror and degradation are not the last word. God is not the problem, man is. God creates roses, man makes bombs. God gives life; man snuffs it out when it stands in the way of his selfish ambitions.

When He came in the flesh to proclaim the forgiveness of man's stubborn resistance to truth and love, the Creator of roses was given a crown of thorns. This was the price He chose to pay to give the world beauty and hope. He has already borne the accumulated malice of the world in his own flesh and has nailed it to the Cross. The current evils of the world are but the "aftershocks" of the great rupture between man and God that was healed by the death and resurrection of Christ. The world just has to wake up to that truth and begin to realize that reconciliation and transformation have since been woven into the fabric of our existence. We have but to say "yes" to the One who makes all things new. We have to walk the way He walked.

Scripture warns us that there will be tribulations and sufferings before the faithful are gathered unto God for everlasting peace. So the disasters we daily witness, while being a cause for concern and an opportunity for prayer, active charity, and Christian witness, should not lead us to discouragement or despair. God is still the Lord of history, of nations, and of your soul and mine. God is still creating beauty, and He would have us notice that—and make the connection with his ultimate plan of the transfiguration of the entire cosmos. Created beauty is like a seed of heavenly glory, planted in hope. It is a sign that the best is yet to come. The existence of a lovely rose in a war-torn world reminds us of the innocent Man on the Cross with the crown of thorns: a poignant figure, veiled glory in the midst of a world steeped in sin. Though the sun hid its light as its Creator gave up his life, and all the world was plunged into darkness, on the third day He arose in divine radiance. He disarmed death by his death, and no one will ever take his glory from Him. "I died, but behold, I am alive forevermore" (Revelation 1:18).

Draw some encouragement from the bits and snatches of beauty you discover around you. There is still hope. Examine a rose, and pray, and you will see what I mean. The plan is not yet fulfilled, the victory is not yet fully manifest. But it's on the way, and nothing will stop it. The roses will reassure you.

Light and Darkness

One of the great themes of the Gospel of John is that of light and darkness. The former refers to all that is good, true, and holy, culminating in the person Christ Himself, who said: "I am the Light of the world" (8:12). The latter refers to all that is evil, corrupt, and false. As if it were enough to explain what Judas was about to do after the Supper, the evangelist simply says: "he immediately went out; and it was night" (13:30). He went into the darkness.

In several places, St. John speaks of the Light "coming into the world." Therefore the Light is essentially not *of* this world, but enters this world from Heaven. The Son of God comes to enlighten us, to save us from our sins, and to take us back to Heaven, to the glory He had with the Father before the world began. He comes as a light in the darkness, so that no follower of his will ever be lost, but will have the "light of life" (8:12).

The world, then, is in a kind of perpetual darkness, to the extent it has not embraced the Light who is Christ. We do know of the "very good" of creation, but let's remember that God said that *before* the fall of man. (Not that creation isn't good *now*, but since the fall it has become, according to St Paul, "subjected to futility" and "in bondage to decay"—see Romans 8:20-21.) After enduring just a few generations of the sins of mankind, God said of human beings: "I am sorry that I have made them" (Gen. 6:7). So He destroyed them all but a tiny remnant, and tried to start fresh, but Paradise was lost till the end of time. There would need to be a Redeemer to salvage the sin-darkened world.

Now, things don't look so dark when I'm at the coast watching the sun sparkle on the deep blue sea, or when I'm taking pictures of colorful flowers or richly-hued sunsets, or even enjoying a good meal. But we're not talking here about material darkness or even emotional gloom. We're talking about the spiritual shadow that has been cast over the world ever since Eve first reached for the forbidden fruit.

Therefore, when the Light came into this world, it would provoke a reaction. Those who were looking for a Redeemer would run to Him; those who were of good will and open heart would recognize and embrace Him. But those who were "of this world" would either flee from Him or attack Him. One of the clearest statements Jesus makes about the incompatibility of light and darkness is something He said in a dispute with his opponents: "You are from below; I am from above. You are of this world; I am not of this world... I came forth from God... you are of your father the devil... He who is of God hears the words of God; the reason why you do not hear them is that you are not of God" (John 8:23, 42-47). *Not of God!* Is there a more stinging judgment, a more grievous indictment that can ever be made? The evangelist comments decisively on the judgment that spontaneously occurs when the Light comes into the world: "This is the judgment, that the light has come into the world, but men loved darkness rather than light, because their deeds were evil. For everyone who does evil hates the light and does not come to the light, lest his deeds should be exposed. But he who does what is true comes to the light..." (3:19-21).

Now we know that "the light shines on in the darkness, and the darkness cannot overcome it" (1:5), so the ultimate and everlasting victory is the Lord's. But the world is still full of those who "love darkness," whose "deeds are evil." These will come face to face with the Light and will, in the end, not be able to flee from it except to Hell, the domain of the "prince of darkness." But it is up to us, now, to make room in this world for the Light, for He has not just come once and left. He is trying continually to penetrate human hearts and minds, and to liberate us from the darkness of sin, ignorance, and unbelief. Those who have experienced the Light must, like St. John the Forerunner, "bear witness to the light" (1:8), so that we all might no longer be "of this world," but by divine grace be "of God."

The Light has come into the world; Heaven has opened its portals to Earth. Let us, then, come to the Light, abide in the Light, and do his will—which is our salvation—"that it may clearly be seen that [our] deeds have been done in God" (3:21).

Dis-Abeled

When Cain killed his brother Abel, he succeeded in his attempt to dis-Abel the new world that God had made. And thus he disabled the moral structure of the world, and it all went downhill until the Savior appeared millennia later. Even now, however, the world often acts as if there has been no Savior, and moral degradation has surpassed anything our forebears could have devised.

Of course, if only his parents hadn't started things with their own sin, chances are Cain would not have had to bear the everlasting stigma of being the world's first murderer. But life is full of "if onlys," and we had better get used to sticking to reality as it is.

It is probably instructive for our own understanding of fallen human nature that murder was one of the first sins committed by man. There seems to be an almost instinctive urge (and this goes well beyond that of self-preservation), when having to deal with a person or situation that incites fear or anger—or that is unpleasant, threatening, incriminating, or just plain tiresome—to simply get rid of it. Cain's anger toward Abel was based on envy, for God accepted Abel's sacrifice and not Cain's—we're not told why, but we can probably assume Cain already had a bad character, if this slight resulted in murder. Abel became an irritant to Cain, so he got rid of him. (And how many of those irritating little "products of conception" are routinely killed by those who simply want to get rid of the problem!) You can kill someone, but if you do, the "problem" doesn't go away. It only gets worse.

Cain's bad character is manifested in several ways. He was arrogant and mendacious toward God when He asked concerning the whereabouts of his brother. "I don't know where he is; am I my brother's keeper?" For the second time the voice of God thundered these words, which Eve first heard in the garden: "*What have you done?*" Cain still didn't repent, but after God passed sentence he started whining: "My punishment is too great!" The story ends with Cain going "away from the presence of the Lord." This is the tragic outcome of sin.

The pattern of sin repeats itself. It was not much different with Cain than it was with Adam and Eve. In each case they sinned, they hid (for as St. John says, those who do evil flee from the Light), they made excuses or tried to misdirect the divine accusations against them, and then had to leave the presence of the Lord. That is a general pattern that still happens countless times today. People today seem not to realize that there are consequences to their actions: the pain and sorrow, the emotional and spiritual damage that evildoing leaves in its wake. They act on the feeling or desire of the moment; they make choices contrary to God's will, and then when the consequences of the choices inevitably manifest, they try to hide, make excuses, or somehow attempt to get off scot-free. Then, when the consequences become evident, they cry like Cain that their punishment is too great. It doesn't work, does it? We've all been there; we've all seen the bad end of submitting to sin. We've thought it somehow unfair that we must be accountable for our actions. But we're so slow to learn the necessary lessons. We're disabled, but our wounds are self-inflicted. When we sin, we gradually kill what is noble and good in us, as Cain killed his brother.

We don't, however, have to flee the presence of the Lord. He has ordained repentance unto forgiveness and salvation. That is a lesson that the Cains and Judases of the world have not yet learned, but one that is imperative for all of us to put into practice. The Lord counseled Cain: "If you do well, you will be accepted. But if you do not, then sin is waiting at your door; its desire is for you but you must master it." In a fallen world, sin is always at the door. But it is not inevitable that we succumb to it, for the Son of God has entered the human condition and redeemed it by his death and resurrection. It should be easier for us to master the advances of sin than it was for Cain, for we have the grace of our Lord Jesus Christ.

We are not only our brothers' keepers, we are the keepers of our own immortal souls. But we can entrust them to the Lord, to Our Lady, to our guardian angels. Thus we have a lot of help. If we really want to do what is right, we are able. Abel was able and did well before God, with only his human good will. We have the grace of the Redeemer, so we are able to do even better.

Altars to an Unknown God

"I perceive that in every way you are very religious," remarked St. Paul to the Athenians. "For as I passed along and observed the objects of your worship, I found also an altar with this inscription, 'To an unknown god'" (Acts 17:22-23). Paul was pleased to find people who were seekers of God, but he wasn't content to allow them to remain in the darkness of their ignorance of the true God revealed in and by Jesus Christ. For he had personally experienced Him who is the Light of the world, and he was commissioned by Him to "be a witness for Him to all men of what you have seen and heard" (Acts 22:15).

St. Paul continued his discourse to the Athenians. "What therefore you worship as unknown, this I proclaim to you. The God who made the world and everything in it, being Lord of heaven and earth...gives to all men life and breath and everything. And he made from one every nation of men to live on all the face of the earth, having determined allotted periods and the boundaries of their habitation, that they should seek God, in the hope that they might feel after him and find him. Yet he is not far from each one of us, for 'In him we live and move and have our being'" (17:23-28). Paul was masterfully opening up the Mystery to them, beginning with creation and providence, and speaking of God's transcendence and immanence. Yet he had not quite gotten to the "punch line," for he was still speaking in more or less general terms.

He went on. "The times of ignorance God overlooked, but now he commands all men everywhere to repent, because he has fixed a day on which he will judge the world in righteousness by a man whom he has appointed, and of this he has given assurance to all men by raising him from the dead" (17:30-31). Now he has made his point. The God whom the Athenians sought but did not know was the Father of our Lord Jesus Christ! They were not exactly overjoyed to hear this, being loath to accept the teaching on the resurrection of the dead (far too coarse a notion for their Platonic idealism!). But some did believe and began to follow the path to salvation that Paul preached.

It is easy to perceive today that many people are indeed very religious (though the preferred term is "spiritual," which lacks the unwanted dogmatic or institutional connotations). It is also not difficult to find altars to unknown gods in the souls of many who may be sincerely seeking God but have not accepted the revelation of which St. Paul speaks.

In a rather popular book of generic spirituality, I found the following passage: "I still find something mysterious in such occasions, as if something unknown, finding us worthy, has used us just as we are to be an instrument of healing." Such passages are not rare in today's spiritual-yet-agnostic milieu. Must it be "something unknown" that finds us worthy to be instruments of healing? Why not the God who has publicly revealed His everlasting love for us in the life, death and resurrection of Jesus Christ? Because of the revelation of Christ, the power and wisdom and reality of God should no longer be regarded as "something unknown."

Some people tend to seek spiritual experiences but may be too impatient or immature to live by faith. The long haul of daily faithfulness in spiritual life lacks excitement and stimulation, so they are on the lookout for loopholes and shortcuts. There are plenty of offers of spiritual experience out there, but they may not lead to the true God. It is convenient then to erect an altar to an unknown god. At least they keep their options open! Others like to be perpetual seekers, but they would prefer not to actually *find* the Truth, because then they might have to make a commitment or accept something that may be contrary to their own current beliefs or preferences. Up goes another altar. Dealing with an unknown divinity (or at least one that can be manipulated or does not make them accountable) tends not to cramp their style so much.

Still others would like the resurrection without the Cross, seeking the rewards of spiritual life but avoiding its demands, perhaps employing the "a la carte" approach to belief and practice. If it suits their spiritual taste, fine; if not, forget it. They tend to conceive of and relate to God on their own terms without acknowledging His absolute rights on their lives, without accepting any authority outside of their own intelligence or intuition. Subjective experience often wins out over objective revelation. The true and manifest God is still not attained, but the unknown one will do fine for now.

It is inevitable then that altars to unknown gods will be going up everywhere, because people need to transcend themselves, to connect with a reality greater than themselves, to encounter God (or, as the case may be, something which they will end up calling God).

By word and example we need to proclaim as did St. Paul that we know the God whom many are seeking without the knowledge which comes from the true faith. While it is true that God is beyond the concepts of any human mind and cannot be wholly confined in any human institution, no one should have to build altars to an unknown god. For "the only Son, who is in the bosom of the Father, has made Him known" (Jn. 1:18).

Look to the Unseen

In an age of rationalism, secularism, and an inordinate reliance on "science" to give us all the answers to the riddles of the universe, St. Paul's advice to "look to the things that are unseen" (2Cor. 4:18) may seem antiquated or irrelevant. Yet it is essential to the life of faith and hope, and hence to salvation.

He says a little further on that we walk by faith, not by sight. Faith is a kind of sight, however, yet not a bodily sight, for it looks to the Unseen. To live merely on the level of the senses is to resign oneself to a life that is ultimately unsatisfying and that leads to disintegration and despair. We are all in a slow process of aging and dying (though more noticeable to some than to others), but we don't want to look at that, don't want to know what our lives ultimately mean and where we are headed. The great health craze of the past couple decades—health clubs, "anti-aging" nutritional supplements, sex-enhancing drugs, and the sort of self-hypnotism by which people positively-think they will be young and healthy for many decades to come—has its deepest foundation in the fear of death, though no one wants to come out and say it. It's a symptom of a widespread loss of faith, loss of hope in the true and everlasting life to come—a giving up on looking to the Unseen. (To be sure, we ought to take reasonably good care of our bodily health, but for too many it is practically an obsession. Physical health is not the primary or ultimate value of this life, as the saints will readily testify.)

St. Paul's Christian realism does not duck the inevitable decomposition of our mortal frames, does not deny the intimations of death that manifest in the sufferings of this life. But he injects them with faith and hope. "We have this treasure [i.e., "the light of the knowledge of the glory of God"] in earthen vessels, to show that the transcendent power belongs to God and not to us. We are afflicted in every way, but not crushed; perplexed, but not driven to despair; persecuted, but not forsaken; struck down, but not destroyed; always carrying in the body the death of Jesus, so that the life of Jesus may also be manifest in our bodies" (2Cor. 4:7-10). What is his response to this state of affairs? "We do not lose heart. Though our outer nature is wasting away, our inner nature is being renewed every day. For this slight momentary affliction [to discover Paul's "slight momentary affliction" see 2Cor. 11:23-28] is preparing for us an eternal weight of glory beyond all comparison, because we look not to the things that are seen but to the things that are unseen; for the things that are seen are transient, but the things that are unseen are eternal" (4:16-18).

Paul was a man who knew where he came from and where he was going. He would be horrified and nauseated (probably in that order) by the moral relativism, self-absorption, godless hubris, and myopic spiritual vision (if there's any at all) of the present age. He was a man seeking the fullness of life, and he knew—by experience as well as by faith—that it could only be found in "the Son of God, who loved me and gave himself for me" (Gal. 2:20). Therefore he wasn't interested in "the things that are seen," that is, the passing attractions, cheap seductions, or material advantages of this life. He strained forward, pressed on, "that I may lay hold of that for which Christ Jesus laid hold of me" (see Phil. 3:12-16).

So, let us not lose heart. Even though we may seem to be wasting away, if we believe in Christ and have hope for eternal life our inner nature is being daily renewed. Know where to look; know whence come peace, courage, joy and eternal blessedness. Look to the Unseen, for before too very long "Christ our life will appear, and you too will appear with him in glory" (Col. 3:4). Then begins the life that is life indeed.

Marshmallows

I read some time ago about a holy priest named Fr. Arseny, who suffered much for his faith in Soviet Russia during the Stalin years. The witness of his life brings me to a further reflection. (By the way, I recommend the book: *Father Arseny 1893-1973: Priest, Prisoner, Spiritual Father*, trans. Vera Bouteneff, St. Vladimir's Seminary Press.)

My conclusion after reading the book is this: I am a marshmallow. Perhaps you are, too. I would wager that at least 90% of Christians in America and Western Europe also are marshmallows. What I mean is that we are marshmallow Christians: soft, spineless, easily crushed, easily melted in the fire of trials and purifications. If we continue like this, we will have to add another marshmallowy characteristic: wholly without nutritional (spiritual) value to those who have any contact with us.

We really have no idea what millions of people consistently had (and have) to suffer for their faith. Of course, we all have our own sufferings, and they are real: illness, injuries, mental anguish, work and family and financial problems, bereavement, etc. This is part of the human condition. But people like Fr. Arseny suffered things above and beyond ordinary human suffering. And it was precisely because he was a believer in Christ that he suffered so— but because of his faith and love for God he was purified like gold in the fire.

He suffered beatings, hunger, sleep deprivation, hard labor, exhaustion. The land itself where he was imprisoned was a kind of Hell on earth: long, frigid winters (temperatures down to 50 below zero, with strong winds), springs characterized by melting snow and rivers of mud, and short, hot, sticky summers in the midst of literal clouds of mosquitoes—and soon it is winter again. He had to work 15-18 hours a day in those conditions, with the most primitive of tools and with the constant cursing and frequent blows of the guards, barracks searches at any hour of day or night, etc. Yet through him God brought peace and hope to many, and he was able to live in gratitude.

Many others among the simple faithful found themselves evacuated from their homes and sent with no money or food to some Siberian village where they knew no one, and told to make the best of it. Women were raped by soldiers, and many people died from intolerable conditions.

Now this isn't meant merely to be a horror story, or something to shame you into realizing how easy you actually have it—though that could still be a salutary meditation! The real point is how these people kept (or found) the Faith in the midst of these severe trials, how they prayed, how they trusted God and the Mother of God, how they were grateful for every kindness, for every divine intervention to keep them alive. They knew what was the "one thing necessary." They believed in miracles and experienced them. God comes to the aid of those who are *really* in need, to those who call on Him with their whole heart.

One thing I found touching was the tender love the faithful had for the Mother of God, especially as she is represented in the famous icon of Our Lady of Vladimir. When they light a candle and pray before her, her sad but compassionate eyes look upon them with love, and she obtains mercy and grace for them from Him whom she carries in her arms. She actually appeared in that form to save a young woman who was about to be raped. Later the man regretted his action and actually went back to that woman to seek forgiveness, and when he saw the icon in her house he exclaimed: "That's her! Who *is* that? She is the one who appeared to save you from me!"

These people lived in an atmosphere, an environment of faith in God, of repentance from sin, of hope for the life to come, in awareness of the constant presence of the Mother of God and the saints, who protected and helped them—even though the society around them was officially atheist, and they could be imprisoned for any manifestation of religious faith. They relied wholly on the mercy of the Lord.

So this is what I'm getting at: they knew what was the meaning of human life, they lived at the heart, the essence of it, because everything that was superfluous was stripped away from them. They knew love and tried to be good for each other, for the world was harsh, and the enemies of Truth were everywhere. In short, they were true Christians, not marshmallows. We see today what happens in free and affluent societies: many members of the Church, including clergy and hierarchs, begin to miss the point of the Faith. They reject some of the teachings of the Church and hence the uncompromising power of the Gospel, they tolerate immorality, wink at peccadilloes, model their spirituality on modern psychology, run the Church like corporate America, and make uneasy alliances with the surrounding society, which is often anti-Christian in its mindset and morality. They don't talk about Heaven and Hell, about the absolute necessity of living to fulfill the will of God, of how difficult and demanding it is to be a true Christian—as if salvation could be attained by presenting one's baptismal certificate, or by merely being tolerant or "nice," and "not hurting anyone."

No, eternal salvation is the ultimate goal, the *sine qua non* of the meaning of human life, and though it is impossible without the grace of God, it will still cost you every ounce of your strength, your blood, sweat and tears. Everlasting life in a paradise of joy is not a "given," a consolation for having merely existed for a certain number of years. It is the fruit of a life of faith and love for God, built up and expressed through trials and hardships, made genuine and unshakable through perseverance in adverse circumstances and even in persecution. To be saved, you have to be a martyr, that is, a witness, with your life, that God is real and is really involved in our world, that He loves us and became man to save us from our sins—yes, those sins which could keep us out of Heaven forever. Marshmallows are for roasting over a fire, and that's exactly where they'll end up.

Human life is a high-stakes adventure. God is with us, and He sends Our Lady and the saints to help us. But our role is indispensable, and the marshmallow Church in America needs our firm support, and our unfailing witness to the truth. We cannot afford to be marshmallows ourselves. "Therefore lift your drooping hands and strengthen your weak knees, and make straight paths for your feet... Strive for...the holiness *without which no one will see the Lord*" (Hebrews 12:12-14). Put *all* your hope in the living God. You will find that He is a wellspring of strength, peace, wisdom, joy, and love. Just ask Fr. Arseny.

Mad Parsons

There is a character in C.S. Lewis' novel *That Hideous Strength* who was sometimes referred to as the "Mad Parson." He was an insider in the National Institute of Co-ordinated Experiments (N.I.C.E.), which was a kind of Orwellian organization whose new-speak propaganda presented the organization as the great friend of mankind that would take human society into a utopian future, but which in fact was doing nothing other than delivering man to the devil and an irrevocable destruction.

The Mad Parson spoke like a parson. He talked of Jesus and the Kingdom and resurrection. But he twisted things around enough—made them fit his particular cultural and intellectual milieu, as is fashionable today—so that his words were actually nothing more than N.I.C.E. propaganda. "The Kingdom of God is to be realized here—in this world. And it will be... The powers of science are an instrument. An irresistible instrument, as all of us in the N.I.C.E. know... That is what I couldn't get any of the Churches to see... I knew that He was coming in power. And therefore where we see power, we see the sign of His coming. And that is why I find myself joining with communists and materialists and anyone else who is ready to expedite this coming... The *real* resurrection is even now taking place. The real life everlasting. Here in this world. You will see it... Get rid of false spirituality. It is all going to happen, here in this world, the only world there is... The Son of Man—that is, Man himself, full grown—has power to judge the world... You shall see. Here and now."

Mad indeed. But the world (and even the Church, to some extent) is full of mad parsons, preaching a "gospel" with familiar words yet with altered meaning. They are not hard to find, those who would reinterpret the Trinity, the Incarnation, the Resurrection, the Holy Eucharist, emptying the rich (and divinely revealed) content and replacing it with vapid samplings from psychology, sociology, and the philosophies or politics of the day. They use the words of Jesus to support their own crooked agendas. But they are leading people astray and ultimately to destruction.

I read recently about an Easter homily given by a Catholic priest. He explained the resurrection as a "spiritual" thing that helps "lift our spirits." *Lift our spirits?* If our religion is that bland, cheap, and vacuous, then we are fools to remain in it a moment longer. You can "lift your spirits" with any new-age self-help book, but only Jesus Christ, the eternal Son of God, can raise you from the dead!

We have to be spiritually and intellectually well-grounded in the Faith, in the teachings of the Church, if we are not to be misled by spurious propagandizing parsons who are trying to insinuate "another gospel" (see Galatians 1:6-9) into the beliefs and practices of the people of God. We must not hesitate to exclaim with the

Apostle: Let their false teachings be condemned!—but at the same time being concerned enough to pray for their enlightenment and salvation, and to try charitably to correct them if it is possible.

I believe that we are going to see more and more of the Orwellian new-speak among theologians and teachers in the Church. We're already seeing much of it in the media, politics, and the educational system (not only about religion, but about morality and truth itself). They are only trying to be N.I.C.E., of course, but there will be Hell to pay for distorting the word of God and turning the message of Christ into something it was never meant to be. The official Magisterium of the Church is our safeguard for the truth about Christian faith and morals. There's no mad parson sitting in St. Peter's chair.

Those Who Do Not See

There are several reasons given in Scripture why the Son of God has come to earth, so his mission is many-faceted. He came that we may have abundant life (John 10:10), to seek and save the lost (Luke 19:10), to preach the Gospel (Mark 1:38), to give his life as a ransom for many (Matthew 20:28), and to destroy the works of the devil (1John 3:8)—just to give a few examples. There's another reason He came: "I came into this world, that those who do not see may see..." (John 9:39).

So many of our failures and sins result from this very fact: we do not see, we don't "get it," we don't grasp the mystery, we fail to see how we are to apply the wisdom of the Gospel to our daily lives. We also generally don't see how the Hand of Providence is at work in the events and experiences of our lives, so we tend to think it isn't. Perhaps in our weaker moments, we don't even see *why* our selfish or disordered desires have to be renounced or overcome for a "higher purpose" like fidelity to truth or even our very salvation. We don't see the radical incompatibility between sin and grace within our souls, and we wonder why there is such inner turmoil, like Jacob and Esau fighting within the womb of Rebekah.

Jesus, as the Light of the world, has come to show us this, to open the eyes of the blind—but also to correct the vision of those who think they can see. It is not a matter of indifference whether or not we know the truth and live by it, for the day of reckoning is coming. Here is the full text of the above quote: "For judgment I came into this world, that those who do not see may see, and that those who see may become blind."

You might ask: what is the point of being able to see, if He has come to make the seeing blind? We have to understand this in the context of the Gospel. He had just healed a blind man, who then professed his faith in Christ and worshiped Him. The Pharisees, on the other hand, refused to believe in Christ and bodily ejected the formerly blind man when he dared say that Jesus was from God, even though He "worked" on the Sabbath.

So Jesus told the Pharisees: "If you were blind, you would have no guilt; but now that you say, 'we see,' your guilt remains" (9:41). The blind man's physical defect was not an impediment to his spiritual vision, for he was open to the grace of God. But the Pharisees, with all their knowledge of the law and supposed righteousness, were blinded by pride and hard-heartedness to the very manifestation of God before them. When Christ came into the world, the Pharisees—those who could see—were shown to be blind, while the blind man was shown to have the superior vision.

In a sense, we have to start out blind in order that we may turn to God to open our eyes. If we think we can see well enough on our own, there will be no healing for us. What did God do to Paul before He enlightened him? He struck him blind! Paul had to realize that he was in fact blind to the truth about Christ, even though he was one of the most educated, zealous, and hence clear-sighted of the Pharisees of his day (yes, Paul was a Pharisee). In a similar vein, the same Paul says that if we want to become wise we had better first become fools. The earliest Christians were mostly low-born, insignificant, poor, of no account. Such are the ones who are able to see clearly. Start at the lowest place and wait until you are called up higher. Don't think you know it all or know it better.

We have to accept, however, that the process of enlightenment is a gradual one. The scales fell off Paul's eyes after only a few days, but for most of us it takes a long time. We're more like the man who was healed in stages (Mark 8:23-25). We know, however, that if we persevere in trusting God, eventually we *will* see, for *that is why Jesus came.* We have to first frankly acknowledge that we really don't see, don't understand, don't get it, but that very admission should restrain us from breaking commandments as if we knew better than God; it should restrain us from acting imprudently on what is admittedly a lack of understanding and clear-sightedness. That's one reason we *have* commandments. We can't figure things out for ourselves, and we would make a mess of everything if all we had to see with was our own cross-eyed or blurred vision. So God says: you don't see it, but I do. Trust Me in the meantime, and do what I say, as I gradually open your eyes.

Along with our own salutary self-distrust, we need to have an openness, a longing, to learn, to grow, to be given the capacity for clear vision and understanding. Better to be among the blind who are just beginning to see than among the "seeing" whose eyes are growing dim...

Do You Want to be Healed?

Jesus healed a paralytic on a Sabbath (John 5:1-17). It almost seems like He deliberately chose the Sabbath on which to work most of his miracles. He says that his Father continues to work, and so, as the Son, He continues to work as well. Even the Jews had to concede that, while God Himself rested on the seventh day and so established the Sabbath, He still gives birth and takes life and keeps the universe in good running order even on the Sabbath. So here Jesus is making an indirect claim to divinity. The claim wasn't lost on the religious authorities, who then and there decided He should die for blasphemy.

But let's get back to the paralytic. We have to make some spiritual applications to what we read here, if this is going to be anything more for us than an edifying story. First of all, let us look at all of the sick people in this account. "A multitude of invalids," it says, were by the healing pool, "the blind, the lame, and the paralyzed." What advantage do they have over most people today? They *knew* they were sick, and hence they sought healing from God. Most people today are more like those Laodiceans whom Jesus reproached in the Book of Revelation: "For you say, 'I am rich, I have prospered, and I need nothing'—*not knowing* that you are wretched, pitiable, poor, blind, and naked" (3:17). The world is full of blind, lame, wretched people claiming their autonomy and indulging in their lusts, as if they were strong and healthy, as if a severe judgment were not awaiting them. The first step, then, toward healing is the awareness and admission that we *are* sick, abandoning our proud self-assessment and embracing the humility by which alone we can see the truth.

G.K. Chesterton was well aware of this. Once the *London Times* asked him to write an essay entitled, "What is Wrong with the World Today?" He sent them a very short one. It went like this: "*I* am." Now there's an honest man. What is wrong with the world today? *You* are. And *I* am. Anyone who commits sin is what is wrong with the world today, for sin produces only corruption, defilement, destruction, and unhappiness.

The paralytic in the Gospel is a rather unattractive character, and he did not learn the lessons that the Lord's goodness should have inspired in him. The Lord asked him, "Do you want to be healed?" That question was rather unusual—and the answer should have been obvious—but since the Lord knew the man's heart, He was aware that the man was not only physically lame, but that his heart had grown sour and bitter over the years. The man answered with a whining complaint. But Jesus in his mercy healed him anyway, though it became clear that while divine grace entered his body, the man resisted its entrance into his soul—unlike the other paralytic Jesus healed, whose sins were forgiven along with his bodily healing. So Jesus gave him a stern warning: "Sin no more, that nothing worse befall you." This man is the only one who ever received this warning from Christ after having been healed.

The first level of healing was insufficient. We can take this to a spiritual level and look at our own lives. If we commit sin, we must go to confession in order to receive forgiveness. While this is necessary and indispensable, it is not enough. Forgiveness must be followed by a deep inner healing. In psalm 40(41), the psalmist does not say to God: "forgive me, for I have sinned against you," but rather "*heal my soul*, for I have sinned against you." Sin creates wounds and vulnerabilities in our souls. A bodily wound can be disinfected and stitched up, but it might take a long time before it is fully healed, and there may be a scar that never goes away.

Forgiveness removes our guilt before God, but there is much work that needs to be done before our souls themselves are *healed*. We need to receive Holy Communion, to pray, to struggle against the temptations that we allowed to enter our souls previously—for every time we sin, we make it easier for the devil to walk that well-marked path into our souls. So we can't just whine and complain to the Lord like the paralytic when He asks if we want to be healed. His question implies a lot. Do we want to do all that it takes to receive and *maintain* the health of our souls, to do the hard work of penance and self-denial and training our wills to do only what is pleasing to God? Be sure that if we persist in sin, something worse will befall us.

We can't wait around for a miracle to happen, for an angel to appear in the troubled waters of our souls and make everything better without any serious effort of our own. We have to work with God; that is the meaning of *synergy*, the process by which divine grace, and human choice and effort, work together to produce the spiritual fruits that enable us to live in communion with God in this life as well as in the life to come.

So let us start by realizing our need for God, and not just in some general, abstract way: "Oh yes, since everyone needs God, I guess I must need Him, too." But really, *feel* and acknowledge your wounds, your emptiness, your sin-sickness, your spiritual paralysis. A perfunctory "Lord have mercy" is wholly inadequate. If there is no deep and sincere cry from your heart to the Physician of souls and bodies, you will remain in mediocrity and hence without the life-giving and transforming power of God, who makes all things new—for those who realize that all things within them *must* be made new, if they are to enter the Kingdom of Heaven. Come to the chalice of spiritual healing, the Holy Eucharist, and begin anew the process of renewal of life. It's not a quick fix, but part of the lifelong program for a complete healing of the soul—that you may get up and walk freely in the Spirit of the living God.

✌ Chapter Two:
In a Word, Repent! ✎

Once we have some idea of the state of affairs, not only in the world or the Church, but also—and especially—in our souls, our next move will become quickly and perhaps painfully clear to us: we must repent. The mystery of repentance is far more profound and spiritually beneficial than mere remorse for wrongdoing or even confession of sins. Repentance, properly understood, is a way of life, a characteristically Christian way of life, one that bears fruit in a lifetime of grace, joy, and communion with God. But it must start with that difficult first step...

The Call of the Gospel: Repentance

Both Jesus and St. John the Baptizer began their preaching with a single word: "Repent!" (Matthew 3:1-2 and 4:17). The Christian life must begin with repentance, as Christ and his Forerunner insisted. You can't even have saving faith unless you first turn to Christ by turning away from evil. Repentance is an act of turning, changing, and even though some have had dramatic "conversion experiences," repentance is not a one-time event, but it is an essential part of the whole Christian life. That is because repentance (Greek *metanoia*) means literally a change of mind and heart, and hence a change of the direction, meaning, and practical expression of one's whole life.

Getting back to the Gospel text, why did Jesus and John first preach repentance? "The Kingdom of Heaven is at hand," that's why! The Kingdom was at hand in the person of the King, who appeared on the scene as a poor working man, but a man with a message from God. He alone could communicate this word of God perfectly, for "in the beginning was the Word, and the Word was with God, and the Word was God" (John 1:1). The fullness of time had come, the *kairos*, the moment that transcends time, the moment when the tired, sinful history of humanity was to experience the inbreaking of the divine. For this, people had to change, to re-turn to the One who had Created them and called them to a covenant of love and fidelity.

Today the call to repentance still graces the pages of the Gospel, yet many do not wish to hear it. They want to hear another "gospel" that is not demanding, that does not hold us accountable, that promises blissful spiritual experience without the carrying of the cross. But you know what St. Paul said about those who prefer "another gospel" to that which we've received from the Apostles (see Galatians 1:6-9).

The Kingdom of Heaven is always at hand. That doesn't mean the world is about to end (though you and I may come to our personal "end" in death at any moment). Christ is always present, always calling us to change what needs to be changed in order for us to live his word faithfully and to fulfill God's intentions in creating us in the first place. Some people, not wishing to embrace repentance with all that it entails (self-discipline, breaking bad habits, standing firm against the seductions of this age, etc.), rest in the affirmation: "God loves me as I am." But there's a better one, closer to the whole truth: "God loves you as you are, but He loves you too much to let you *stay* the way you are."

The Christian life begins with repentance, and repentance remains an integral part of the Christian's entire life. Repentance isn't only about being sorry for our sins and confessing them (though that is part of it). It is also—and most fundamentally— about change. That is why if we express sorrow for sin at one moment and go out and do it again shortly thereafter, we have not really repented. We will be known by our fruits. That is why the Baptizer exclaimed to the Pharisees: "Bear fruit that befits repentance!" (Matthew 3:8).

We have a petition in one of our litanies that reads: "That we may spend the rest of our life in peace and repentance..." This does not mean a life of remorse or of wailing "woe is me!" but rather a vigorous embracing of the truth of the Gospel and an equally vigorous rejection of all that comes to us from the "father of lies."

Repent. Repent again, and still. Continue in repentance and rejoice in the Lord, who has called you out of darkness into his marvelous light. The Kingdom of Heaven is at hand. That's the Gospel; that's the Good News.

Not the Righteous but Sinners

Jesus, the Son of God, the All-holy and sinless One, gave the lion's share of his attention to sinners. Not that He necessarily enjoyed their company more than anyone else's, and still less did He condone their lifestyles, but He was a Man with a mission. This mission was an expression of his everlasting love, which thirsted for the salvation of souls whom He had created in his own image, and with whom He desired to share eternal life and joy.

The concept of sin has fallen into disfavor in recent generations. All ages have teemed with sinners, but in the "old days" sinners at least accepted the fact that they were sinners, whether or not they wished to do anything about it. Nowadays people don't even talk about it, don't want to deal with it, want the whole idea to go away. I just read an interesting article on the "theology" of Woody Allen (despite everything, he's one of my favorites), which presented a scene from the movie Annie Hall: "Her parents ask what his parents will be doing for 'the holidays'. 'We fast, to atone for our sins,' his mother explains. Annie's mother is confused. 'What sins? I don't understand.' Alvy's father responds with a shrug: 'To tell you the truth, neither do we.'"

But God does. That's why He sent his only Son to offer Himself in sacrifice for us, so that our sins might be forgiven. It's a serious and fundamental issue. "Sin" and its derivatives appear over a thousand times in the Bible, so it is something that is a constant, both in human experience and in the divine response to it. This is why Jesus had to suffer and die for us. When He offered his Body and Blood at the Last Supper, Jesus told us the reason for his sacrifice: "the forgiveness of sins" (Matthew 26:28). And we say those same words every day in the offering of the Holy Eucharist. If Christ could ever be said to have had an obsession, this would be it: He had to forgive our sins. We discover this repeatedly in the Gospels.

This is what he told his "righteous" critics as He dined with tax-collectors and other sinners: "Those who are well have no need of a physician, but only those who are sick. I came not to call the righteous, but sinners" (Mark 2:17). He was eating and drinking with sinners who, within a relatively short time, would be eating and drinking the price of the forgiveness of their sins at the Eucharistic assemblies of the early Church.

In this we should take heart, that Christ came to forgive sinners and was willing to bear unimaginable sufferings so that we

25

might not have to endure the just (and everlasting) consequences of our sins. In the book about Fr. Arseny that I mentioned in Chapter One, we find two different responses to God's offer to forgive sinners, something like that of Peter and Judas. Fr. Arseny listened to the outpouring of the hearts of two criminals, both of whom had committed unspeakable crimes, repeatedly. The first one humbly confessed his sins with many tears and sincere repentance, while the other, though haunted by his sins, said, "I am not sorry. What happened, happened. There is no forgiveness for me." The former was liberated from the crushing weight of his sins, while the other died in anger and despair.

Jesus is trying to tell us: I *came* for precisely this—to take the burden of your shameful wickedness upon Myself. Accept it! You are sick and I am the Physician. There is no sin you can commit that will forever drive Me away from you—except the refusal to repent. I am with you always; I love you even in your vileness, because I have created you in My image, and I can still rescue that image if you turn to Me.

Let us throw off any pretense of righteousness, acknowledge our sins and our utter need for the mercy of God every day. The Lord has come to call sinners to repentance, to feed us with his sacrificed Body and Blood, to cleanse us of our iniquities and to unite us to Himself in an undeserved communion of grace and love. Hell counts among its inmates many who considered themselves righteous. Heaven is populated with grateful, repentant sinners.

Lost and Found

Lost sheep. Lost coin. Lost son. The fifteenth chapter of the Gospel of Luke is the Bible's "lost and found" department. Happily, everything that is lost in this chapter is eventually found.

Being lost is a metaphor for being in sin, separated from God and from the righteous. Thus the sheep that wanders away from the flock is lost, the coin that has disappeared is lost, the son who leaves home for a dissolute life is lost. But what rejoicing there is in heaven when what was lost is found! Jesus says something quite startling about this: "There is more joy in heaven over one sinner who repents than over ninety-nine righteous persons who need no repentance" (Lk. 15:7). This will have its application in the parable of the Prodigal Son, over whom there is more rejoicing than over his less troublesome and "righteous" brother (who, however, still was in need of some repentance).

As Joni Mitchell would say, "You don't know what you got till it's gone." That means that we rarely (or insufficiently) appreciate what we have while we have it, and only realize how precious it was when we no longer have it. Such was the case with the father of the prodigal son. We can tell, by the words of the elder son, that the father more or less took his sons for granted, although it's also clear that they were well provided for. The departure of the younger son was a shock, a loss, a bereavement—for the father didn't know if he'd ever come back. When he did return, it was like finding something precious that was lost, even like resurrection from the dead: "this my son was dead and is alive again; he was lost and is found."

Now our heavenly Father lovingly provides for us, though we can't say that He takes us for granted. But we can perhaps say that his concern for us increases when He sees us straying, when we become lost through our sin and heedlessness. Therefore we can say that He is more concerned about the lost sheep or children than about the faithful ones who are already doing his will and who will be generously rewarded for so doing. (One gives more attention to a sick child than to a healthy one who doesn't need it.) But when the lost ones return—then you will see the rejoicing begin! It's not only God but even the angels, Jesus says, who will be celebrating the return of the repentant sinner. There is so much happiness in heaven because they know how much horror there is in hell. They know how urgently important it is (for his own sake) that the lost sheep return quickly to the arms of the Good Shepherd, who will carry him home to the Father.

Repentance is an important theme in the New Testament. The words "repent" and "repentance" show up about 60 times, but the theme or concept of the change of heart and life that repentance indicates is found almost everywhere in the Bible. "Lost and found" refers to sin and repentance. Jesus came "to seek and to save the lost" (Lk. 19:10), which means he came to "call sinners to repentance" (Lk. 5:32). Repentant sinners tend to be humbler than the righteous; they tend to be more grateful and to love more ardently, for they know how far they have fallen, they know from what they have been mercifully saved. The one who is forgiven much, loves much (see Lk. 7:36-50).

Let us pray for those who are still "lost," that they may be "found," that the grace of repentance will be granted, especially to the worst of sinners, those who have wandered farthest from the Father's house. And let us rejoice, not only over the returning sons and daughters, but let us be grateful ourselves, for I can probably safely say that you who are reading this were once dead and are alive again; you were lost and now are found. Give thanks to the Lord, for He is good; his merciful love endures forever!

Lo Siento

At least twice in the past ten years or so I have unsuccessfully attempted to learn Spanish. I had learned enough by 1997 to hold a very rudimentary conversation, which helped when I was on a pilgrimage to see *Nuestra Señora de Guadalupe*. But because of a shortage of time and of people to practice with, I've unfortunately forgotten most of what I had learned. Since I'm busier now than ever, I despair of ever having the time to try it again. But I do remember a few things.

Spanish is a language of music and passion. When you want to say "I'm sorry," for example, you say *Lo siento*, which literally means "I feel it." Perhaps this expression has something to teach us about our own experience of repentance. Do we "feel it" in our souls, in our guts, when we have offended God or another person? Are we *moved* to repentance? Or do we merely say "I'm sorry" the same way we might say "excuse me" when bumping into someone in a crowd?

Repentance begins with an awareness that we have turned from God, spurned his commandments and counsels, and grieved his loving heart. To confess our sins is not (or shouldn't be) merely the more or less indifferent acknowledgement of having violated one or another of the divine precepts, saying a perfunctory prayer, and then going away with a "clean slate." To sin is to pierce the Heart of Christ, who willingly made Himself vulnerable to our wickedness out of his everlasting love for us. On the Cross, Jesus uttered, in effect, the *Lo siento* of all mankind before God, and He felt it in every cell of his tortured body, in the depths of his anguished soul. Therefore repentance is not a small or routine matter. He felt the sting of our sins. We have to feel our contrition.

This doesn't mean that we have to try to generate a lot of emotional sorrow (especially if that would be merely a pious façade). But it means that we must be sufficiently aware of what we have done, of who it is we have hurt or offended, and how important it is to repent—that is, to resolve to change our hearts and behavior—in a genuine and sincere manner.

I went to confession during the time that I had all this on my mind. While the ritual itself wasn't (and need not be) an emotional or dramatic experience, I was more aware of the need to be attuned to the gift of grace and mercy, to feel something stir within the soul. We must realize that God doesn't "owe" us the forgiveness of our sins just because we more or less reluctantly show up at the confessional. He forgives us because He loves us, and the crucifix is a perpetual testimony to that self-sacrificing love. All of our complaints, arguments, and excuses wither before the image of the crucified God. He has a right to expect from us a heartfelt recognition of the defiling, destructive nature of sin, as well as of the healing, saving nature of his immeasurable compassion. When his merciful love comes to our sinful yet contrite hearts, we "feel it."

As I was leaving the church where I made my confession, I stopped for a moment at a large crucifix, trying to understand a little more of the love that drove Him to suffer so that my sins might be forgiven. I approached and gently touched his pierced foot, one of those wounds by which we are healed. Softly, I said: "*Lo siento.*"

Dust We Are

When Abraham dared to argue with the Lord over the fate of Sodom, he used this humble introduction: "I have taken upon myself to speak to the Lord, I who am but dust and ashes" (Genesis 18:27). Dust he was, and to dust he would return, as the Psalmist also knew: "What profit would there be in my going to the grave? ...can dust sing your praise or proclaim your truth?" (Psalm 30:9). It has been said that, materially seen, we can be reduced to a few dollars worth of chemicals, and we know what a small pile of ashes one can become if he passes through the crematorium. Ashes to ashes, dust to dust. Are we ultimately nothing more than a mound of dirt?

Let's first remember that there is, even in the Old Testament, a good side to being dust. The fact that we are dust actually spares us from punishments that would be due to nobler substances. God has compassion on us, we learn from Psalm 103, because "He remembers that we are dust." If we were angels we'd only have one chance to get it right, but being dust makes us eligible for repentance and forgiveness. God knows our humble origins and the limitations of people made of dust, and so He makes allowances for our lack of wisdom and fortitude. He knows that we struggle with "grievous weakness and painful passions"—as one of our liturgical texts laments—and that we have much difficulty finding our way clear of all kinds of besetting (or besotting) plagues. Being dust ought thus to make us humble, and grateful for God's forbearance. Yet we can't seem to learn the simplest of lessons. "Why are dust and ashes proud?" (Sirach 10:9).

Though our bodies shall return to the dust from which they came, there is more to humanity than the assembling and disassembling of bodies of dust. How do we know? Pull your old dusty Bible off the shelf and read Genesis 2:7. You will see that once God formed man from the earth, He breathed the breath of life into him. This dust is sustained by the very breath of God! We're onto something here. We also learn that we are created in God's image, which immeasurably ennobles this humble dust. But the greatest thing (and this—for better or worse, depending on your perspective—is the destroyer of all our excuses) is that God Himself has taken our dust upon Himself by becoming man in our Lord Jesus Christ. He has united the dust of our human nature to Himself and—descending even farther, into Hell—He has also taken on the filth of our sins and nailed them to the Cross. Through faith in Him and obedience to Him, come what may, we will discover that we are more than mere dust, and are destined for the glory God has prepared for those who love Him.

So dust yourself off and get busy with the work of your transformation! God does the lion's share, but He still requires our free co-operation. Can dust sing his praise? Yes, when it is animated with an immortal soul and the grace of the Holy Spirit. Being dust we shall return to dust, but being united to God we shall rise again and forever sparkle like diamond dust in the Sun of Righteousness!

Cleansing the House of Prayer

There's a story about Jesus that is rather unusual. Usually, He welcomes people; here He drives them away. It must have been something terrible that they were doing to incite Him to drive them away. He wouldn't do such a thing merely to defend Himself from his attackers, for we know that He patiently endured much abuse, and even went like a silent lamb to the slaughter. Here, however, He was defending his Father's honor, for his Father's house was being profaned (He would defend the honor of the Holy Spirit, too: "whoever says a word against the Son of Man will be forgiven, but whoever speaks against the Holy Spirit will not be forgiven").

The story is very short: "Jesus entered the temple of God and drove out all who sold and bought in the temple, and he overturned the tables of the money-changers and the seats of those who sold pigeons. He said to them, 'It is written, "My house shall be called a house of prayer," but you make it a den of thieves'" (Mt. 21:12-13). It is clear that this was a thorough cleansing: He not only drove out the merchants, but he overturned both tables and chairs! Now it is sometimes objected that these people were engaging in a standard practice, a necessary service, changing the gentile Roman coinage into that which was acceptable for temple offerings, and providing animals for sacrificial worship. But two things were wrong: this business did not have to be done inside the temple precincts and, to add insult to injury, those engaged in this business were cheating their customers in the presence of God—otherwise, Jesus would not have called them "thieves." Jesus had no tolerance for those who would do evil in his Father's house.

Let's indulge in a bit of allegory here, though based on Scripture. St. Paul says that we are temples of the Holy Spirit, and therefore these spiritual temples are meant to be, following Jesus' quotation from Isaiah, houses of prayer. But it may be that our house of prayer needs to be cleansed, may even need a radical upheaval. We have to see if we have allowed thieves into the house of prayer—not just the occasional unworthy thought, but perhaps we have become habituated to some "standard practice" that is not acceptable to the Lord. Jesus surprised the money-changers as well as the authorities, because they saw nothing wrong with "business as usual." But we may also be surprised to find that the "business as usual" of our own inner lives needs to be cleaned up, to reflect better what it means that we are temples of the Spirit and houses of prayer. We ought to ask ourselves if the things we think or fantasize about, or allow in through our senses, are things we would bring into a house of prayer, even before the Blessed Sacrament—for Christ dwells within us.

What has to be driven out ruthlessly is all malice, hatred, impurity, rage, vengeance, falsehood, and anything else that is in itself contrary to the will of God. But even though the Lord is tough on evil, He is always compassionate with our weakness and inability—despite our sincere efforts—to be all that his grace enables us to be. Note that in the very next verse (21:14), Jesus resumes his usual practice of welcoming: "The blind and the lame came to him in the temple, and he healed them." Our weaknesses and defects can be healed, once we drive out evil through repentance, absolution, and persevering self-discipline. The Lord will always have some pleasant surprises for us, even if initially we have to experience the unpleasant surprise of discovering "thieves" in our house of prayer. Notice that it was the ones who by law were allowed to be in the temple that Jesus drove out, and the ones who were forbidden by law to be in the temple—the blind, lame, or otherwise disfigured or diseased were considered ritually impure— were the very ones He welcomed! So it is that, for the sake of fidelity to Christ, we may find ourselves having to reject what the world accepts and to accept what the world rejects. As long as we are honestly seeking the will of God, we will know what the Gospel requires of us in every situation.

So be aware that you are a house of prayer. Be aware that some things are appropriate for houses of prayer and some things are not. When Jesus comes to us we want Him to reach out his hand of healing, and not overturn our tables and chairs! Let us turn to Him now so that He can reveal what still needs to be done to purify the inner temple. Then He can say of us: "These I will bring to my holy mountain, and make them joyful in my house of prayer" (Isaiah 56:7).

Unrepentant

Even though the Lord's mercy is boundless, we cannot afford to be presumptuous. We seem to have stubborn (and sometimes clever) ways of avoiding genuine repentance, and hence, despite our supposed piety and our superficial or perhaps even self-deceiving "trust in God's mercy" (which can degenerate into little more than presumed permission to sin), we may be in fact living unrepentant lives.

The following is an excerpt from a prayer by St. Augustine, who had no illusions about human nature:

"Before Thine eyes, O Lord, we bring our sins, and compare them with the stripes we have received. If we examine the evil we have wrought, what we suffer is little, what we deserve is great. What we have committed is very

grievous, what we have suffered is slight. We feel the
punishment of sin, yet withdraw not from the obstinacy of
sinning. Under Thy lash our inconstancy is visited, but our
sinfulness is not changed. Our suffering soul is tormented,
but our neck is not bent. Our life groans under sorrow, yet
amends not in deed. If Thou spare us, we correct not our
ways; if Thou punish, we cannot endure it. In time of
correction we confess our wrongdoing; after Thy
visitation we forget that we have wept. If Thou stretchest
forth Thy hand, we promise amendment; if Thou
witholdest the sword, we keep not our promise. If Thou
strikest, we cry out for mercy; if Thou sparest, we again
provoke Thee to strike."

I can hardly say more. This is such an incisive commentary on the human spiritual condition. It exposes not only our weakness, but our deviousness as well. We are given an insight into why we don't really change or grow very much. The prayer reveals that we live, more often than not, as hirelings or slothful servants instead of sons and daughters. It manifests our self-interest, our desire only to escape punishment, but not to return love for love. It also makes clear the psychology of the modern creators of the "non-judging God": they're only looking for an excuse to persist in sin. He spares us (they assume), so we correct not our ways.

That prayer of St. Augustine may be a revelation for us, perhaps a painful, though salutary one. We might wish to incorporate it into our examination of conscience. We may find, to our dismay, that after having blithely consigned the unrepentant to the flames, we ourselves are shown to be unrepentant, at least by the Saint's criteria. I've usually considered myself to be repentant, but I think I have to re-examine myself in the light of that prayer. High-profile examples of unrepentance abound in today's news, but we have to make sure there isn't one hidden in our own souls.

It's time to get serious about the spiritual life: not merely about its external rites or about superficial practices that don't reach the soul, but about true repentance. Christians, we must be different, the word of God must be *life* to us—or else let us be honest enough to hand in our baptismal certificates and retain only our secular IDs. Those who truly belong to Christ will not be found unrepentant.

A Deeper Turning

We can learn a little more about the person and mission of John the Baptizer, the great preacher of repentance, from two prophecies—the first one made by the Archangel Gabriel and the second by John's father at his birth. I will first summarize the elements of the prophecies: He will be great before the Lord, He will be filled with the Holy Spirit (therefore he shall abstain from lesser spirits, wine and liquor); He will turn many to the Lord their God, in the spirit and power of Elijah, turning the hearts of the disobedient to the wisdom of the just, and preparing the Lord's people for his advent. He will be a prophet, who will give people knowledge of salvation through repentance and forgiveness of sins, as the Light of God dawns on those who sit in darkness and the shadow of death. What a marvelous litany of graces! Only Christ Himself had greater things said of Him before his birth.

I want to focus on the word "turn," for this is at the heart of John's mission. He will turn many to the Lord their God, and turn the hearts of the disobedient to the wisdom of the just. He will do this ultimately by turning them toward the Lamb of God, who takes away the sin of the world. But first he has to turn them inward, that is, he has to get the people to recognize and acknowledge their sinfulness, so that they can turn away from evil and selfish behavior. One can turn to God only after one has turned away from evil—if you try to skip the repentance part and go directly to God, the first thing He will show you is your sins, so there's no short cut! God is a God of truth, and sin must be dealt with before a personal and intimate communion can develop. This double turning is the knowledge of salvation through forgiveness that the prophet was born to declare.

But this turning from sin and turning to God is, in its fullness and depth, a rather complex and profound matter. That is precisely because it is a spiritual, ontological matter and not a legal or merely ritual one. It's easy enough to say "I repent," and even mean it, and then receive absolution, but still not be wholly turned toward God. It's not enough simply to perform the proper ritual. If you repent and honestly confess, you will be forgiven the guilt of your sin, but it may be that the necessary transformation still has not taken place. It may be that the will itself has not yet been reached by grace, for the will has not sufficiently *reached out* to grace. It still keeps it self-ward orientation, still is not sufficiently turned. Forgiveness is ours for the asking, but the deep healing of the soul can be a long process.

This mystery is profound but has been well-expressed in poetic form by Kathryn Mulderink in a sonnet entitled, *De nocte*, i.e., Of Night. What she's saying is that what Scripture calls "the mystery of iniquity" goes so deep into the human soul that no superficial or even standard treatment can fully turn toward God that which was first turned away by original sin and later through numerous choices. The remedy must be a radical one. She writes:

> *"There's a dark that illumines the darkness we are*
> *In the subterranean chambers beyond sin,*
> *Where subtler poisons deface, debar,*
> *And unravel every hard-won discipline.*
> *Below repentance's smoothly finished frame*
> *Lurk nature's will and inward contradictions*
> *Though we've immolated sense in puring flame*
> *And submitted to our cleansing benedictions.*
> *More contrariety with God have we*
> *Than sin which once we chose but now reject;*
> *He is more than sinlessness and we*
> *Cannot sublimate through force or intellect.*
> *We must let go of us, arms cruciform,*
> *To expose our hearts to Fire that transforms."*

Our genuine and deep healing, turning from sin and toward God will only come through a radical "yes" to God that takes us straight to the Cross, and only in that cruciform abandonment to God will the divine Fire be able to enter the darkest depths of our souls, purifying us of all the hidden sticky residues of our habitual sins, of all the ways that throughout our lives our saying "no" to God has profoundly disfigured us within.

This is why the prophetic mission of the Baptist is so important, so crucial. His work of turning hearts to the Lord, turning the disobedient to the way of wisdom, is not a mere correction of a few faults. It is preparing the way for God to reach down into the depths of the human soul, to the hidden place at which we are all connected to the primal rebellion of Adam and Eve, and to *turn it back*, uniting to the obedience of Him who became man for our salvation, who humbled himself unto death on the Cross in radical obedience to the will of the Father. To the extent that we all thus turn radically back to the Father, the power of the devil is utterly vanquished in this world.

This is the knowledge of salvation through the forgiveness of sins; this is the Light from on high entering the hidden places in our souls that are still in darkness and the shadow of death. This is guidance into the way of peace. But this way of peace and light, of mercy and salvation, is not an easy way. It is the way of the Cross, but it is the only way truly to know the mystery of God. We can't live on the surface; we can't think that we will ever enter into a rich and genuine union with God if our hearts aren't turned all the way back to Him, if we haven't let the searching Light of his grace and truth illuminate every dark recess of our souls, if we haven't allowed the key of the Cross to open every locked and sealed inner chamber.

To have our hearts wholly turned to God is not a matter of our simply saying "I'm sorry," and God saying, "Don't worry, it's OK." That is not salvation; that is not transformation. Rather, we must cry out from the depths, "O God, save me! I am lost!" as He reaches down and pulls us from the jaws of the dragon. It is being willing to mount the altar of the Cross and to allow fire from Heaven to consume the sacrifice. If we don't know how evil sin is, we can't know how marvelous mercy is. If we don't tremble at the prospect of damnation, we cannot appreciate salvation.

So let us ask the Forerunner to intercede for us, to prepare the way of the Lord, to turn our hearts toward Him who longs to purify, heal, and transform us by his grace, for He loves us more than we can imagine. To us is offered the beginning of a new life in profound communion with the saving mystery of Christ.

Judge of the Living and the Dead

One of our preparatory Sundays for Lent is that of the Last Judgment (Matthew 25:31-46). If we haven't heeded the call to repentance on the previous Sundays, the Church gives us the "bottom line," the outcome of our repentance—or lack of it. If you read the liturgical texts for Vespers and Matins of the Sunday of the Last Judgment, you'll get the clear impression that no one gets away with anything. These Offices have not submitted to the scalpel of post-Vatican II political correctness; they do not manifest "sensitivity" to the updated outlooks of "Easter people." They are filled with lamentations and cries of woe, while unquenchable fires roar in the background, and the "worm that dieth not" is prepared to devour the unrepentant. Yet it is also filled with recourse to the divine compassion, with confidence in God's love for mankind, while still begging Him to place us with the righteous elect and not with the unregenerate damned.

Now I don't have a particular affinity for fire and brimstone, but I tend rather eagerly to pray this Office. It's a bracing tonic, a wake-up call, something we all need to hear, at least from time to time. It's not the whole of the Gospel, but the whole of our lives are leading up to that decisive moment, and if we end up on the wrong side for that Final Separation, then we have completely missed the reason for our existence, and we'll have a *really long* time to think about it.

Many people these days have lost the sense of sin, believe in a "non-judgmental" God (even though that's not the One of Scripture and Tradition), and are generally heedless to the call to repentance, not believing in the consequences thereof. But I'd rather believe the truth, even if that makes life a little harder. I'd rather confess my sins and do penance than believe that God doesn't bother with such things, as if all things are going to turn out well in the end, no matter what. But there's a great difference between *not* admitting sin because you believe God is merciful, and *admitting* sin for the very same reason. The sin that is forgiven is the one that is confessed, the one for which there is genuine repentance. Mercy is granted only to the one who knows how desperately he needs it.

There are many prayers in the Liturgy, for both priest and laity, in which we beg that our offering of the Sacrifice and reception of Holy Communion will be "without judgment or condemnation." It's not without reason. St. Paul said that the Corinthians were sick and even dying because of unworthy reception of the Body and Blood of Christ (1Cor. 11:27-30). We must live with the awareness that our lives are going to be judged, that there are definite standards that we are expected to meet, that there are heavenly consequences for doing good and hellish ones for doing evil.

It's rather strange, perhaps, that on one occasion, after preaching rather forcefully on this mystery—reiterating the Church's faith and pointing out the error of those who don't even believe that Christ is coming again as Judge—I experienced a temptation about that very thing. As the Liturgy went on, I became distracted by the thought: "After all that, is He *really* going to come at the end to judge us?" Instantly, the choir and the entire congregation sang out: "He will come again in glory to judge the living and the dead!" We happened to be singing the Creed at that moment, and it jarred me, for I was listening to the tempter more than to the Liturgy and wasn't paying attention to the words. But at the very moment I entertained my foolish question, it was immediately countered by the profession of faith of the great assembly. The Lord was not going to let me stray for a second! Later that day, I looked back at the word I noted from my morning's Bible reading, and I saw: "they believed the Scripture and the word that Jesus had spoken" (John 2:22).

He doesn't want anyone to doubt the truth of his words in Scripture, especially when they concern such an essential and crucial matter. It's good to hear the hard word about the great and fiery judgment, if that will keep us on the straight and narrow. In the final analysis, salvation is the only issue, and everything in our lives *must* (directly or indirectly) lead us toward that end—and woe to us if we move in the other direction! So hear the word of the Lord, know that there will be a final reckoning, and do whatever it takes—for Heaven's sake—to secure your place at the right hand of the Awesome Judge!

God Resists the Proud

Both St. James and St. Peter quote this text from Proverbs: "God resists [or opposes] the proud, but gives grace to the humble." I thought that perhaps I should reflect on that, for though this seems self-evident, there may be more to it than we see at first glance.

I've said before that this is one of the most chilling texts in Scripture, that is, if we are among the proud (and if you think you're not, by that very fact you probably are). For what more terrible thing can there be than for God to *resist* you? But are we speaking here only of the ultimate separation of the proud from the presence of God, or is the issue more subtle?

I had a dream some time ago, of which I remember nothing except that (oddly enough) I was writing a poem. All that survived the return trip to consciousness was this:

> *Some people live*
> *And some people die*
> *Beneath the indifferent sky.*

I was somewhat dismayed to discover this rather dark and faithless expression lurking in the labyrinthine corridors of my unconscious mind. But it is merely an all-too-human response to the unseen mysteries of life. I profess faith in God and all that He has revealed, yet if left to my own passions I would demand proof of them. This is a subtle (or perhaps not so subtle) form of pride. And God resists me in this. He is not going to prove anything to me, but is going to leave me free. I just read one author who said that the greatest act of human freedom is the act of faith. This is a rather complicated issue, but it should be at least fairly clear that the act of faith is, by definition, free, i.e., not forced by compelling evidence.

Many today who are champions of "freedom," at the expense of moral and spiritual laws and obligations, actually make their choices under the strong compulsion of lust, greed, gluttony, self-interest and egoism. So they are hardly free. As for believers, there is much *support* for faith in our observations and experiences, but nothing like a mathematical proof. So to choose to believe is a free choice; we are not obliged to accept the claims of faith by sheer weight of evidence or by any internal or external compulsion.

The demand for proof is arrogant, and the Lord resists it. He resisted those who said to Him as He hung on the Cross: "Let him come down now from the cross and we will believe in him." He did not come down, for He resists the proud and insists that our faith be free and not coerced by overwhelming miracles. We tend to be like those who also said to Him: "What sign do you perform, that we may see and believe in you?" (John 6:30). The Lord resisted requests for signs as proof of his claims, when He knew that those who asked were of bad will, were among the proud. His response? "No sign shall be given..." (Mark 8:12).

On the other hand, the Lord gives grace to the humble. Now the humble ones are not the self-denigrating, the lugubrious, the timid, the weak, or the gullible. Rather the humble are those who simply live in the truth—about themselves, about others, about God—and so live in peace, in evangelical childlikeness, and can more easily recognize the signs of God's presence that He does in fact give to those who demand nothing. In a text that I've heard hundreds of times (it is one of the common readings in Vespers for the feast days of monastic saints), I just realized recently that "those who trust Him will understand truth..." (Wisdom 3:9). To humbly trust without demanding signs and proofs will open our hearts and minds to what God wishes to reveal to us. It increases our capacity for truth, because humility is the virtue that most easily receives it.

So don't set yourself up for resistance from God. He wants to give, but not as a response to our arrogant demands. He will give on *his* terms, so we are to make our acts of faith and trust with the freedom of the children of God—for God gives grace to the humble.

❧ Chapter Three:
Grace is Sufficient ❧

The mystery of divine grace encompasses our struggle to respond to it in creative and fruitful ways. We discover another paradox: grace is sufficient, yet without our sincere and wholehearted response, grace will bear little to no fruit in our lives. Then again, it is when we are weak that divine power is perfected in us. Then again, without effort and self-discipline our spiritual life languishes. Then again...

Strength in Weakness

I've always found it somewhat difficult to understand the concept of strength in weakness. This was Jesus' answer to St. Paul's pleadings for deliverance from his thorn in the flesh: "My power is perfected in weakness." So the conclusion was, "My grace is sufficient for you" (2Cor. 12:9).

It is a paradox, a mystery, as we often find in divine revelation. I think that if we're even going to begin to understand it, we have to know what weakness is not. It is not *moral* weakness, as if God's power could be perfected in, say, a man's weakness for frequenting prostitutes (though God's power can certainly be manifest in one's valiant struggle *against* the moral weakness). It seems to me that the human weakness that divine power works through is simply our physical, psychological, and emotional inadequacies, afflictions, and limitations—which ought to give rise to the awareness of our radical dependence upon God. Our weakness seems to make us unable to rise to the occasions for which greatness is required, unable to bear the burden and heat of the day, unable to be what we know we ought to be if we wish to live as faithful servants of God.

Our weakness, though real, is not absolute. What, then, is the strength God requires of us in our weakness? One author puts it this way: "The strength [God] asks of us is the decision to trust him in all things, especially in the moments of greatest abandonment...knowing our weakness and trusting to the point of rashness in his Fatherly goodness" (Michael O'Brien, *A Cry of Stone*).

That's it, I believe: *the decision to trust Him*. It doesn't take a lot of strength, but it does take a significant measure of faith. God can exercise his strength in our weakness only and insofar as we trust Him to do so. We don't know the particular form his power will take when it is manifest through our weakness. But we trust that his grace is sufficient, and so we live another day. St. Paul didn't say precisely *how* he experienced God's power in his weakness, but look at the result: "For the sake of Christ, then, I am content with weakness, insults, hardships, persecutions, and calamities; for when I am weak, then I am strong" (2Cor. 12:10).

It is a sublime power indeed that can make one "content" with weakness, hardship, and calamity. Decide to trust, then. There's nothing to lose, and sufficient grace to gain.

Grace: a Two-way Street

Ever wonder why you sometimes seem to get no response from God in time of temptation or trial? Ever call on the name of the Lord without results? Before you conclude that God is hard of hearing or unconcerned with your needs, reflect a little on the meaning of divine grace.

Grace, as you know, is God's life, God's love flowing into us. It is the divine gift of his own indwelling presence. So if God's love (and hence his power) is flowing into us, why doesn't much happen? Maybe it's because nothing is flowing *back*.

Grace isn't a drug, a magic potion, or an automatic solution to our problems. Our relationship with God has to be just that: a relationship. This means that Love requires a response of love from us. If God's grace is to bear fruit in our lives, we have to love Him back. What is it that we love? In times of temptation, it may be that we secretly love whatever the temptation promises, though we half-heartedly turn to God because we know that sin is wrong. In times of trial or suffering, perhaps what we really desire is simply deliverance from the affliction and not a richer encounter with God.

What if we were to send back love to the Lord in times of trial or temptation? What if we decided that we were going to love Him in the midst of our afflictions, and trust his love to be the strength and comfort we need? Grace bears fruit when we respond to God's love with ours. We may just discover that there's more strength in our love than we thought, because it has given us access to the inexhaustible grace of God. It has created a place for Him to work within us. When that place is created in our hearts, God knows that He has an open invitation, and He will come when He pleases. He will see that it is good. And we will know that He is the Lord. And Love plus love will bear fruit.

So go ahead, call on the name of the Lord—but not as you would call a plumber or a mechanic, for his job is not merely to fix things. Rather, He makes all things new. Open your heart to Jesus' love, and know that his heart is open to yours. Then ask, and you shall receive.

God Knows Your Heart

It is a comforting awareness. God knows our hearts, knows what makes us tick, knows our sorrows and sufferings, capacities and incapacities. The fact that God knows our hearts is, however, a two-sided coin, as the Scriptures reveal. Let's take a look first at what we might call the negative (though still salutary) side of this divine knowledge of our innermost selves.
God knows our bad will, our secret sin, whatever darkness or duplicity there may be within us and, to use a phrase of St. John of Kronstadt, whatever "unrighteous movements of the heart" He may find as well. In one of his stern rebukes to the Pharisees, Jesus said: "You are those who justify yourselves before men, but God knows your hearts; for what is exalted among men is an abomination in the sight of God" (Luke 16:15). So the fact that God knows our hearts means that we cannot hide anything from Him. We cannot pull the wool over his eyes: "You have kept...our hidden sins under the light of your scrutiny" (Psalm 90:8). Nor can we appease Him with external acts or rituals when we are unreconciled to Him within. His harshest criticisms were leveled at those who presented a righteous exterior but who were interiorly corrupt: "You outwardly appear righteous to men, but within you are full of hypocrisy and iniquity" (Matthew 23:28).

On the other hand, we find consolation in God's thorough knowledge of us, because we can "reassure our hearts before Him whenever our hearts condemn us; for God is greater than our hearts and He knows everything" (1John 3:19-20). Often we don't even know what is in our hearts, and our inner life is in turmoil or confusion. After lamenting the inexplicable dark mystery of the human heart, Jeremiah cried out: "Who can understand it?" But God immediately replied: "I, the Lord, search the mind and try the heart" (Jer. 17:9-10). We are not stuck forever with the limitations and defects of our hearts, if we confidently entrust them to Him Who Is Greater Than Our Hearts. They may need a lot of healing, a lot of changing, but we can still rest in his providence and mercy.

In one of our prayers of preparation for Holy Communion, after acknowledging our sinfulness, we say that we run to Him for refuge. See, when we sin, we shouldn't run *away* from God in shame but *toward* Him in repentance, like the prodigal son hastening to his father. For where else can we find forgiveness and healing for our wounded and reckless hearts? Adam and Eve hid from God after their sin, but He found them out anyway. Better for you to confess right away and get it all on the table, for God already knows your heart.

Sometimes we come before God trying to explain or excuse ourselves, or even trying to tell Him what we know is best for us! Be still and know that He is God. He knows your heart; He knows what you need before you ask. Take courage and consolation in that. He is with you; He understands. He won't let you wallow in self-pity or mediocrity, though, because his compassion is based on truth and on what He knows you can do with the help of his grace. So reach out for that divine hand that is reaching out to you. God knows your heart, and if you let Him, He will make it one with his own.

Laws of the Spirit

Early in the 20th century, Fr. Basil Maturin undertook a noble but near-impossible task: He tried to figure out what St. Paul was saying in the inscrutable seventh chapter of the Letter to the Romans. Actually, he didn't produce a word-by-word commentary (not that I know of, anyway), but rather made some sense of the spiritual laws of which the Apostle spoke. These spiritual laws reveal much about the mystery of grace and human effort. The quotes from him are taken from his excellent little book, *Christian Self-Mastery*.

He discerns four spiritual laws: the "law of the members," the "law of sin," the "law of the mind," and the "law of the Spirit of Life" (this last one actually appears at the beginning of chapter 8, but Paul didn't divide his own work into chapters; that was done by editors centuries later). The first two laws are related, as are the second two.

The law of the members is at work in our acts and desires that are not in themselves sinful, but that end up preparing the way to sin. The very lack of discipline evident in our indulgence in them is a sign that sin is not far away. "The man who determines that he will not do what is positively wrong, but will do everything else he wishes, will find that, in the long run, he cannot stop short of actual sin." Yield to the law of the members, to "harmless" acts of self-indulgence or to habitually taking the path of least resistance, and you will soon be captive to the law of sin.

The law of sin brings the destruction of moral and spiritual life. Once you pave the way for sin by lack of discipline in regard to things in which you may tend to pamper yourself or prefer your own way instead of making a sacrifice for another, then the law of sin gains ascendancy and ultimately brings spiritual death. "Once admitted and indulged, sin lives, grows, and develops by its own law. Its growth is like that of an organism that feeds on the very life of the soul, absorbing its strength... We cannot bargain with it and say it shall go so far and no farther." Once sin becomes habitual, we have to make extraordinary and painful efforts to uproot it. The idea is to discipline ourselves in the "neutral" things, things that may not be evil in themselves but that have a real potential to take us there if we continue in them. Learning how to say "no" in small matters will strengthen us to do likewise in large ones. Faithful in little, faithful in much.

On the other hand, the "law of the mind" is the counterpart to the law of the members. Living by the law of the mind is a preparation for living by the law of the Spirit of Life, just as living under the law of the members sets us up for living under the law of sin. The law of the mind acts in our reason and conscience: "to lift up the soul to all that is best in it." It leads us to do what is right, encourages us to discipline ourselves in things that can lead to sin. But because the law of the members (and perhaps also the law of sin) are simultaneously at work in us, the law of the mind is not always successful in helping us to see and do what is right and pleasing to God. But it does point us to the One who can liberate us from sin.

By the power of divine grace, the law of the mind leads us to choose the way of Christ, whose Spirit then brings us under his own law. "Conscience is, as it were, a valve through which the stream of grace flowing forth from the Spirit of God floods the soul... if conscience is open, the stream rushes forth in a mighty torrent, refreshing, invigorating, and uplifting all the powers of the soul." Then we can cry out with St Paul: "The law of the Spirit of Life in Christ Jesus has set me free from the law of sin and death" (Rom. 8:2). This liberation, however, must be diligently maintained, for those other laws still have potential to regain power if our vigilance falters.

The battle doesn't begin with the law of sin and the law of the Spirit. It begins in the little grey areas, with the law of the members and the law of the mind. Here is an extended quote that puts the struggle in perspective: "Thus, the great moral battle, whether the soul is to be ruled by sin or by the Spirit of Life, depends upon the victory of the law of the members or the law of the mind. About the trifling acts of self-indulgence or self-will against which conscience so vehemently protests, from the first waking in the morning when the law of the members cries, 'Rest a little longer,' and the law of the mind cries, 'Arise and prepare for the work of the day,' on through every hour, almost every moment of the day, the tide of battle ebbs and flows. And behind these two combatants, whose conflict is over things so trifling that they scarcely seem to have any moral value at all, stand the two mighty powers of life and death, of sin and righteousness, awaiting the issue."

Let us realize that there are mighty powers behind our daily choices. The way to our eternal destiny is paved with little daily choices.

The Treasure and the Pearl

I'd like to continue with Fr. Maturin's reflections on spiritual life from *Christian Self-Mastery*. Here it will be in the context of two of Jesus' shortest parables, which are among his best, in my opinion: the parable of the hidden treasure and of the pearl of great price (Matthew 13:44-46).

Let's start with the pearl, for the seeking comes before the finding. Notice first, though, that in the parable of the treasure, it is clear that the Kingdom of Heaven is the hidden treasure ("the Kingdom of Heaven is like a treasure..."), and we can probably assume that the precious pearl also represents the priceless value of the Kingdom. But that's not exactly how Jesus presents it. He says: "The Kingdom of Heaven *is like a merchant in search of* fine pearls..." So the search itself is part of the mystery of the Kingdom. We have to have the proper dispositions, the willingness to make necessary sacrifices, not only in order to actually *possess* the pearl of great price, but even to undertake the quest at all.

If we truly seek, we will find. A merchant sought and found the priceless pearl. A man found a hidden treasure in a field (he couldn't have found it if he wasn't looking for it; buried treasures don't rise to the surface of their own accord). But in order to possess that treasure he had to buy the field. And the field cost precisely the value of everything he owned. So he sold everything to buy that field.

Fr. Maturin gives us the spiritual principle and application: "To acquire anything...we must part with something we already possess, which we value less than that which we would acquire. If we do not think it is worth the price, we do not pay it. The law of gaining possession is the parting with what we value less for what we value more. A man cannot keep his money and at the same time get what he has his heart set on having. The question is which he values most... He who values this life more than the life beyond the grave will purchase its pleasures and enjoyments at the price of that life. He who believes that he was made for eternity, and that his home and happiness are in that other world, will be ready to sacrifice this world for it."

Both the man who found the treasure and the one who found the pearl sold all they had to acquire that which was of surpassing value. This is like the spiritual "dying" that is mortification or self-discipline, accepting a loss for the sake of a greater gain. Was the man who sold all he had grudging or bitter over the price he had to pay? No, for it says: "*in his joy* he goes and sells all he has..." He forgets his loss in the joy of his gain.

This is what Jesus offers us when He asks us to deny ourselves, take up our crosses and follow Him. He is asking us to value less what perishes, and especially what leads us to sin, and to value more the hidden treasures of the spiritual life and of the Kingdom of Heaven. He asks us to let go of that to which we cling for security or pleasure, and to open ourselves to that which is promised but not yet fully possessed. For we, like the merchant, are on a search, but Christ guarantees—by the Blood of his pierced heart—that if we don't give up the search we will find the precious pearl, the hidden treasure. Then, in our joy, we will easily relinquish the passing fancies of this temporary life.

Be willing to pay the price. If you give all, you will receive all—and God's "all" is infinitely greater and more precious than the relatively insignificant "all" we are asked to sacrifice. Give up what is of less value for that which is of more. You will gain possession of the treasure, the pearl—the Kingdom of Heaven.

Do It Again

C.S. Lewis had a way of gaining and expressing insights into dimensions of our lives that perhaps we do not give sufficient attention, if any at all. He wove them into his novels almost in passing, so that you really have to be listening in order to "get it." But he knew what he was doing, and those who have ears will hear. The following is from *Perelandra*, and it describes one of the experiences of Dr. Ransom as he was exploring for the first time that paradisal planet—tasting its indescribably wonderful fruits. "He had meant to extract the smallest, experimental sip, but the first taste put his caution all to flight... It was like the discovery of a totally new *genus* of pleasures... As he let the empty gourd fall from his hand and was about to pluck a second one, it came into his head that he was now neither hungry nor thirsty. And yet to repeat a pleasure so intense and almost so spiritual seemed an obvious thing to do. His reason, or what we commonly take to be reason in our own world, was all in favor of tasting this miracle again... Yet something seemed opposed to this 'reason'... For whatever cause, it appeared to him better not to taste again. Perhaps the experience had been so complete that repetition would be a vulgarity—like asking to hear the same symphony twice in a day... He stood pondering over this and wondering how often in his life on earth he had reiterated pleasures...in the teeth of desire and in obedience to a spurious rationalism...

"Looking up at a fine cluster of the 'bubbles' [another type of paradisal fruit] which hung above his head, he thought how easy it would be to get up and plunge oneself through the whole lot of them and to feel, all at once, that magical refreshment multiplied tenfold. But he was restrained by the same sort of feeling which had restrained him over-night from tasting a second gourd. He had always disliked the people who encored a favorite air in the opera— 'That just spoils it' had been his comment. But this now appeared to him as a principle of far wider application and deeper moment. This itch to have things over again, as if life were a film that could be unrolled twice or even made to work backwards…was it possibly the root of all evil? No: of course the love of money was called that. But money itself—perhaps one valued it chiefly as a defense against chance, a security for being able to have things over again…"

Lewis has here hit on something to which most people probably wouldn't give a second thought, but which is actually quite important. The desire to repeat pleasurable experiences, simply for the sake of the pleasure—for in the above passage "he was now neither hungry nor thirsty"—may truly be at the root of all evil, at least of all greed and lust and hedonistic self-absorption. The "do it again" mentality also makes it difficult for people to receive God's gifts precisely as gifts—which are regulated by the wisdom and generosity of the Giver and not by the unrestrained desire of the recipient. To receive something from God in the measure that it is given is to live in peace, gratitude, and self-control. To always want more for the sake of pleasure or of luxuriating in superfluous abundance is to merit the censure of the selfish man who "grew rich for himself but not in the sight of God" (Luke 12:21).

The principle applies in spiritual life as well as with material goods and pleasures. If one has a powerful or profound experience of the presence and love of God, upon returning to prayer one may wish to re-create the experience, to have it over again because it was so blessed. But that is not within our power, nor is it within the will of God, who remains the Master of his gifts and of the revelation of his presence, according to the inscrutable designs of his will for our spiritual growth and salvation. We simply try to dispose ourselves to be open to *whatever* He wishes to give—and to make sure we are presenting no inner obstacles that would impede his lavish bestowal of grace.

All good things come from God and are to be received with thanksgiving, and also with the wisdom that waits on his providence and doesn't try to *take* something that is meant only to be received. Don't try to have it again, whatever it is. If it is good for you, it will be given again, according to the Lord's mercy and goodness. For even good things can become a source of evil if abused. But the delights of Paradise await those who receive life as it comes from the hand of God.

I Press On

"Whatever gain I had, I count as loss for the sake of Christ. Indeed, I count everything as loss because of the surpassing worth of knowing Christ Jesus my Lord" (Phil. 3:7-8). I think I would be both eager and afraid to meet St. Paul in person. The man is so intense, so focused on Christ, so ready to trash everything if only he could be with his Lord—and therefore so uncompromising when it comes to slackers, "Sunday Catholics", or stubborn pagans.

But he also has a salutary lack of self-confidence, not resting on his laurels (nor being self-righteous) but putting all his hope in the Lord. "Not that I have already obtained this [i.e., the power of the resurrection] or am already perfect, but *I press on* to make it my own, because Christ Jesus has made me his own" (3:12; I prefer a translation from some older Bibles: "I press on, that I may lay hold of that for which Christ Jesus has laid hold of me"). He continues, driving home the point: "One thing I do, forgetting what lies behind and straining forward to what lies ahead, *I press on* toward the goal, for the prize of the upward call of God in Christ Jesus" (vv. 13-14).

We can see in almost all of Paul's writings that he is pressing on to attain the goal of his life, of every human life: eternal happiness with God in Heaven. Many of us need to heed his exhortation to forget what lies behind and to strain forward to what lies ahead. "What lies behind" is often a history of failures, regrettable or humiliating experiences, and sins. Once we bring all this to the Lord in sincere repentance, and receive absolution through his Church, we should forget it—or remember it in general only for the sake of humility and a reminder of our utter need for God. Morbid dwelling on past sins does not move us toward the Lord. But once having received forgiveness, we cannot slacken the pace toward the finish line. We "strain forward" with all that is within us, to obtain "what lies ahead," that for which Christ has forgiven our sins, that for which He has "laid hold of us."

I think we need to hear this word as an encouragement when we get bogged down in all the burdens and troubles of daily life, and perhaps may be tempted to give up, throw in the towel, or just lapse into a tired mediocrity, numbly going through the motions of living. We may not always feel the joy, the exuberance, the liveliness of faith and hope (which ought to accompany the astounding revelation of what God has prepared for those who love Him), but we can press on, we can persevere, we can fix our eyes on

Jesus and the goal, the "outcome of your faith, the salvation of your souls" (1Peter 1:9).

So let us press on and strain forward to what lies ahead. There are no runners-up in the race of life—only winners and losers. "Run so as to win the prize," the Apostle exhorts (1Cor. 9:24). Again he says: "Let us not grow weary in doing what is right, for in due season we shall reap [eternal life], if we do not lose heart" (Galatians 6:8-9). Things sometimes get very difficult or discouraging, and sometimes the finish line seems very far away, but I press on...

Abide in the Vine

Jesus calls Himself "the true vine" (John 15:1). His disciples are the branches. Sounds good so far, but we soon realize that his Father is the vinedresser who wields the pruning shears. Every fruitless branch is simply cut off and thrown into the fire, but the fruitful branches are pruned so as to bear even more fruit.

While being aware that we can persist in sin so as to become wholly unfruitful and then cut off, I prefer to focus here on the branches that are pruned unto greater fruitfulness. There's a little wordplay in this text of the Gospel: Jesus says that the Father prunes (*kathairei*) the fruitful branch, and then immediately adds, "you [the disciples] are now clean (*katharoi*) because of the word I have spoken" (vv. 2-3). The word *katharos* means clean or pure (thus a "catharsis" is a purifying experience). The verb form *kathairo* therefore means to cleanse or purify, but it also means to clear by pruning.

So Jesus is telling the disciples that in their case his own words are the pruning shears of the Father, the action of which will produce more fruit. "You are clean (pruned) because of the word I have spoken" (v. 3). Having been pruned through enlightenment by the word of the Lord, the disciples are now invited to "abide" in the Vine.

Jesus makes it clear that if pruning is necessary for bearing more and better fruit, abiding in the Vine is necessary for the very possibility of bearing fruit in the first place. "As the branch cannot bear fruit by itself, unless it abides in the vine, neither can you, unless you abide in me" (v. 4). Then He makes his point, without any more allegorical language: "Without me you can do nothing" (v. 5).

Is it literally true that without Jesus we can do *nothing*? The answer is yes and no and yes. Yes, first of all, because without the creative and sustaining power of God we would not even be able to *exist* for an instant, let alone do anything. But then no, if we mean doing anything without the direct spiritual action of Christ upon us. We can certainly sin without Christ (and if we wish to be without Him, that's exactly what we'll end up doing), for He does not support or enable our evil. Nor do we need explicit reference to Him for tying our shoes or making a sandwich. As long as his divine power keeps us in existence, He allows us to make our choices and go about our lives freely, with or without acknowledging or relying on Him. But finally, yes, because without Jesus we can do nothing that is ultimately worthwhile. We cannot do good, become holy, keep his commandments, or do anything that leads to our salvation without the explicit gift of his divine grace. Whatever good we *think* we can do without Him will ultimately amount to nothing.

So we must abide in the Vine, draw our sustenance, strength, wisdom, peace and joy from Him. He gets more personal a few verses later: "Abide in my love" (v. 9). How do we abide in his love? Do we just luxuriate in the thought or feeling of it, or simply claim that we do so without really knowing what we're talking about? Jesus makes it clear: "If you keep my commandments, you will abide in my love" (v. 10). Love is always about willing and doing, not about wishing, fantasizing, or talking: "Let us not love [merely] in word or in speech, but in deed and in truth" (1John 3:18). It should be consoling to us that without Jesus we can do nothing, for the other side of that coin is: "I can do all things in Him who strengthens me" (Phil. 4:13). The Vine is the source of our life, and our abiding therein is the assurance of our salvation. Let us not be afraid of being pruned by the sharp edge of the word of God (see Heb. 4:12). That is infinitely better than to be made barren, diseased, and withered by the world, the flesh and the devil. Keep the Lord's commandments and thus abide in his love. In this the Father shall be glorified, and in this your joy shall be full.

All

We're all familiar with the Great Commandment of Christ (actually, the two of them). What we're probably not so familiar with is putting it into practice, perhaps because it may seem to be an impossible (or worse, impractical) ideal, but God does not command the impossible—though He may command the impractical!

The question came up in a simple rabbinical discussion about the commandments of God. A scribe asked Jesus: "Which commandment is the first of all?" Jesus gave the unabridged version: "Hear, O Israel: the Lord our God, the Lord is one; and you shall love the Lord your God will all your heart, and with all your soul, and with all your mind, and with all your strength" (Mark 12:28-30). He added loving one's neighbor as oneself, with the concluding comment: "There is no other commandment greater than these."

When I read the Scriptures (usually in the wee hours of the morning), I often write down a passage that particularly speaks to me, something that I will try to carry with me through the day. When I come to the above passage in the Gospels, I seem always to write that one down, despite whatever else may be in that particular chapter. Perhaps this is because it is something of which I always need to be reminded, something that is so essential to Christian faith and life that it shouldn't be forgotten for a single day. Perhaps also this is because I seem daily to fall short of the "all" required by Jesus in this greatest of commandments.

One can make a general (or even formal and specific) consecration of one's life to God and still not be giving all—loving Him with *all* our heart, mind, soul, and strength. I'm not loving Him with all my mind, for example, if I expose it to words or images or thoughts that are contrary to his truth, justice, mercy, holiness and purity. I'm not loving Him with all my strength if I tend to be lazy, procrastinating, or sluggish, especially when it comes to my obligations for prayer, fasting, worship, or active charity.

While it may be a long process to reach the point of "all," as the saints did, the Lord requires our constant efforts (in co-operation with his constant outpouring of grace) to attain to this level of love and fidelity to God. This will entail not only a "cleaning up of our act" regarding the obvious or gross violations of his commandments, but also a sincere and penetrating examination of conscience—of heart, mind, and soul. Where is our treasure? There will our heart be also. What do we find attractive or interesting? There will be our mind. To whom is our allegiance, and how many masters do we serve? There will be our soul. What do we find most worthy of the commitment of our time and energy? There we will apply our strength.

I heard recently in a reading from a Bible commentary that we cannot simply devote part of our time to God and part to worldly affairs. All must be for God. That doesn't mean there are no more worldly affairs to deal with (even monks, alas, have to deal with some), but all affairs, divine or human, must be caught up into our relationship to God, must somehow be a part of our service to Him. If we are involved in something that could in no way be considered a service to Him, that cannot be offered as a sacrifice or cannot be done in good conscience under his watchful eye, then we shouldn't have gotten involved in it in the first place! All the duties (and the legitimate leisure) of our state in life can be taken up into our wholehearted love of God.

But we have to *make* it so, more and more consciously. To have a vague, general intention of living for God is insufficient to fulfill the Great Commandment. We really have to pray and work to make the "all" an experienced reality, something that drives us from within, that energizes, enhances, and graces our thoughts, words, and actions of each day. What a beautiful life it would be, if we could live it while loving the Lord our God with all our heart, mind, soul, and strength. We would then realize what it means to be a child of God, with all the riches of grace.

That's the life He wills for us, makes possible for us, and to which He calls us. It prepares us for the life of Heaven, the fullness of loving God with *all*… If we don't do it during this life, we won't be able to start doing it in the next. Begin now. God created your whole heart and mind and soul. Offer them back to Him with love.

Sufficient Grace

That famous passage in St. Paul's letters with which I began this chapter seems always to require further reflection for fuller understanding. It's a word from the Lord at once disturbing and consoling, peace-giving and perplexing: "My grace is sufficient for you, for My power is made perfect in weakness" (2Cor. 12:9).

This seems to be the most common answer to my prayers, at least those concerning myself. I tend to want to pray in hope that God's grace *will* be sufficient, but He's telling me that it already *is*. My next move is to pray that it will be *manifest* or *experienced* as such! Then He sends me back to the "is" without further comment.

Sometimes I think that if the Lord would have consulted me first about how to deal with "thorns in the flesh" or other weaknesses of human nature or character, or various stubborn circumstances, we would have come up with a more satisfying solution. But since He chose to bypass my input, I have to conclude that He has foreseen something in His infinite wisdom and serenity that I may have missed amid my frantic cries for immediate deliverance.

Probably most of us have some "tragic flaw," some sort of besetting temptation or sin, some nagging weakness or vulnerability that we'd like simply to be rid of once and for all. We don't know what St. Paul's was, but he described it metaphorically (I hope that's all it was!) as "a messenger of satan to beat me." So then, looking at our own problems, we must conclude that things could be worse. All the same, we do experience inadequacy, the inability to be vibrant with virtue in flawless fortitude and unflagging faith. Somehow it seems, though, that this is precisely what God has come to expect from us—at least in this present life before we are to "shine like the sun in our Father's Kingdom."

Not that God wants us to wallow in sin or to give up efforts to overcome our failings, for indeed He hates evil and loves holiness, but He wants us to learn something first. He says his power is perfected in weakness, a weakness that is translated as utter dependence upon divine mercy and assistance. So his grace is sufficient, though He may not choose to wipe out every trace of our weakness, but He will carry us through with equanimity and trust, as we learn to walk with Him one step at a time, learning the necessary lessons along the way. Human beings tend to get proud and arrogant if they have no humiliating weaknesses of body or soul to serve as reality checks.

Still, we wrestle with the mystery. Paul repeatedly begged the Lord for deliverance but received only the "My grace is sufficient" response. As we progress in the spiritual life, we may go through many stages of knowing and "unknowing." We may come to know God in a certain way, and then later realize that He is not really what we thought, or that He is, but much more, or in a different way. Life will always be a struggle, but with divine grace it will be a rewarding and enlightening one. An old monk from Mt. Athos was once asked if he struggled with the devil. He replied: "I struggled with the devil for many years, but I no longer need to do so. Now I struggle with God." That means that he had succeeded in overcoming temptations, but now he was hurled headlong into a Mystery beyond all comprehension, without any compass but radical faith and trust. It was as if he were learning about God all over again, only at a much more profound level.

We see, then, that it is not acceptable for us (at least in the long run) to ask God merely to fix what is broken, heal what hurts, or pull out those painful or humiliating thorns in the flesh. Jesus has some perfecting of his power to accomplish, and our weakness is his workbench—just as his Cross was his Father's. "He was crucified in weakness, but he lives by the power of God." Life is not so much about personal perfection as it is about letting Christ live in us. "Do you not know that Jesus Christ is in you?" (2Cor. 13:4-5). God has mysteries into which He would lead us, but we have to learn how to trust and abandon ourselves to Him absolutely, even while apparently hamstrung by our defects. He has taken everything into account.

So turn the reins over to the Lord. He will meet the insufficiency of your will and efforts with the sufficiency of his grace. Then, because of his loving care for your life and salvation, and despite all appearances (or even agonies), all manner of things shall be well.

❧ Chapter Four:
The Key to the Narrow Gate ❧

That key would be the Cross of Christ, as you surely know. The Cross is alternately embraced and fled by most Christians, for even though we know it is our only hope, we find ourselves—with willing spirits and weak flesh—struggling with a kind of ambivalence about it. If only there were some other way! Jesus had the same thought in the Garden, but He set it aside in favor of his Father's will. If we are willing to carry our crosses as we follow Jesus, we will find that his Cross will carry us—straight to his pierced heart, from which all blessings flow. He wants us to be where He is, and to share his glory. But we must begin by learning to say a very important word...

Learning to Say the Y-word

The word really is one of the simplest words to say, and we do it all the time in various contexts and in various slang renderings. But in certain contexts the word is feared, shunned, or fled from in terror—even though the most important of these contexts is one of love and gentleness. Still, it is a word one dreads to pronounce because of what the implications may prove to be. The y-word, of course, is "yes."

To be sure, there are many contexts in which we rightly refuse to say the y-word. To "just say no" to the many evils offered to us in our promiscuous and thrill-seeking society is surely the best thing to do. But I'm talking about something else here. I'm talking about saying "yes" to what is most noble, most profound in our human life and experience, which for that very reason is most demanding. I'm talking about saying "yes" to God—which is the perfection of saying "yes" to truth, beauty, goodness, virtue, and love.

In some ways it is not hard to say "yes" to God. If He says, "I want to bless you," we say, "Yes!" If He says, "I want to make you strong and peaceful and joyous," we say, "Oh, yes!" And if He says, "I want to make you eternally ecstatic, utterly fulfilled, and forever overflowing with gladness," we say, "YES!!" But when He says, "OK, here's how," and shows us the Cross, we say, "Y-y-y... M-m-maybe... Uh, I-I-don't know about that..."

One of our core problems here is that we're willing to say "yes" to something (happiness, blessings, etc.) but not to some One, the One who sets the conditions to the attainment of these things, or better yet, the One with whom a personal communion infallibly produces all blessings as a consequence thereof. If we want the gifts but not the Giver we will ultimately end up with neither. But if we desire God even to the point of an unconditional "yes" to his will, then happiness will naturally result. Jesus said it best: "Seek first the Kingdom of God and his righteousness, and all else will be given as well."

But let's go a little deeper. I'll give you the benefit of the doubt that you are really seeking God and not just a handout of happiness. There are still levels of "yes" that must be ascended. We can rather painlessly say "yes" to the minimum requirements of sacramental life and whatever it takes to qualify as a card-carrying Catholic. With a fair amount of struggle we may even be able to satisfy the basic requirements of Christian morality. Some may even follow the call to a life designed explicitly and directly to serve and worship God—that may take a near-heroic sacrifice, if one is to live such a life authentically. But there's a deeper level still.

Allow me to employ a little computer terminology here. Sometimes you are given series of options as you are managing files or programs and have to make a decision. Your choices look something like this: No, Yes, Yes to All. We can say "yes" at various levels of love, fidelity, and commitment, but what God is ultimately seeking from us is a "yes to all." This is the deepest level at which we hold nothing back, at which our lives become an oblation to God, at which He is free to do with us as He wills, knowing that our "no's" are now behind us. This is the level at which we embrace the Cross, indeed, at which we come to the point where we *must* embrace the Cross as our only hope, which paradoxically leads us to our ultimate and only joy.

Blessed Charles de Foucauld was a man who said "yes to all." I pray his famous "Abandonment Prayer" daily, but in my own case (true confessions here) I have to amend it a little. Where he says "I am ready for all, I accept all, let only Your will be done in me..." I *pray for the grace* to be ready for all, accept all, etc. I have to be honest with God and myself, for I know that pious veneers don't impress Him in the least. I may not yet be ready and accepting of *all* (since I usually imagine the worst and most drastic interpretation of what that could mean), but I *want* to be. I want to be so surrendered to his will that I am fearless, at peace, ready to walk into the lions' den if that is his good pleasure.

God gives us plenty of opportunities to practice saying the y-word in small ways in our daily lives. It's a school, a training ground for the times when a more difficult "yes" will be required. But no saint has ever made a complaint that his "yes" was ill-advised, that he got less for his "yes" than he bargained for (not that saints bargain at all). We have to get over our tendency to count the cost, calculate the short-term liabilities, or fear the sting of self-sacrifice. It is God we're dealing with here, remember? The Generous Father, the Heart-pierced Son, the Spirit of Love? An unconditional "yes" to God will bring untold (as well as told) benefits, both now and forever.

So don't follow your "no's"; that only leads you away from truth and love, from the God who is Truth and Love. Get proficient through practice at saying "yes." Go even to the deepest level, as the Lord leads you. He knows your capacities (better than you do, I might add, so don't complain if you think He's working you too hard), and He will make your sacrifice of loving obedience fruitful a hundredfold.

Called to... Suffer

I think that most of us would probably have to admit that, even with the joyous inbreaking of Easter grace and glory, life on earth is more or less a continual Lent. I find that while Easter brings hope and the courage to persevere, it doesn't fix all the problems and pains of our lives. On the level of the liturgical year, it seems to work better: we fast and struggle all during Lent, and then, behold, when Easter arrives we can eat freely, wear bright-colored vestments, and sing hymns of glory instead of penitence. The dark sorrows of Good Friday are swallowed up in the bright rejoicing of Easter Sunday.

But daily life is not like that. If you are suffering from say, cancer, on Good Friday, it will most likely still be there on Easter Sunday. The same can be said for any illness or the pains of any injury, whether physical or emotional. If you are an alcoholic during the sorrowful days of Holy Week, you will most likely still be one on the joyful day of Easter. Similarly, all the rest of the daily problems, frustrations, worries, responsibilities and difficulties will remain, and they are there waiting for you after you clean up the dishes from Easter dinner. (Nature is indifferent to the liturgical year as well. Sometimes it is warm and sunny on Good Friday, and cold and rainy on Easter Sunday.)

What are we to make of this? It's a point I've often made: we're still living in the "not yet" of earthly exile. We're not yet in Paradise, not yet dancing about in glorified bodies. The grace of Easter is a foretaste, not a fulfillment, the promise but not the reward. Yet our sufferings in this life are not random, meaningless, or fruitless. They are not something we are supposed to flee while marking time as we ever-so-slowly move toward the end of our exile. Why? Because we are *called* to suffer.

This is spelled out for us in the First Letter of Peter. He describes himself as "a witness of the sufferings of Christ as well as a partaker in the glory that is to be revealed" (5:1). A witness does not necessarily mean an eye-witness, but one who testifies to what he has experienced. The apostles are all witnesses of the Resurrection, though no one saw it happen. But they testify to it because of what the risen Lord revealed to them. Note also that the glory that St. Peter speaks of is *to be* revealed; it is not yet revealed, that is, not yet fully manifested. At the same time—and here is one of the paradoxes of Christianity—he calls himself a *partaker* of this yet-to-be-manifested glory.

But on to suffering. No one likes to suffer or to be punished, even when he deserves it. We rail and rebel against it. But the Apostle silences our complaints. He says not that we ought to pride ourselves on bearing our *deserved* punishments patiently—there's no credit in that—but that we should bear *undeserved* sufferings patiently. "If, when you do right and suffer for it you take it patiently, you have God's approval. For *to this you have been called*, because Christ also suffered for you, leaving you an example, that you should follow in his steps" (2:20-21). This life is perpetual Lent and not perpetual Easter because we are *called to follow in the footsteps of Christ in his sufferings*. This also silences those superficial Christians who say that since Christ suffered for us, we are not supposed to suffer. That obviously contradicts the word of God. He suffered not only to take away our sins, but to leave us an example to follow.

Again, the Apostle reminds us of another difficult duty: to bless those who curse or hate us. "Do not return evil for evil, or reviling for reviling; but on the contrary, bless, for *to this you have been called...*" (3:9). When he counsels us to firmly resist the devil, he reminds us that "the same experience of suffering is required of your brotherhood throughout the world" (5:9). Therefore suffering in this world is not merely inevitable, it is *required*. But it is not without end, and the Lord will show us that He is risen indeed: "After you have suffered a little while, the God of all grace, who has called you to his eternal glory in Christ, will himself restore, establish, and strengthen you" (5:10).

So we see that the call to suffering is part of a double call, the other part being a call to "eternal glory in Christ." You can't choose one and reject the other. It's all or nothing—though if you choose nothing instead of all, you're going to suffer anyway, both here and hereafter, so you might as well accept and respond to the call to suffer in this life, keeping your heart set on the call to glory in the next.

We must realize that the primary mystery of this life is that of the Cross, and the primary mystery of the next life is the Resurrection. God in his mercy sweetens our exile with both the promise and the foretaste of future glory and joy—through the grace and beauty and love He allows us to experience even in this Valley of Tears. But let us not cling to the moments of joy, and fear the times of suffering, for to suffering we have been called. If we accept and consider it precisely as a calling, one that will be fulfilled in the calling to everlasting life, we will count it all joy and become steadfast in our faith, as we await the full manifestation of God's "precious and very great promises" (2Peter 1:4).

Redemptive Suffering

That's a rather misunderstood and even intimidating term, and perhaps could be more clearly expressed some other way, but certainly not as concisely. Of course, Jesus Christ is the only Redeemer, and only his sufferings can take away the sin of the world. But there is still some "redeeming value" (if you will, in a less strictly theological sense) to offering our own sufferings in union with the Lord's.

Many souls cannot be moved or converted by word or example, usually because they have chosen a path contrary to the

Gospel, or because there is some other impediment not of their own making. The Lord wishes to save them, too. But they can only be touched from within by the hidden dynamism of grace working through the spiritual connections within the Mystical Body of Christ. Thus one soul can influence and positively affect another, through the power of the Holy Spirit. It seems that God expects us to pray and offer sacrifices for the salvation of our brothers and sisters, and that He even waits for this before intervening in another's life. This is because God is love and wants to teach us to love as He does, that is, sacrificially. "Offer spiritual sacrifices..." (1Peter 2:5). "Such sacrifices are pleasing to God" (Hebrews 13:16). Loving is giving, offering oneself for the sake of another. Pope John Paul II said that it is only in the gift of ourselves that we discover ourselves and the meaning of our lives. Intercession, therefore, is a commitment of love, an offering of oneself for the good of others, especially for their eternal salvation.

The mystery of offering pain as loving intercession is expressed simply but powerfully by Michael O'Brien in *A Cry of Stone*: "She had loved him well, offering the hurting to Jesus who joined it to his own hurting and poured it like a cascade into Tchibi's hurting so that he no longer hurt so much... Soon he would hurt only a little, and in time there would be no more hurt. Then he too would love, and the rivulets would spill into creeks, and creeks into rivers, and rivers into lakes that spilled into great rivers, and across the wide world all moving waters, all pure water, would pour into the sea which was Love. Yes."

Another author said that Christ did not only offer Himself to the Father *on behalf of* mankind, but *in union with* mankind. The Lord does not save us without our co-operation. We make a difference. That is why St. Paul could say: "I rejoice in my sufferings for your sake, and I fulfill in my own flesh what is lacking in the sufferings of Christ, for the sake of his body, the church" (Colossians 1:24). How could something be lacking in Jesus' sufferings? Christ is the Head, but the Church is his body. We are members of Christ. If we do not offer ourselves to God in union with Him, bear our crosses with Him, then something is lacking, for then there is a withered branch on the Vine. Nothing can diminish the efficacy or perfection of Christ's sacrifice, but what is lacking is the full number of the saved, or the personal application of the fruits of redemption. The more members of Christ who join themselves to Him in self-offering to the Father, the more the Church is healed, purified, sanctified, and its members saved. St.

Paul said his sufferings were for the sake of the Church, so obviously he believed there was some benefit to be gained by the members of the Church through the offering of his own sufferings in union with Jesus. The power of love connects us in ways that we can scarcely imagine.

Dostoyevsky wrote the following in *The Brothers Karamazov*: "Every day and whenever you can, repeat within yourself: 'Lord, have mercy upon all who come before you today.' For every hour and every moment thousands of people leave their life on this earth, and their souls come before the Lord—and so many of them part with the earth in isolation, unknown to anyone, in sadness and sorrow that no one will mourn for them, or even know whether they had lived or not. And so, perhaps from the other end of the earth, your prayer for his repose will rise up to the Lord, though you did not know him at all, nor he you. How moving it is for his soul, coming in fear before the Lord, to feel at that moment that someone is praying for him, too, that there is still a human being on earth who loves him. And God, too, will look upon you both with more mercy, for if even you so pitied him, how much more will he, who is infinitely more merciful and loving than you are. And God will forgive him for your sake."

Suffering in this life is inevitable. Wherever love is required, sacrifices are required. We can help others open to the grace of God and find salvation if we join our prayers, labors, and sufferings to the Lord's, by the hidden means of love in the Spirit. If even one soul finds its way to God through your offering, it is more than worth it.

On Bearing Burdens

St Paul encourages us to "bear one another's burdens" because this will "fulfill the law of Christ" (Galatians 6:2). How are we to understand this? In the most basic sense, and one of which all of us are capable, it simply means to help others in their needs, for Jesus' sake. We can all "be there" for others when they need us, and offer whatever material aid or spiritual consolation it is within our power or charism to give.

But there are deeper levels. In Charles Williams' novel, *Descent Into Hell*, he calls this bearing of burdens "the doctrine of substituted love." He means that one can, on a spiritual level, out of love for another—and in conscious reliance on God's grace—will to experience another's fear or grief or other burden of suffering, and thus help free them from it, provided they believe it can really happen. (This isn't the same thing as psychic "sympathetic suffering," for that generally does nothing to help relieve the original sufferer of his pain.)

Williams calls it "picking up another's parcel," of which they first have to let go. In the case recounted in the novel it was worry and fear. After Pauline agreed to let Peter Stanhope "carry her parcel," we read the following: "Her mind leapt back to Stanhope's promise, and she knew that, whatever the explanation might be, she had been less bothered for the past ten minutes than ever before in any solitude of twenty years... She had promised to leave it with him... she only had to keep her promise... She wouldn't worry; no, because she couldn't worry... She was, then and there, incapable of distress. The world was beautiful about her, and she walked in it, enjoying. He had been quite right; he had simply picked up her parcel. God knew how he had done it, but he had." Not everyone can do this, because not everyone has the capacity for it. But that does not mean that the capacity cannot be developed.

In his book on anxiety, Hans Urs von Balthasar notes the difference between "sin-anxiety" and the anxiety (or angst) of the Cross. The former is the one that plagues most of us, the one that Jesus forbids his followers in the Sermon on the Mount—the one that has its source either in a lack of trust in God, in a culpable psychic or emotional malaise, or in unresolved guilt. One would vainly attempt to glorify sin-anxiety and call it the angst of the Cross (as people often confuse psychological depression with the "dark night of the soul"). There is a vast space between the two: the space of Christian faith, hope, and love. If one cannot rid oneself of sin-anxiety through divine grace and the practice of Christian virtue, one can never reach the spiritual maturity and radical openness of spirit needed to embrace the angst of the Cross and bear fruit thereby.

One can enter into Christ's redemptive sufferings only if one is already immersed in a profound joy, trust, peace, and genuine Christian love. Then he is prepared to bear, with Jesus, others' burdens, and that only insofar as it is the explicit will of God. We can "pick up the parcels" of others through the power of the Cross, once we are free from anxiety and rooted firmly in grace. At this point we are no longer mere servants or disciples of Christ, but friends and lovers. At this point it is no longer we who live, but Christ who lives in and through us.

There's really only one way to advance beyond sin-anxiety, to enter into the joy of grace and love, and to be strong enough to share the Cross of Jesus for the sake of others: "Come to Me... Take My yoke upon you and learn from Me, for I am meek and humble of heart. Your souls will find rest, for My yoke is easy, and my burden is light" (Matthew 11:28-30).

Faithful in Little, Faithful in Much

When the Master returned after having entrusted his servants with various sums of money (talents), those who multiplied his "investment" were granted this blessing: "Well done, good and faithful servant; you have been faithful over a little, I will set you over much. Enter into the joy of your Lord" (Matthew 25:21). The one who hid his talent in the ground, however, was cursed and cast out for being "wicked and lazy." Why? Because there is a spiritual principle involved here, one He'd like to share with us: "He who is faithful in a very little is faithful also in much; and he who is dishonest in a very little is dishonest also in much" (Luke 16:10). If the slothful servant was unfaithful in a simple task entrusted to him, the Master surely couldn't trust him with anything really important, so he could no longer be counted among the Master's servants.

The same principle applies in our own lives. We can't expect to cut corners in small matters, be a little lazy, tell a few "white lies," get a little curious about forbidden things—and at the same time think that when something really serious or important comes up, we'll surely rise to the occasion and do the right thing. It doesn't work that way. Why? Because the way we think and act, even in small things, forms our character in a certain way, perhaps imperceptibly in any particular situation, but if we become habitually unfaithful in little things, we will also be unfaithful in the big ones. Some people think that the prime of life is for making money and engaging in various forms of self-indulgence—they can repent and "get religion" when they are old and unable to enjoy their former pleasures anyway. But if you disregard the commandments all your life, chances are you will not repent in old age, either.

On the other hand, our fidelity in small matters (avoiding scrupulosity, of course) will form our character in such a way that we will also be faithful in greater things. Our lives are composed mostly of a long series of relatively little things, so how we handle them indicates what kind of person we are and how we are likely to handle other things. Ultimately, it is not our accomplishments themselves that really matter, but *how the things we do make us who we are*, that is, how what we do forms our character, either as faithful or unfaithful. Do we sacrifice ethical principles for the sake of success? Do we allow the Gospel and the Church to form our conscience in truth and love, in morality and justice—or do we learn all the ways to get an advantage through little compromises? The little ones will soon turn into big ones.

St. Francis de Sales once said: "We shall soon be in eternity; then we shall see how unimportant were all the things of this world, and how little it mattered whether they were accomplished or not." What does it profit someone to gain the world and lose his soul?

Start small. Be faithful in little things. There will come a time when God will entrust you with much. When more is given, more is required in return. On the other hand, he who has (that is, who has been faithful) will be blessed still more. The main thing is not to be unfaithful, even in a little. That begins the moral and spiritual degeneration that ends in the outer darkness. Rather, be a good and faithful servant, and enter into the joy of your Lord.

Cross Purposes

We see so many images of the Cross: in icons and other holy pictures, on churches, around people's necks, and other places as a sort of Christian "logo." It may be that we get desensitized to it, comfortable with it, perhaps even get a little fuzzy about its true purpose. The image of the crucified Christ should make you more *un*comfortable than comfortable, at least at first, until you experience the love that flows out of Jesus' wounds along with his Precious Blood.

What is the purpose of the Cross? Huge volumes, and many, have been written down through the centuries, and probably more are yet to come. Here I just want to take a brief look. The reason for the Cross is that "God so loved the world that He sent his only Son..." (John 3:16). Human sin was the reason that the gate of Paradise was locked, and the Cross is the key that re-opened it. But was God so mad at us that He demanded nothing less than the bloody sacrifice of his own Son to appease his wrath? Was the purpose of the Cross the satisfaction of God's offended honor? Some writers (even saints) have said so, and there is a grain of truth to it, but that is not even close to telling the whole story.

God could have forgiven all our sins with a simple *fiat*, "Let it be done." But if He did that, we might have ended up mistaking Him for a sort of benign divine Administrator discharging the day's duties in a calm and detached manner. But God is a Lover (read the Prophets to discover some of his passion), and nothing short of the utterly complete manifestation of his love would have sufficed. Love is most perfectly manifested in sacrifice (that is why the two-becoming-one sacrifice/ecstasy of married love is an image of divine love), and only a complete and perfect sacrifice would manifest the love of God and communicate his power to forgive, heal, and save. The sacrifice began with the Incarnation, the Son's incomprehensible sacrifice of his eternal divine glory for the sake of becoming a lowly human being like us. The agony and ecstasy of his sacrifice was consummated on the Cross (Latin for "It is finished" is *Consummatum est*). If to suffer for the beloved is the highest form of selfless offering in love, then Jesus had to take human suffering to the limit (and beyond), to pour out his lifeblood fully, that we would find forgiveness in this love, and return to Him with our whole heart. Scripture says not only that He loved us, but that He loved us "to the end" (John 13:1), that is, to the utmost.

Pope Benedict XVI has reminded us that this awe-inspiring and profound mystery of the Cross is not simply good for a reflection on what God has done for us long ago. This very mystery is present to us daily in the Eucharistic Sacrifice, in Holy Communion. He says: "The Eucharist is the memorial of the whole paschal mystery...and the Cross is the tangible manifestation of the infinite act of love with which the Son of God has saved man and the world from sin and death. Because of this, the sign of the Cross is the fundamental gesture of the Christian's prayer. To make the sign of the Cross is to pronounce a visible and public 'yes' to Him who died for us... When we receive Holy Communion we also...embrace the Wood which Jesus with his love has transformed into the instrument of salvation, and we pronounce our 'Amen,' our 'yes' to crucified and risen Love."

That is the purpose of the Cross, yesterday, today, and up to the moment we meet Him face to face and enter his intimate embrace in the Kingdom of Heaven. Then we will know the meaning of everlasting love, and we will glory in the eternal fruitfulness of the Cross of our Lord Jesus Christ.

Fruit of the Spirit and Crucified Passions

Most Christians are familiar with St. Paul's list of the fruit of the Spirit (or at least with a few items on the list). Just to refresh your memory, here it is: "The fruit of the Spirit is love, joy, peace, patience, kindness, goodness, faithfulness, gentleness, self-control" (Galatians 5:22-23). The first thing to notice about this is that these elements are not nine *fruits* of the Spirit, but rather the nine-fold *fruit* of the Spirit (in the original Greek it is singular, as well as in any accurate translation). You can't have a few perfect fruits and simply decline to have a few others. If you are lacking in any, then your spiritual fruit has a rotten spot on it, or is still somewhat sour.

The first three elements of the fruit of the Spirit are probably the ones most people remember. Yes, everyone is all for love, joy, and peace, especially of the superficial variety. Such fruit is rather tasteless, however, even if it isn't rotten. In modern America's insipid culture, love, joy, and peace have been too often reduced to common greeting-card sentiments that don't really require a whole lot from anyone (though if genuine they are quite demanding). What if you were to receive a card that said: "Wishing you a bit of serious self-control during the holidays"? Yet this is just as much a part of the fruit of the Spirit as all the others.

It is clear that St. Paul is not concerned with greeting-card wishes or superficial piety. Immediately after he describes the fruit of the Spirit he says: "Those who belong to Christ Jesus have crucified the flesh with its passions and desires." (See Galatians 5:19-21 for a list of the "works of the flesh.") It is clear, then, those who have crucified the flesh have united themselves to the sufferings of Christ—nailed sin to the Cross—in order to be freed from sin by his grace. This is not merely an option for those who tend to go for that sort of thing. If you belong to Christ, then you must crucify the flesh.

How do you know if you really have crucified the flesh? Obviously you haven't if you are still engaging in mortally sinful behavior. But most of us are somewhere between mortal sinners and saints, and we would perhaps like to see some sort of evidence that we do in fact belong to Christ. It's fairly simple: if you are bearing the fruit of the Spirit, you most likely have crucified (or are crucifying) the flesh, for good fruit can only come from a healthy tree.

The fruit of the Spirit is great material for an examination of conscience. How well (how consistently, selflessly, deeply) do you love—God, other people, and (rightly understood) yourself? Do you manifest joy and experience inner peace? How's your score on patience (probably low for most of us), kindness, etc.? Then, if you really want to crucify the flesh, how well do you practice self-control, in thought, desire, speech, and action? The fruit is one because you are one. We can't allow ourselves to bear good fruit sometimes and rotten fruit at others, for then we must conclude that the tree itself is diseased and may need some radical surgery. The various elements are all meant to work and grow together, so we have to pay attention to them all. If you are kind but not patient, your fruit has not matured. St. James says that if you break one of the commandments, but not them all, you are still guilty, because it is the same Person who has given each of the commandments, and any individual offense is not excused merely because it isn't a multitude of offenses. The same Person has been offended.

So let's hope and pray that the (near) future will find us bearing the fruit of the Spirit and crucifying the flesh. After all, you want to be found to belong to Christ Jesus, don't you?

Punished—For Now

I hope I'm not scaring you with this title, but it's time to look at an issue that most people these days discount, undoubtedly to their spiritual peril. The idea of a God who punishes sin seems to have flown out of the Church when the Vatican II windows were opened. But a rejected idea does not mean the reality behind it ceases to exist.

Too sharp a distinction is often made between the God of the Old Testament and the God of the New, as if they were two different Gods. The Old Testament God is a punishing God and the New Testament God is a loving, merciful God, they say, so we can discard those archaic images of inexorable divine judgment. It is true that you can find numerically more expressions of divine wrath in the Old Testament, but you can also find much tenderness there. On the other hand, you will also find the wrath of God in the New Testament.

"When Israel was a child, I loved him... I drew them with human cords, with bands of love; I fostered them like one who raises an infant to his cheeks... My heart is overwhelmed, my pity is stirred..." (Old Testament God, Hosea 11:1-8). "Then in anger his master handed him over to the torturers until he paid back everything. So will my heavenly Father do to you, unless you forgive…" (New Testament God, Matthew 18:34-35). So, it's the same God in both: loving by nature, severe when circumstances demand it.

Why, then, have we decided that Jesus and his Father are merciful and that other God is harsh and vindictive? Sure, Jesus revealed God as a loving Father, and even sacrificed Himself out of love for us. But the divine nature hasn't changed just because now there is a Jesus. There's still no free pass for sin: "Whoever disobeys the Son will not see life, but the wrath of God remains upon him" (John 3:36, the same chapter in which we read: "God so loved the world…"). I could overload you with more citations, but I think you get the point.

There's a description of God in Psalm 99 that seems to hold together the two sides of this divine coin. I used to have some difficulty with this, but I don't anymore: "For them you were a forgiving God, yet you punished all their offenses." We seem to want forgiveness to mean merely looking the other way, saying everything is OK without any honest accounting. And somehow punishment (or correction, or discipline) seems to be little more than a vindictive demand for the satisfaction of justice. But both of those are wrong. So is the image of God (explicit or implicit) as a benign old Grandfather who sits in his rocker saying, "There, there, everything's OK; I wouldn't hurt a fly."

Punishment and forgiveness are both bound up in the mystery of the Cross. There is no punishment we could endure to atone for a single sin. We are utterly incapable, so we would not be able to satisfy divine justice by any sort of punishment or discipline from God that He may require. We received forgiveness because Jesus offered Himself as a sacrifice, enduring all that was due to us, atoning for every sin ever committed. Therefore God doesn't punish our offenses as a way for us to atone for them; He does it for didactic and therapeutic purposes—because He loves us.

You see, we have a lot of lessons to learn, and our tainted nature tends to resist the path of righteousness and hence needs constant instruction and correction. This our Father graciously supplies, though sometimes it is in the form of a punishment. Certain "punishments" are administered not directly by God but as a result of the nature of things or the structure of society. If you jump off the roof of your house, you will likely break some bones; if you rob a bank, you will likely get caught and go to prison; if you commit sodomy, you will likely contract AIDS or some other related disease (yet other punishments may be forthcoming); if you have an abortion, you will likely suffer physical and emotional (and definitely spiritual) harm. Probably you who are reading this rarely, if ever, do any of those things. But there are a host of smaller sins that we commit all the time which, even though atoned for by Jesus (God is a God who forgives), require that we bear the fruits of repentance and accept divine discipline. "The anger of God I accept," cries the prophet, "for I have sinned against Him." Yet once we acquiesce to God's judgment, "He will bring me forth to the light; I shall behold his deliverance" (Micah 7:9).

Remember this important passage from Hebrews: "Do not regard lightly the discipline of the Lord, nor lose courage when you are punished by him. For the Lord disciplines the one whom he loves, and chastises [literally, scourges!] every son whom he receives" (12:5-6). So rather than deny that God punishes—thinking that He somehow has evolved from a strict God to a lenient one, a punisher to a forgiver—let us simply embrace the truth: He is a merciful Father who, out of love for us and concern for our spiritual well-being and salvation, has recourse to punishments, corrections, and whatever it takes to help us learn the lessons of life that are essential to our lasting happiness. Easy forgiveness without clearly-felt correction may not reach deeply enough into our hearts and minds to effect the required change. We must not take the horror of sin or the gift of divine mercy lightly. God intends that we be fully aware of what we have done and the price of the atonement thereof. If we just say, "Sorry about that!" and dance off happily, without having felt the painful reality of sin in our hearts and our very bones, chances are we won't learn our lesson and won't think twice before offending Him again. But thus we flirt with blasphemy.

To accept that God may be disciplining us because of our sins, even if we have repented and received forgiveness, is not to have a false or negative image of God (you'd have to deny practically the whole of Scripture to assert that). The authors of the Wisdom Books of the Old Testament are always saying that if a wise man accepts reproof, discipline, and correction, he becomes wiser still. For everything that comes from God bears good fruit—if we allow it. If it is *God* who punishes, then it is a blessing, for God is love. We can reduce our confusion and anxiety over the events and sufferings of our lives if we simply accept that we are in God's hands, and that even his punishments are advancing our salvation.

But we have to co-operate; we have to say "yes" and prove that we are learning our lessons. If we're on the way to salvation we'll only be punished for now. Next I'll have something to say about those who are punished forever—quite a different state of affairs.

Punished—Forever

We must go even deeper now into the mystery of divine punishment, but again, it does us no good to try to deny it. Better to learn the hard truth now, when we can do something about it, than when it's too late, and we can't.

From reading the previous reflection, some could get the impression that since Christ atoned for our sins, our salvation is thereby automatically assured, though we might have to be taught a few painful lessons in the meantime. That sounds too much like the erroneous "once saved, always saved" idea put forth by some Christians. But Scripture makes it clear that we have to endure to the end if we are to be saved—enduring in faith, hope, and love, in obedience to the will of God, which alone is the way to salvation. It's true that we ought to have confidence in God's mercy, but confidence is not the same as presumption.

So let's look briefly at what happens when God's therapeutic punishments go unheeded, when we don't learn our lessons, persevering in sin and refusing to repent. God will do everything He can to bring us to salvation. He already cleared out the biggest obstacle—our absolute banishment from Paradise due to sins for which we are essentially and radically unable to atone—by sending his Son as a sacrifice for our sins, reopening Paradise to all who would believe and follow Him. But during the span of our earthly lives, that work of believing and following has to be accomplished. Part of that work involves the divine discipline or temporal punishments that open our eyes and help us to know and do God's will, that we may change whatever needs to be changed—with the help of grace—so that we may be found fit for the Kingdom when Jesus returns in glory to judge the living and the dead.

But what about that atonement for every sin? How can we lose our souls if all our sins are already atoned for? Since Christ's sacrifice was not some mechanical act that produces a pre-determined or universally-guaranteed result, we have to choose to *accept* his sacrifice, allow it to mark our lives, that is, we must personally appropriate his gift, for He wishes to grant it personally to each of us. If we do not say "yes" to the atonement of our sins, then that atonement will not apply to us personally, even though it is objectively available to the whole world.

Therefore I submit the following, rather speculative, explanation (you may not find this in the Catechism, but just think about it and discern for yourself). The question is often raised why the damned have to be punished *eternally*, when, say, a few billion years of torment ought to suffice. Well, look at it this way. Those who die in a state of unrepented mortal sin have willfully cut themselves off from God, have spurned his repeated offers of mercy and hence of salvation, and have therefore *rejected the atonement of their sins* that Christ accomplished on the Cross.

Man is utterly incapable of atoning for sin; only the God-Man could do it. So the punishment of the damned may perhaps be understood like this: since they have rejected Christ's atonement for their sins, they now have to do it themselves, as it were. Hell is being forever burdened with your own sins, knowing—all too late—that Christ was willing to take them all away and receive you into Paradise, but you said NO. The damned have to bear intense sufferings for their sins, but all eternity won't suffice for it—try as they might, human beings cannot atone for their own sins—yet they still have to stay in Hell until their sins are atoned for. You can't enter Heaven if you are still in your sins. That's why Hell lasts forever.

That's also why *eternal* punishment has such a different character than *temporal* punishment. God's punishments in our lives are actually graces, helps, instructions, and purifications, but none of that applies in Hell. Hell's punishments are just that—punitive; they cannot be remedial or therapeutic. That time is past. The definitive rejection has been made toward God (God doesn't reject us; He just accepts the consequences of our freedom, even if we use it to permanently reject Him). Now all that remains is the impossible task of suffering for one's sins, which will never result in atonement.

So let us soberly examine our lives. It's not sufficient that we once make a profession of faith and then live in sin, blithely talking of God's mercy but ignoring the better part of Scripture. "Do not be deceived; God is not mocked," says the Apostle. "Whatever you sow, that you will also reap" (Galatians 6:7). He goes on to say that only by sowing according to the Holy Spirit will we reap eternal life.

Let us also be willing to accept divine punishments now, so we don't have to endure them forever. Life is not to be taken lightly or carelessly, even though we are called to live in joy and gratitude. Christians are happy and thankful that they've been warned beforehand! We are then to bring the Good News of salvation to others, so that they do not waste and destroy their lives and have to hear the Bad News of damnation. The choice is ours; God has done and is doing his part. God does not desire the death of a sinner, but that he repent and live—so say "yes," repent, endure to the end, and be saved!

The Next Level

Hopefully by now you have come to a greater understanding and acceptance of the presence of the Lord in our lives that manifests as necessary correction and even therapeutic punishments for our failures to be faithful to his will. Now we have to go a step further and see things in the most profound and positive light.

Jesus Christ "bore our sins in his body on the tree, that we might die to sin and live to righteousness" (1Peter 2:24). Bearing our sins means not only "absorbing" them in Himself to neutralize their evil, but experiencing the penalty or punishment for them. The punishment that would last all eternity for us was concentrated in the body and soul of Christ for a relatively short time. When we today are required to endure any sort of divine chastisement because of our sins, it is not only instructive or purifying: it can also be granted to us as a share in Christ's own sufferings for the same sins.

We have first to realize that all suffering has some relationship to sin. It is true that some people suffer innocently, that is, not as a consequence of their own sins (little children, for example). And it is not always easy or even possible to connect one's suffering with a particular sin. Yet it remains true that the only reason there is suffering in the world is because there is sin in the world. There was no suffering in Paradise before the fall. But there has been ever since, and it is given in the Book of Genesis as a curse because of sin. "Suffering cannot be divorced from the sin of the beginnings, from what Saint John calls the 'sin of the world,' from the sinful background of the personal actions and social processes in human history... one cannot reject the criterion that, at the basis of human suffering, there is a complex involvement with sin" (Pope John Paul II, *Salvifici Doloris*).

So the fact that we suffer at all—whether it be a divine discipline, or simply a result of causes built into the nature of things, or the result of other circumstances beyond our control—still has some relation to sin, which is at the root of the "fallenness" of this world. That means that you and I do not suffer innocently as Christ did on the Cross. Yet God in his mercy gives us the opportunity to make even his chastisements fruitful for us, and for those for whom we may offer our sufferings.

Since God laid on Jesus the iniquity of us all, and since *He* was wounded for *our* transgressions, bruised for *our* iniquities, and upon *Him* was the chastisement that makes *us* whole (see Isaiah 53:5-6), the penalty for our sin was transformed into the sacrifice of our redemption. Thus the meaning of suffering has changed. "In bringing about the Redemption through suffering," writes Pope John Paul, "Christ has also raised human suffering to the level of the Redemption. Thus each man, in his suffering, can also become a sharer in the redemptive suffering of Christ."

We don't really have to deal with the issue of whether we suffer innocently or not (and hence whether or not our sufferings are worthy to be united to Christ's), because we are all guilty and hopelessly in arrears. But the gift of God in Christ is that, having made Christ's suffering the means of our redemption, all further sufferings of mankind can be elevated to a new and fruitful level. The Pope continues: "The Redeemer suffered in place of man and for man. Every man [henceforth] has his own share in the Redemption. Each one is also called to share in that suffering through which all human suffering has also been redeemed." All human suffering has been redeemed, i.e., carries the potential for great spiritual fruitfulness—if accepted as such through faith and love for Christ, who loved us and gave Himself for us (see Galatians 2:20). Therefore even what we suffer from divine punishments—administered as discipline or to help us learn life's lessons and avoid future sins—can share in the redemptive power of Christ's sufferings.

That is a great gift, so St. Paul could say to the Philippians: "It has been *granted to you* that for the sake of Christ you should not only believe in him, but also *suffer for his sake*" (1:29). This brings what may have been our rather reluctant acceptance of the discipline of the Lord to a higher level. From the irksome daily annoyances to the most intense pain we may be called to endure, "all human suffering has been redeemed," so we should be willing to offer it to God in union with Christ, grateful that He has given it a power, a value, and a meaning far beyond what it has in itself. Nothing we suffer is useless, nothing is wasted, if we choose to unite it to the redeeming sufferings of Christ.

Uniting our sufferings (regardless of their cause) to those of Christ is an act of faith and love, and only through this act are they spiritually beneficial and powerful. To paraphrase the Pope from the same Apostolic Letter: Faith enables us to know the love that led Christ to the Cross. And if Jesus loved us by suffering and dying for us, then with this suffering and death He lives in those whom He loved in that way. He lives in us. And Christ thus unites Himself to us to the degree that we, conscious of this through faith, respond to his love with our love.

We've now come a long way from merely resigning ourselves to the necessary and inevitable "punishments" of God which we suffer. Guilty and deserving of much more than He imposes on us, we still are granted further gifts by being allowed to increase the value of our sufferings by uniting them, through our faith and love, to those which secured our redemption. "Christ has led us into his Kingdom through his suffering. And also through suffering, those surrounded by the mystery of Christ's Redemption become mature enough to enter this Kingdom." Amen.

Shall I Not Drink the Cup?

When Peter suddenly sliced off the unsuspecting ear of Malchus the slave in Gethsemane, Jesus reproached him: "Put your sword into its sheath; shall I not drink the cup which the Father has given me?" (John 18:11). What is this "cup" that the Father had given Jesus? We know it refers to his passion, but why a cup?

This image has been used frequently in Scripture, usually referring in some way to one's allotted portion or destiny, either for weal or for woe. Thus we find a scorching wind as the allotted cup of the wicked, and the Lord himself as the portion and cup of the righteous. There's a cup of salvation and a cup of wrath, a cup of consolation and a cup of judgment. We find a cup of blessing and a cup of dismay, a cup of the Lord and a cup of demons. The most precious cup is that of the New Covenant in the Blood of Christ.

Jesus' allotted cup was his passion and death (we often hear of "tasting" death in the Scriptures), and ultimately his resurrection. The first taste of this cup was that of suffering, and this image turns up several times in the Gospels. When James and John wanted the places of honor in the Kingdom of Heaven, Jesus asked them: "Can you drink the cup I shall drink?" Having no idea what He was talking about, they said they could. Then He prophesied that indeed they would, but it would not come to pass until they had been filled with the Holy Spirit. Before that time, they would not have the courage to suffer with or for Him.

The cup Jesus had to drink was a cup no one else could, except as a small share in his. For Jesus had to drink the cup of the suffering and sin of all mankind, and then pour out his own blood on the Cross. The cup of God's wrath that the prophets declared was reserved for the wicked was deferred, for now it was to be given to the sinless Lamb. "All the wicked must drain it," said the psalmist, to the full measure of their sins. So horrifying was this cup that it even daunted the Son of God for a brief moment in Gethsemane. "Take this cup from me!" He cried to his Father in agony. But deeper than his fear of torture and his loathing of sin was his love and obedience toward his Father. So He chose to do his will. He Himself would drink the cup that was justly reserved for sinners. By the time Judas and the mob had apprehended Jesus, his courage was restored. When Peter tried to spare Him the cup with brandished sword, Jesus responded that He was nevertheless going to drink it.

We tend to choose the consoling cups, the peace and the blessing. We readily drink from the Eucharistic chalice, the sweet Wine of divine love and grace. But we tend to flee from the cup of suffering, as the disciples deserted their Master in the garden. We have to realize, though, that life brings a mixed cup for us to drink, sometimes bitter, sometimes sweet. But since it is from the hand of the Father, we must drink it all, for it is our allotted portion. Sometimes it is our just punishment; sometimes it is an unexpected blessing. But let us go forth with steadfastness and trust, accepting the cup that the Father gives us in the various times and circumstances of our lives.

Whether it is unto suffering or joy, it is still the cup of salvation, for God desires the salvation of all, and He works all things toward that end. Our willingness to accept what the Lord sends or permits will strengthen our character and increase our courage and devotion. So take up the cup of salvation and call upon the name of the Lord. In the end, we'll see how both the bitter and the sweet will be transformed into one great cup of blessing at the eternal banquet in the heavenly kingdom.

Not Happiness But...

After reading a biography of Alexander Solzhenitsyn (*Solzhenitsyn: A Soul in Exile*, by Joseph Pearce), I was quite impressed with his vision and conviction. He is a man seeking, both intellectually and spiritually, the most profound awareness of what it means to be a human being, on many levels of life—political, cultural, spiritual. He speaks out against what threatens the dignity and nobility and true freedom of our humanity, and he has suffered much for standing against the prevailing winds of a shallow, self-absorbed consumer society.

He said something that he admitted would be considered, in the modern world, "something strange, something almost insane." Yet it is a bombshell, and it jarred me into a more awakened state. It is extremely simple, perhaps almost a truism for people who seriously follow the Lord, yet it is outrageous to many: "the goal of Man's existence is not happiness but spiritual growth." Go back and read that again. Simple. Simple as dynamite.

How dare he tell modern man that his goal is not happiness! Sure, everyone wants to be happy, there's nothing evil in that, but the kind of "happiness" that most people seek will actually *deprive* them of spiritual growth, while true spiritual growth will produce the only happiness worth the dignity of man.

He's telling the world that there is something more important than feeling good, more important than living in luxury, more important than making the fulfillment of one's needs and desires the goal of life. To discover one's spiritual nature, one's capacity for courage, self-discipline, and for embracing truth and inner freedom even at the price of much suffering, and to learn the profound lessons of life which alone make it truly worth living—all this is infinitely more important than the "happiness" hawked by the mass media, for which they demand that we barter our better judgment and all that is most noble in our souls. The illusion of happiness through immediate gratification is coveted and pursued by the mindless masses of a high-tech, low-culture society. But modern-day prophets like Solzhenitsyn stand up and say that man's moral greatness consists in, among other things, "standing before the things which are temptations to him and showing himself able to overcome them."

How often do we find (if we are paying attention) that even in our daily lives we are ruled by self-interest? We seek our own advantage, our own happiness, in the choices we make, we habitually assess persons and situations according to their effect on *us*, and we judge our day a success if we end up feeling happy or if we gained some advantage. Do we ever ask ourselves if, in the decisions of the day, we chose spiritual growth over happiness, if indeed it came down to that?

One reason we don't choose spiritual growth (and here I don't mean in the abstract—"Oh sure, I'd like to grow spiritually") is because it means denying ourselves, taking up our crosses and following Jesus. The way of spiritual growth is the way of the narrow gate, but it is the only truly meaningful way to live your life—and not just meaningful (that term can be ambiguous), but manifestly fruitful in blessing others and preparing for the fullness of life to come.

For Solzhenitsyn, the path to spiritual growth was "repentance and self-limitation." He wrote the following about spiritual growth in the context of freedom and on the level of society, but it has its applications to personal spirituality as well: "Here is the true Christian definition of freedom. Freedom is *self-restriction*! Restriction of the self for the sake of others! ...this principle diverts us—as individuals, in all forms of human association, societies, and nations—from *outward* to *inward* development, thereby giving us greater spiritual depth... If in some places this is destined to be a revolutionary process, these revolutions will not be like the earlier ones—physical, bloody, and never beneficial—but will be *moral revolutions*, requiring both courage and sacrifice, though not cruelty—a new phenomenon in human history..."

It should be clear that such a development toward spiritual depth through courageous self-sacrifice is far from the agenda of the "if it feels good, do it" crowd. What will our lives mean—both now and in view of the day we stand before God—and what will be the judgment of the time granted us on earth to live as images of God, if we only live for ourselves, for passing pleasures and ephemeral "happiness"?

To live a life in preference of spiritual growth and all it requires does not mean the renunciation of all legitimate recreation, simple pleasures, family joys, etc., for these too are blessed by God. But we have to be clear on what is the goal of our lives, and what are the means we employ to attain it. If we seek first the Kingdom of God, Jesus told us, everything else we need will be graciously given. But if we run after the things the unbelievers run after, we will not only ultimately come up empty in human satisfactions, we will be found unworthy of that for which we were created—and we will be eternally frustrated and miserable. Better to practice a little self-denial now, seeking to know the will of God and to do good to others as we grow in the wisdom of the true meaning and goal of life, than to seek happiness at all costs and thus to degrade our own humanity. Self-seeking dulls spiritual awareness, but the wisdom of "repentance and self-limitation" sharpens it, and opens the door to deeper self-knowledge and spiritual growth.

I'm really just scratching the surface here. We have to reflect on these matters carefully and at length, and make the necessary changes in our perspectives and behavior. Our attention to spiritual growth today will ensure a joy that no one can take from us, beginning now but fulfilled only when our humanity is fully revealed in that of the One who became man in order to enable us to live with God.

Take Your Cross, Find Your Life

I've been writing quite a bit here about the Cross, that inescapable monument to divine and sacrificial love, universal reconciliation, human hope—and the inexorable demands of a God who will stop at nothing until we are eternally secured in his life-giving and all-captivating embrace.

Let's go again to the Gospel. In the tenth chapter of Matthew, I notice that Jesus says if we love parents or children more than we love Him, we are not worthy of Him—there's a good point for your examination of conscience! And here's another: "He who does not take his cross and follow Me is not worthy of Me" (v. 38). Now we know that in an absolute sense, no creature can ever be worthy of God, but Jesus is speaking in a different sense (just like He often does in the Book of Revelation, where He does say some people are worthy). So, in a relative sense, our obedience and faithfulness to the will of God, which is a fruit of his grace in us, can make us worthy of Christ and his Kingdom.

The implication above is that one who *does* take up his cross and follows Jesus *is* worthy of Him. But this entails a whole life of purification, perseverance, and dogged fidelity to the One who calls us to a joy and fulfillment beyond all comparison with our sufferings in this valley of tears. The Lord gives us a general and succinct maxim for cross-bearing unto worthiness: "He who finds his life will lose it, and he who loses his life for my sake will find it" (v. 39). These verses, by the way, are part of the Gospel reading for the Sunday of All Saints (in the Byzantine liturgical calendar), so this is how the Church views the way to sanctity.

A common excuse for immoral, irresponsible, or otherwise self-serving behavior—be it in adolescence or mid-life—is that one is trying to "find himself." But this kind of self-absorbed quest usually ends in quite the opposite way, for the Lord warns that such self-seeking will end up with the loss of the only thing that really matters: one's immortal soul. Perhaps if someone would ask me what my goal is, I could say, as a Christian, that I'm not trying to find myself but to *lose* myself.

But how is it that Jesus wants us to lose our lives in order to find them? First of all, we have to notice that He said we are to lose our lives *for his sake.* That excludes all kinds of imprudent, negligent, and self-destructive behavior, and centers our quest to lose ourselves wholly on the will of God. One translation, which is literally inaccurate, but which does help somewhat with understanding the meaning of the passage, reads "he who loses his life for my sake discovers who he is." So there's something about taking our crosses and following Christ that enlightens us as to our true identity, and hence the meaning and destiny of our lives.

But something has to be lost in the process, and this is something that the Cross prunes away from us. We have to "lose our lives," that is, live no longer for ourselves but for Him who died and rose for our sake (see 2Cor. 5:15). And we have to do that not in theory or pious sentiment, but in all the practical details of life. There's something about the self-denial and even the suffering that taking one's cross entails, which teaches us lessons that cannot be learned in any other way. Alexander Solzhenitsyn describes as one of the defining moments of his entire life his arrest and subsequent imprisonment in Soviet gulags—because it was only through this harsh, self-stripping experience that he finally learned the truth about himself—he had been somewhat egotistical and intellectually proud—and the truth about the radical evil of the Communist system—he had been a fervent communist. Despite the severe suffering, he later looked upon that experience with a certain gratitude, because in losing his life he found it, discovered his true identity and recovered his faith, which he had abandoned for the communist illusion. He learned the lesson of "profit from loss."

We may never be put to such a terrible test, but we have to continually remind ourselves that we are here to "lose our lives," to relinquish our self-centered vision of life, to learn to serve and to be always available to do the will of God, convenient or not. If we are always trying to find ourselves we will become absorbed in ourselves and eventually become quite good at deceiving ourselves—with the end result that we lose the very thing we sought in the first place. The better part is to take up our cross and follow Jesus, losing our lives for his sake, so as to find them back in Him, with his image in us fully restored. And then, guess what? Having discovered who we really are by (sometimes painfully) discarding who we really are not, we will discover that He finds us worthy of Him...

✌ Chapter Five:
Loving in Truth and Truthing in Love ✌

Truth and love ought to be things that everyone wholeheartedly seeks, supports, and practices. Most people don't pride themselves on deception and hatred. Yet we find today that many people don't agree on these fundamental elements of human living and relating. Truth is relativized, love is trivialized or degraded. To whom then shall we turn? To the One who has the words of eternal life—the One who is Truth, who is Love.

Truthing in Love

There is a lot of talk these days, and even some heated arguments, about truth and love. The champions of truth are without love, their opponents aver, and those who speak only of love are told that they ignore truth in order to embrace a fuzzy, sentimental brand of love that isn't really love at all.

So who's right? It's not a simple matter of right and wrong. In such debates, it is rare that one side would be wholly right and the other wholly wrong. So let us lovingly try to discover the truth.

Truth and love are not options for us to choose when we are deciding how to live, to believe, and to relate to others. Both are equally essential. Truth without love is tyranny, and love without truth cannot be genuine, because love and falsehood are mutually exclusive. We can't even do right by accepting some disproportion between the two. We can't be 60% for truth and 40% for love, or 30% truth and 70% love. We have to be *all* truth and *all* love!

This is a daunting feat for fallen humans, but the saints did it rather well. We ought to look especially to Jesus and his Mother as ideals. St. Paul gives us an appropriate expression for this most genuine Christian way of being. The passage I'm referring to (Ephesians 4:15) is usually translated "speaking the truth in love" or, somewhat more accurately, "doing the truth in love." But the literal translation is simply "truthing in love." Since "truthing" isn't a proper English word, the translators gave us the next best thing.

But I prefer "truthing" because it covers everything: speaking, doing, *living* the truth in love. Christians are the ones who are supposed to go about truthing in love. We *must* speak the truth as written in the Gospel and proclaimed by the Church, even if it causes some pain or distress to those who hear (those are signs that they need the grace of repentance). But we cannot use the truth as a weapon of self-righteous superiority, taking pride in shaming others by having bettered them with a more cogent argument.

On the other hand, when we say we love others or have compassion for them, yet refuse to bring the truth to them on the pretext that it might upset or trouble them, we are doing them a grave disservice. Sometimes the failure to speak the (sometimes hard) truth to those we love can result in damage to or even the loss of their souls. How is that love? It is then nothing more than mushy cowardice.

St. Paul continues his exhortation: "...truthing in love, we are to grow up in every way into Him who is the head, into Christ..." So, if we're going to be "loving truthers," we have to grow up! We have to mature by the grace of God so that we know how to place equal value on truth and love, for one cannot exist without the other. We have to learn, in the Holy Spirit, when and how to speak and act in such a way that both truth and love are equally served, and thus that God's will is done. Only then will we be truthing in love, and loving in truth.

Who is Truth?

Nearly 2000 years ago, Pontius Pilate immortalized himself as the Patron Sinner of all relativists. He acquired this dubious distinction by uttering his infamous question: "What is truth?" The problem was, he asked the wrong question. He should have asked instead, "*Who* is truth?" for the Answer was standing right before him.

Pope Benedict XVI has lamented the "dictatorship of relativism" in modern society. The very existence of objective truth is dismissed in many intellectual circles, and this attitude trickles down to the average person, who thus confuses truth with subjective preference or feeling. It is rather arrogant (to say the least) for people today, who are the latest of the latecomers in the history of the universe, to think they can decide for themselves what is true. "True," in most cases, usually means what suits them at the time, or perhaps it is identified with the majority decisions of fellow relativists.

But God has spoken, and when God speaks the universe must listen. It can try to turn a deaf ear, but it will not succeed forever. The Word that God spoke was incarnate in our Lord Jesus Christ, who said: "I am the Truth" (John 14:6). Truth is ultimately a Person, not a formula or an abstraction, still less an opinion or a collection of data or ideas subject to human manipulation. If a word, an idea, a teaching, can be rightly considered true, it is because it corresponds to the One who is the Truth. That is why we have to pay very close attention to the words of Christ. These are the words of God, for He is the Word of God. Here is where we find the truth. Christ is foreign to nothing that is true, and nothing that is true is foreign to Christ. But to be known as truth, everything must find its source, its resonance, its fulfillment, in the Incarnate Word of God.

Admittedly, in the words available to us in the Gospels, we do not find direct answers to all of our pressing 21st-century issues. That is why Jesus, having ascended to his Father, sent us the Spirit of Truth, "who will guide you into all the truth" (John 16:13). The Holy Spirit guides the Pope, and all the leaders of the Church who are in union with him, to proclaim the truth to the world. The truth that is proclaimed is not "the Pope's truth," as opposed to "your truth" or "my truth." Those are the categories of today's deceptive relativism. The truth is one, for God is one, and what the Church proclaims is what God has revealed. The Spirit of Truth guides our hearts and consciences as well, and we will know for sure that we have the Spirit if our conscience does not reject or refute divine revelation.

We ought to be grateful that we don't have to grope in the darkness in the search for truth. Even though truth is, in a certain sense, limiting, for it draws the line beyond which is falsehood, it is at the same time liberating, because Jesus, who is the Truth, sets us free. We become free from the darkness of ignorance and of evil, and free for the abundant life of joy and blessedness that Christ came to give—here, and especially hereafter. He makes us secure in the truth of his words, the truth of his very being as the eternal Word of God.

The issue of truth is essential to our salvation. Among those who are denied entrance into the Kingdom of Heaven are "all those who love and practice falsehood" (Revelation 22:15). The words of Christ are valid forever. He does not swing with the times; He does not follow the latest trends, nor is He evolving into a more enlightened consciousness. He doesn't have to, for "His wisdom made the heavens" (Psalm 136:5). Christ speaks and angels fall prostrate. It is only his stiff-necked people who refuse to hear and believe. "Lo, they have rejected the word of the Lord; what wisdom can be in them?" (Jeremiah 8:9).

God's word is all-powerful, yet He does not condescend to compete with the shrill noises of this world; He doesn't attempt to shout down the garrulous deceivers. But listen carefully, and you will hear. The Truth will reach open hearts, and those who have ears to hear will hear. "Those who trust in the Lord will understand truth, and the faithful will abide with him in love" (Wisdom 3:9).

Do We Really Want to Know?

The Scriptures and the Church teach us about "the life of the world to come," but I wonder if we think about that very much. I think many people take a more or less unarticulated "heaven can wait" attitude, as they go about their busy lives. But what if it's all *true*? What if this life is but a brief preface to the infinite story of our everlasting existence? That is precisely what the Scriptures do teach us, so maybe we ought to investigate it a little more closely.

But people are *afraid* to know, partly because of a generalized fear of the unknown, but also because that knowledge might make it imperative that they change their lives. And many seem to be not ready to do that just yet. Charles Williams captures that mentality well in his novel, *Descent into Hell*, in which he dares to speak what we leave unspoken: "'Grant to them eternal rest, O Lord. And let light eternal shine upon them.' Let them rest in their own places of light; far, far from us be their discipline and endeavour. The phrases of the prayers of intercession throb with something other than charity for the departed; there is a fear for the living. Grant them, grant them rest; compel them to their rest. Enlighten them, perpetually enlighten them. *And let us still enjoy our refuge from their intolerable knowledge*" (italics mine).

But we won't be able to enjoy it for long. Williams continues: "Men were beginning to know, they were being compelled to know;

at last the living world was shaken by the millions of spirits who endured that further permanent revelation." The lively awareness of eternity, of immortal souls, of Heaven and Hell, cannot fail to mark our earthly lives profoundly.

Someone recently sent me a little booklet with a singularly uninteresting title: *An Unpublished Manuscript on Purgatory.* I had heard of it before, but never had any desire to read it. I assumed it would be full of pious scare-tactics, stories of souls who return from purgatory to burn their handprints onto the walls of their intended intercessors (but souls don't have hands). Yet it is not that at all. It is about a soul, a nun, who was in purgatory and was permitted to speak to one of her Sisters in religion and to ask for prayers.

What strikes me about it is the *lack* of scare tactics and pious embellishments. She speaks as do the angels in Scripture: rather tersely and quite to the point, in an utterly no-nonsense style, as if time were pressing and she had to say only what was essential. Her message is clear, serving only to emphasize what the Church has already taught us (if our whole life hasn't been a post-Vatican II one): life is short, eternity is long; if you waste or ignore the graces God is offering you now, you will pay for it later; nothing is more important than loving God and doing his will; all things will quickly pass, except for the life after death; now is the time for detachment, purification, prayer, sacrifice, and charity, for soon it will be too late and you will desperately wish that you had been less selfish and realized that God alone was worth all your love and effort; God is bending over backwards to bless and save you, but you must offer a free response to his love and grace.

You may think that the above summary is rather scary after all, but it is said without drama or intimidation, only as plain and sober fact. Do we really want to know all this? I think we darn well *ought* to want to know, because in this case ignorance is *not* bliss, but could result in precisely the opposite. Maybe you don't want to know, because after you go to work, take the kids to the soccer game, pay the bills, do the housework and weed the garden, you have no time or energy to think of crossing the threshold of eternity and gaining a vision more vast and profound than you could ever imagine. So start by bringing God into every event of your day, asking Him to help you see all things in their proper perspective. You will begin to recognize superfluous or worthless things or activities as such. You will also realize that you need to make some sacrifices; you will have to make some choices that express your faith that the fullness of life is yet to come and that it wholly depends on God and your present relationship to Him.

Let us not flee or play the agnostic when it comes to the knowledge of things that bear on our salvation. The souls who have left this world now see everything *very* clearly. We still wear the blinders of our self-centered or narrow-minded perspectives, held fast in this world and afraid to look toward the next. But if a soul came to you, speaking wisdom from the world of God, would you want to know? Could you afford *not* to know?

His Word is Truth

I came across a rather ill-considered footnote (though typical for modern biblical "scholarship") in a Bible I've been reading. The translation is actually a very good one (RSV), but the annotations suffer, at times, from the "debunking disease" of commentators who have evidently lost a significant degree of their faith. It was an explanatory comment on the holy prophet Elijah's raising to life of a dead boy in 1Kings 17. Here's the comment: "Some have argued that the child was not really dead, and hence that no miracle was involved. This is beside the point. The writer meant to portray a powerful God and a worthy prophet."

Allow me briefly to demolish this argument. Who the "some" are is not indicated. I suppose if I were prone to making ridiculous statements I would hide behind a shield of anonymity as well. How they could know (or think) that the child was not dead, when the text says he was, is sheer (and dishonest) speculation. The boy's mother lamented "the death of my son," and Elijah questioned why God would afflict the woman "by slaying her son." Hard to see how "some" can argue that the child was not dead. The last phrase of that sentence in the comment betrays their agenda: "and hence that there was no miracle involved." They come to the biblical text with an *a priori* disbelief in miracles; therefore miracles must be explained away. If miracles can't happen, then this story that describes a miracle must be interpreted so as to deny the miracle. Again, dishonest scholarship, based on a personal or communal (i.e., the unbelieving academic community) presupposition.

After saying that there was no miracle in the biblical account of the miracle, they assert: "This is beside the point." Sorry, but the miracle is *precisely* the point. This is like what I once said about those who think they can have Christian faith if Jesus' bones were to be found in a grave. They think *that* is beside the point, too! But again, that is the whole point. It's also like what "some" say when they assert that the words of Jesus in the Gospels are not literally his own but what his disciples put in his mouth as they wrote their accounts for the edification of the Church. Weren't the things that He actually *did* say worth writing down? I guess, then, that Jesus must not have said anything noteworthy, and his disciples were better at expressing the revelation of God than He was. (One group of "scholars" actually *votes* on whether or not Jesus actually said certain things written in the Gospels!) I don't see how the sheer idiocy of this approach escapes some otherwise intelligent people.

The commentator goes on to say that the alleged miracle—which wasn't a miracle, and which is beside the point anyway—is "meant to portray a powerful God and a worthy prophet." This comment is lame in the extreme. In what sense is God portrayed as powerful if there was no miracle? And how is the prophet worthy if he is a liar and a charlatan—for he said the child was dead, prayed to God, and returned him to his mother alive? God is only portrayed as powerful if He *did* raise the dead child, and Elijah is only worthy if he is the faithful mouthpiece of God's word and instrument of his power.

We should allow God's word to speak for itself, for his word is truth. I don't deny that some passages are obscure or too profound for a facile interpretation, and hence we need the guidance of the Church to properly understand God's word. What we *don't* need are the speculations of scholars who are either trying to make a name for themselves with "original" or controversial interpretations, or those who have simply lost their faith and are trying to look respectable in the eyes of secular colleagues, or those who really do have an agenda to contradict or dilute the Church's Scripture-based doctrines. If the Bible says Elijah or Jesus worked a miracle, then the burden of proof (and it's a heavy one) is on those who would deny it. Let us read the Scriptures with an attitude of faith and humility: "standing under" them that we may under-stand them, responding to the inspired authors like the woman who received her son from the dead and said to Elijah: "Now I know that you are a man of God, and that the word of the Lord in your mouth is truth."

Grains of Truth

As I've said above, the question of truth is an important one these days. Not only are we faced with distortions of truth in the media, big business, and government, we have still more important questions concerning truths about ourselves and that which has been revealed by God. On the other hand, many are saying there really is no such thing as truth (in any absolute or objective sense, anyway), that truth is only what seems true for us according to our subjective perceptions or preferences.

The entire issue of truth is far too large and unwieldy to treat adequately in a brief reflection, so I will limit myself for now to a few words about religious truth, that is, that which God has revealed for our salvation. Truth is embodied in the word of God, and the word of God is found in Holy Scripture and Holy Tradition. Scripture and Tradition together are the foundation of "the church of the living God, the pillar and bulwark of the truth" (1Timothy 3:15). The Catholic Church, in her self-understanding as the Body of Christ, the Bride of Christ, has declared in her official teaching (*Lumen Gentium*) that the fullness of revealed truth subsists within her. Is the Church trying to say that all truth about everything in found in her? No. The Church knows the parameters of her authority and competence. The Church is simply stating that—since she has faithfully preserved the heritage of Christ and the Apostles—all the means of grace and salvation, and the fullness of God's revelation to man concerning God, man, and our salvation, is to be found in her.

The Church also states in her official teachings that elements of truth can be found in non-Catholic Christian churches and even in non-Christian religions, and does not deny the possibility of salvation to those who sincerely seek God and strive to live a righteous life, insofar as they know what that means (see Romans 2:12-16). Grains of truth have been liberally scattered all over the world.

Yet even within the framework of God's revelation as received and interpreted by the Church, there is room for legitimate variations, emphases, and approaches to the mysteries of God. And here is where we ought to have respect for the various grains within the Church herself. I have read, for example, writings of hermits who insist that prayer in solitude and silence is the only way to God, and I've also read writings of activists who say that solitude and silence have to be set aside for the sake of active compassion and service to the poor and needy, and in this God is discovered. Both possess some grains of the whole truth, but neither has it all, and problems enter in when controversies or even animosities develop between those who insist that their way is the only way. We ought to be working together, supporting one another with contemplative prayer and active labors. We are members of each other in the Body of Christ, as St. Paul says, so the full truth is realized when each member contributes his or her unique gifts and talents for the spiritual and material well-being of the whole Church.

Each of us has our own grain of truth to contribute to the whole. We all ought to be willing to be ground and mixed together like flour for the bread of heaven, a Eucharist offered to God in truth and love, grace and beauty, peace and unity. The grain of wheat must die to itself to bear fruit, said the Lord (John 12:24), and our self-sacrifice in charity and mutual understanding will make it happen. This will be the great revelation of the Last Day for all the faithful, but we are called now to embrace truth where we find it, and at the same time to realize that the Church bears the fullness thereof.

There *is* absolute and objective truth. It comes from the God who is love, who sent his only Son, who in turn said: I am the Truth. And the Church is entrusted with the mission to hand on, interpret, teach, and live the Truth who is Christ. We pray to God in every Divine Liturgy for the leaders of the Church, that they may "rightly impart the word of Your truth." Amen, let the grains be gathered.

Reason Has a Wax Nose

That is a saying of some medieval theologians concerning rational argumentation. It means that if one is clever (or perhaps devious) enough, one can come up with a kind of logic or reasoning that can turn an argument in any direction one pleases. We can be left with a series of endless inconclusive disputes on various issues, as debaters on both side turn reason's wax nose this way and that. This can be somewhat exasperating, and may result in the kind of relativism that Pope Benedict XVI has decried, for people end up refusing even to hear solid arguments but merely say: "That may be true for you, but not for me. I have my own truth." End of rational discourse. This, of course, implies a brand new definition for "truth."

An important remedy that God has given to reason's wax nose is this: Revelation. When God speaks, He is not merely taking one side of a debate. He doesn't have to argue his way to a satisfactory conclusion. He speaks, and his word is truth. Jesus came to reveal definitively the mystery of God, not to engage in endless debates, which is why the Pharisees were indignant (and the common people delighted) that He spoke with authority, "and not like the scribes."

But in the hands of heretics even divine revelation (the Scriptures, at least) can be made to seem to have a wax nose. This is not because the word of God is itself susceptible to manipulation, but because different interpreters assign different meanings to it, and not always with the most honest or noble intentions. Most of the heresies in the history of the Church were based on some sort of misreading of the Scriptures (or at times a failure to acknowledge the divine revelation contained in Holy Tradition).

God has also given us a remedy for that: the *Magisterium*, or teaching authority of his Church. The *Magisterium* firms up the "nose" of Revelation that some would like to turn to wax, and leaves no room for contradictions of essential dogmas—but theological reflection to deepen our understanding of Revelation and application of it to daily life is still fostered. So there needn't be any doubt or confusion (or self-interested, deceptive trickery) concerning what God has revealed for our salvation.

But you know what? There are still many in the Church today that think even the *Magisterium* has a wax nose! Here is where their bad will and rebellion are manifest. God reveals his truth and his will in Scripture and Tradition, and the Church authoritatively interprets and promulgates it, but some go to great lengths to deny or distort it. For example, take the Vatican instruction on the admission of homosexual men to seminaries. In many places, where the response was not outright rejection or mean-spirited protest, we find a number of bishops, priests, canon lawyers, and seminary officials scrambling to find loopholes or ambiguities in the document so that they don't have to obey it. The highest authority in the Church has spoken, so their first approach is to try to justify disobedience to it! Something is rotten at the core of this approach. If they don't understand it (as some of them say) it is because they do not *want* to understand it. The Vatican is making a serious attempt to break up the "gay" network in the clergy and hierarchy, so those with vested interests or agendas are enraged and indignant that someone has finally pulled back the curtain and turned on the light.

There are other churches and communities where doctrine and morality do have wax noses. The Catholic Church isn't one of them (manifest infidelities to her faith and morals notwithstanding). Those whose standard response to the *Magisterium* is rejection or devious re-interpretation of her teachings ought to find a church with a more malleable nose, and then go there. The Church is not meant to be a hideout for morally-challenged rebels, but a sanctuary for those who seek salvation from the living and true God—who speaks the words of truth and life, and isn't interested in clever stunts and mushy reasoning. We see it often in the Scriptures: "I, the Lord, have spoken." To Peter He has given the keys of the Kingdom. And what Peter binds or looses on earth is bound or loosed in Heaven.

Fear of Truth

There's a certain "sickness" going around that can be called the fear of truth. When people fear the truth, they want to get rid of the one who speaks it to them. Thus the prophets and the martyrs were killed. Christ Himself said, "I am the truth." Therefore, He had to die at the hands of those who feared the truth.

There are different kinds of fear of truth. One is found among those whom you might call the "seekers," who always say that they are seeking the truth, but they don't really want to find it—because if they did find it (and if they had any integrity), they would be obliged to embrace the truth. The truth would require them to change their lives. It's much easier to go on seeking but never finding. Then you never have to convert and conform yourself to the truth because you always have this excuse: I'm still searching. Well, eventually you have to find, and start *living* the truth.

The same thing can be said for those who are simply lukewarm or culpably ignorant. They'd rather not know what the Gospel says and what it requires, because if they do they will have no excuse for their sin. They are, in effect, choosing to live in the darkness and turning away from the light, perhaps not realizing how foolish and dangerous a thing that is for their souls. Others fear the truth not because they might have cold feet about embracing it, but because to embrace the truth will put them at some sort of disadvantage. By living a lie, they have some advantage, some economic or political or social advantage—perhaps even ecclesiastical advantage. What comes to mind are the abortion industry, the "gay" movement, corrupt politicians and corporate heads, and the high-profile dissenters in the Church. These are the "men who by their wickedness suppress the truth" (Romans 1:18). They all have a stake, a vested interest, in not embracing the truth—and actually trying to suppress it—because their own agendas are more profitable for building up their egos or their economic or political fortunes if they continue the lie. Therefore they fear and hate those who would unmask them.

Now there's another kind of fear of truth, which I discovered in a book by Jean Vanier, entitled *Drawn Into the Mystery of Jesus through the Gospel of John*. He says that this type of fear is found among those who have grown up in severely dysfunctional or abusive situations, and who learned as children that truth is harsh or painful. Therefore they learned to flee reality for self-protection. Their unfortunate experiences are not their fault, but the answer is not to hide in the darkness, for Christ calls us into the light. Fear of truth can be overcome, and it must, or else one may stay in the darkness his or her whole life, and maybe for all eternity.

Vanier writes both of the truth that we find among the Pharisees in the Gospel and that which we may find in our own lives:

> "They are frightened of Jesus, frightened of reality and truth. They want to get rid of the one who announces the truth and who offers to bring them into reality. They cannot hear the words of Jesus or recognize who He is. They are cemented in fear and in hate. They refuse to see and accept the facts of the miracles of Jesus, because if they did see and believe, then they would have to change their ways.
> "Who are those we refuse to look at, listen to and accept because they make us see our own brokenness in such a way that we would be forced to change our ways? ...We do not want to see our own inner reality, our brokenness and fear. We pretend that everything is all right and that we are all right. Why are we frightened of the truth? Is it because...if we see reality too clearly we will fall into despair?
> "[The conflicts, abuse, or rejections experienced in childhood can make people] hide away in their shell,

and flee from all the pain and from reality. They find a welcome escape in illusions... They cannot or do not want to name the truth... Truth and reality can be too dangerous, too terrible for some people... We can be frightened of uncovering certain truths about ourselves...frightened of the consequences, afraid that we might have to change... We hide behind walls that we have created for ourselves to prevent us from looking directly at the facts, from listening to others...who may reveal to us other truths about life and what it means to be human."

We have to let Christ into our lives, into our infirmities, into our bondage. We must have the courage to hear the truth about God and about ourselves through the Gospel, through the Tradition, and through those whom God puts in our lives to speak the truth to us. The word of divine truth is a two-edged sword, as we read in Hebrews (4:12-13). One edge of this sword is like a scalpel for cutting away the disease of error, self-deception, unhealthy defense mechanisms, and the self-interest that leads us to embrace lies. The other edge is for liberating us from bondage to falsehood and sin, cutting through the fetters that bind our souls to the powers of darkness.

Therefore be not afraid of truth, for Christ Himself is the Truth, and He has the words of eternal life. We are called to be courageous in speaking and receiving and living the truth, following Him who said: "If you continue in my word, you are truly my disciples; and you will know the truth, and the truth will make you free" (John 8:31-32).

The Call of the Gospel: Love

When we speak of love, we are at the heart of the Gospel. In the famous John 3:16 that is emblazoned all over Christianity, as the offer of salvation to those who believe, the reason for our faith and hope is given: "For God so loved the world..." The Gospel is essentially a testimony to God's love for us, as well as a call for us to return that love and then spread it around.

There are many commandments and counsels in the Scriptures, but only one is called "the great and first commandment" (Matthew 22:38). This is: "You shall love the Lord your God with all your heart, and with all your soul, and with all your mind" (other evangelists include: "and with all your strength"). Jesus immediately says that the second great commandment is like the first: "You shall love your neighbor as yourself. On these two commandments depend all the law and the prophets." These commandments of love fulfill the law and the prophets, just as Jesus Himself does in his own person and teaching.

Love is thus meant to be all-embracing, all-pervading, demanding all our attention and effort: *all* your heart, mind, soul, strength. Whatever Jesus said or did (even his severe reproaches of the Pharisees) flowed out of his everlasting love for those He came to save. Jesus does not appear "loving" in the Gospels in the way that many people today are "loving." The word has been terribly abused and distorted almost to the point of meaninglessness in many cases. It is not loving to be blindly or lazily tolerant of evil, to condone sin for the sake of smoothing out conflicts, or to act as if human happiness can be achieved by acceptance of or indulgence in that which jeopardizes one's eternal salvation. That is why Jesus' love is "tough" love: He came to save us, to preach the truth that leads to salvation, and He would do whatever it would take so that we would hear the word of God and keep it—that's how much He loves us. He even gives us extreme examples to show how utterly important it is to prefer nothing to the Kingdom of Heaven: "If your right hand causes you to sin, cut it off and throw it away; it is better that you lose one of your members than that your whole body go into Hell" (Matthew 5:30).

Jesus calls us to love as He loves: loving unto salvation, unto truth and righteousness, not the phony "love" that is emotional excess, lust, misguided tolerance, or any other aberration that contradicts the word of God or endangers one's (or another's) immortal soul. Read St. Paul's magnificent hymn to love in First Corinthians 13 for some practical applications (patience, forgiveness, endurance, etc.), and then remember Jesus' words: "By this all men will know that you are my disciples, if you have love for one another" (John 13:35). Christians who hate or fight or denigrate or condemn one another are a scandal to the whole world and a counter-witness to the Gospel.

To love another is to will the other's good, ultimately to will the other's ultimate good: salvation from sin and the gift of eternal happiness in Heaven. Lesser goods should be willed only insofar as they serve or work toward (or at least do not contradict) the ultimate good. Among the most important "lesser goods" are those which our brothers and sisters need just to survive on this earth: food, clothing, shelter, basic medical care, etc. Christian love is manifest in a special way through sacrificial and compassionate service to the poor. Love and sacrifice are two sides of the same coin. It is a prominent theme in the Gospel: Jesus' preference and love for the poor and for those who are of no account in the empires of man.

To love is one of the most natural and at the same time one of the most difficult things to do. We tend more easily to love those who love us and do good to us, but Jesus says: What credit is that to you? Even sinners do as much (Luke 6:32-36). The call of the Gospel is to love even our enemies, to do good to those who do evil to us, to pray for those who persecute or slander us. This is loving as Jesus loved, for He prayed, "Father, forgive them," as the nails tore through his flesh. He dramatically manifested at that moment these words: "Love covers a multitude of sins" (1Peter 4:8). St. Peter declares at the beginning of that verse: "*Above all*, hold unfailing your love for one another." Indeed, the Gospel is the Good News of love: God's and ours, or better, God's *in* ours.

We need much reflection, probably much repentance as well; there is much to resolve and to change if we are to live as Jesus' disciples and friends. To believe is necessary but inadequate. Faith must work through love, says the Apostle (Galatians 5:6). Love God wholly; love others as Jesus loves. It will take you to the Cross, but it will also take you to Paradise.

The Asceticism of Charity

In reading the ascetical literature of spiritual writers (especially monastic ones) of past ages, one will find much emphasis on corporeal penances and acts of self-denial. Fasting, vigils, and other bodily austerities were understood to be the path to the weakening or taming of the body and hence of the liberation of the spirit. This is true, to a certain extent, despite their platonic misunderstanding of the nature of body and soul and of their relationship. The emaciated, unwashed saint was often held up as the ideal. But something important is missing when the focus of the spiritual life is on bodily renunciations.

"Asceticism" simply means training, such as an athlete would engage in when preparing for some important contest. So it has been understood that severity to the body constitutes a kind of training for the life of the spirit. Again, there is some truth in this, for self-discipline undertaken for Christ's sake will always have some benefit. But there is much more. The Pharisees also fasted and prayed, but they lacked charity and wisdom, so they received only reproach from the Lord.

It is usually easier to fast or pray than to love one's neighbor in practical ways. It is easier to accept some sort of bodily discipline than to, say, forgive or be kind to an arrogant or obnoxious person. So it is not always a great feat of holiness to practice corporal penances. It is often a much greater feat to practice the asceticism of charity.

Not eating does not necessarily make us holy. The demons don't eat, and look where they are. Depriving oneself of sleep is not necessarily sanctifying, either. The demons don't sleep, and that doesn't make them holy. But the demons do not love, and here is where we can enter upon the road to holiness. Neither are they humble, and here again we have an asceticism that can bear much fruit.

The asceticism of charity (and humility) is a deeper kind than that of bodily penance. We ordinarily get enough bodily penance through the illnesses and injuries that we all sustain more or less regularly. Offering these to God without complaint, while making an effort strictly to follow (at least) the fasting prescribed by the Church, is for the average person sufficient bodily penance. The greater work of Christian asceticism is learning to live with others in peace and mutual charity and forgiveness, refusing to judge or condemn, to gossip or hold others in contempt, and being willing to set aside one's own interests or activities for the sake of helping or comforting another in need. Jesus also said that our reward would be great in Heaven if we accepted misunderstanding, revilement and persecution for his sake. How much harder it is to swallow our pride than to refuse to swallow some extra food!

So if you say you cannot be a holy ascetic because you can't fast or do vigils or afflict your body in other ways, take courage, for there is a whole range of ascetical practices within your reach (with the help of God's grace). But if you think you *are* a holy ascetic because of your fasting and vigils, etc., then be aware that you are far from it if you are not actively loving, forgiving, and serving your brothers and sisters. All forms of asceticism are difficult and demanding (and important) in their own way; some bear more fruit than others. Choose the better part, along with St. Paul, who said: "the greatest of these is love."

In the Absence of Knowledge

The asceticism of charity finds a specific application here. What happens, for example, when your spouse or child is expected home at a certain time, and they are still not back an hour later than that, and there has been no call to notify you of any change? Many people would think the worst has happened, or at least would begin to worry. Why is that, when they have not a bit of concrete evidence that anything went wrong? Why think there must have been an accident or some other bad experience instead of the half-dozen other possibilities that bode no evil? There is a psychological principle that goes something like this: in the absence of knowledge or of facts concerning a given situation, the mind will automatically create some scenario to fill the gap—usually a more or less pessimistic or negative one.

What does that have to do with the asceticism of charity? Well, think about it. How often do you judge another person before you have all the facts concerning the issue? How often do you hold people under suspicion based on a hunch or vague feeling about their character or intentions? How often do you think you know how another person regards you, or what he or she is thinking about you? "So-and-so doesn't like me, and so when I say such-and-such to him, he will probably say this, and then I'll say..." And so the self-generated (and usually groundless) scenarios go on.

In many cases charity consists simply of giving the other person the benefit of the doubt, not making any judgments in the absence of knowledge or facts. We tend to assume the worst intentions and motivations in others, but the asceticism of charity would have us assume the best. It really is a type of asceticism, a training, to get ourselves to regard and treat situations and persons differently than we've become accustomed to doing.

We have to question ourselves carefully to see if our speculations or judgments or suspicions have any solid basis in reality and fact. *Why* do we think that someone doesn't like us or is out to get us? *Why* do we attribute base motives to another? *Why* do we assume malice instead of human frailty or an honest mistake? Perhaps we've been hurt or wronged in the past, and so we're "once bitten, twice shy." But everyone has been hurt or wronged in some way at one time or another. We can't let that set the course for our whole life and turn us into pessimistic, fault-finding, untrusting people. Obviously, we also don't want to be so gullible as to be an easy mark for every con-artist, but let's at least begin to trust and give the benefit of the doubt to people we know. The unfounded negative assumptions about others are the first steps toward paranoia, not to mention straying from the Gospel.

It's too easy to fail in charity by creating mental scenarios about other people—or giving their actual words or deeds the worst possible interpretation—and then acting accordingly as if it were the truth. Decide to attribute honorable intentions to others—in the absence of contrary knowledge—and to look for the face of Christ in them. "...think with sober judgment... let love be genuine; hate what is evil, hold fast to what is good; love one another with brotherly affection... live in harmony with one another... so far as it depends on you, live peaceably with all" (Romans 12:3-18). "For the whole law is fulfilled in one word: 'you shall love your neighbor as yourself.' But if you bite and devour one another, take heed that you are not consumed by one another" (Galatians 5:14-15).

The world is already filled with hatred, suspicion, ill will, and malice. Do not feed the flames, but rather take the initiative to be good to others and thus draw goodness out of them; think well of them and thus create an environment in which they are encouraged to think well of you. That doesn't mean we'll never be deceived or betrayed or hurt by another—but if, in the absence of knowledge, we assume the best instead of the worst, we'll be following in the footsteps of Christ and will have his blessing.

Astonishing Love

There has been a lot written in recent years about what they call "Near Death Experiences" (NDEs). I certainly believe in the possibility of such things, because I certainly believe in eternal life after death. But I do question many of them, for they can come from sources that are not God, and hence people can be deceived by them. If someone writes of having a NDE in which they float into some sort of non-judgmental "light" that tells them all is well and to go back to earth and enjoy life, I will find it hard to believe.

But there are some that correspond to what has already been revealed by God about the afterlife, even though we don't have many details in Scripture or Tradition. One thing is clear, however:

there will always be a judgment. And there will always be love. The two are inseparable in an encounter with the true God.

I recently read an article on certain aspects of a book I had read years ago about the NDE of Dr. George Ritchie from Texas. He was "dead" for nine minutes after a serious illness, and he met the Lord Jesus. There are several elements about his experience that resonate with the truth.

The articles states: "When he saw Jesus...it was a far more masculine power than he expected, not the meek image so often presented to us through artwork, and yet at the same time a Presence filled with 'astonishing love.'" It was, in his words, "a love beyond my wildest imagining." We can hardly imagine such a love—since it is beyond imagining!—but we ought at least be aware that it is infinitely greater than anything we have considered or experienced thus far.

Yet "this love knew every unlovable thing about me," Dr. Ritchie said. This is the judgment that goes with the love. He wasn't condemned at that time for his sins, but he learned that they were unacceptable to the God of Love, who calls and enables his children to live in his love and to extend it to others. As scenes from his life passed before him, there was an underlying question: "What have you done with your life? What have you to show Me?" This doesn't mean personal accomplishments or achievements, for when he tried to offer something important that he did, the Lord simply said: "That glorified *you*." He realized through many other scenes of his life how he had indeed served and glorified himself instead of the Lord, how he had not loved as Jesus requires.

The doctor then became afraid. How could he have known? How could he have prepared for this unexpected revelation? The Lord answered: "I told you by the life I lived. I told you by the death I died." Even though this hard truth was announced to him, he still felt only love from the Lord. It is this incredible combination of the uncompromising light of truth with the warm support of love that indicates a genuine spiritual experience.

"This was not the Jesus of my Sunday school books. That Jesus was gentle, kind, understanding—and probably a little bit of a weakling. This Person was power itself..." Yet not a threatening or inimical power, but the power of Truth and Love incarnate.

What can we learn from this? First of all, that we have no excuse not to live a life of love, of obedience to the word of the Lord. We can't say we didn't know. There's a saying: "Ignorance is bliss, but it won't stand up in court"; still less will it stand in the court of the divine Judge and King. When that searching light of Truth illuminates our souls, we will see ourselves as clearly as God does, and we will have nothing to say in our defense. Yet Christ is not a "hanging judge," eager to punish us for our sins. Rather, He is eager to forgive us. He wants us to experience his "astonishing love," the overwhelming, penetrating, joy-giving, and healing love that He can't help but communicate to all. It is up to us, however, to receive that love and respond to it with our own, however feeble it may be in comparison.

Don't wait for a NDE to wake you up to the astonishing love and all-illuminating truth of the Lord. He wants us to experience it now, through faith, prayer, the sacraments, and through living the kind of life that opens us to recognize, receive, and give love. Christ is not the mild, effeminate figure of greeting cards and children's prayer books. He is the Holy, Mighty, and Immortal One who reigns over heaven and earth—and He will demand an account of our lives when we at length stand before Him. Let us love now, so that when Love examines our lives He will find some correspondence with his own—and we will rejoice forever in a love beyond our wildest imagining.

Learn That I Have Loved You

This is something that the risen Lord said to the members of one of his faithful churches in the Book of Revelation (3:8-13). He was encouraging them in the face of persecution by their enemies. But it is something we have to learn too, and learn well.

I experienced a very fruitful meditation on this point, a moment of grace (an extended "moment," for it lasted several hours), and I'd like to share a bit of what was given me at that time.

The first point is that we really have no idea how much Jesus loves us. It will take a lifetime of prayer and meditation on the Scriptures even to scratch the surface, to begin to comprehend. His love for us is not merely an excess of feeling, beyond what we are capable of feeling. It is manifested in what He has done for us, sacrificed for us, endured for us. Read carefully through the Gospel narratives of the Passion. See how Jesus knew what He was going to suffer for us, how He embraced it and went towards it willingly, despite the terror that seized Him in the garden. He gave us his precious Body and Blood for our spiritual sustenance; think of what

He felt when all of his chosen apostles forsook Him and fled in his hour of need.

Jesus knew what He was doing, why He was enduring it all. He loved you, so He let them spit in his face for you. This means not only enduring it for you, but they spit in his face "for you," that is, in anticipation of your doing the same through your sins—I share the guilt with you, and I have wept over it, but you have to hear the "you" to know that He did it not for generic "humanity" but for you and me personally. He loved *you*, so He let them strike Him across the face, mock Him, drive thorns into his head and strike Him again—so that you would not have to pay the ultimate and eternal price for your sins. He accepted the scourges and the nails for you, and He forgave you for rejecting Him and crucifying Him. He entered into an agonizing desolation such as no human being will ever experience in the way He did: "My God, my God, why have You forsaken Me?" He did that for you. Learn that He has loved you.

We must begin to forgive as Jesus has forgiven. We think perhaps that because He was divine it was easy for Him. It wasn't. But He wanted to do it; his everlasting love compelled Him. We are like the official who was forgiven a huge debt and then refused to forgive a pittance that was owed him (Mt. 18:23-35). But others must learn that we love them (or are trying to love them) as Jesus does. We cannot stop short of this, after all He has endured to forgive us out of the abundance of his love.

All too often, people (even Christians) find ways to criticize or complain about God: his "silence," his "absence," his seeming inability or unwillingness to clean up our messes and make all things right in the world. He loves us even in our blind ignorance, in our own inability to perceive his presence and the wisdom of his plans for us. It is not right for us to require Him to fix everything we've broken—while we still rage at Him in our obtuse stubbornness and refusal to open up to his grace and truth. Before we think we have reason to rage at God, we must learn what He has done for us out of love, while suffering for our sins. He stood there, loving us, while we denied and betrayed Him, forsook Him and fled from Him, insulted, tortured and killed Him. If we do not acknowledge this with profound repentance, the world will continue to self-destruct. But floods of grace, peace, and divine love are just barely restrained, waiting for us to open our eyes and hearts, to confess our betrayals and then receive his infinite, merciful love. He is ready to renew the face of the earth.

Learn that He has loved you, that He goes on loving you. Do not wait a moment longer to rush to Him in love and gratitude, offering yourself to Him who has offered Himself for you. For *you*. He waits, quietly, yet with all the impatience of a rebuffed Lover. The wounds we have given Him are so deep that He will manifest them for all eternity—not as a reproach of our wickedness, but as a testimony of his love. He considered that those wounds were worth bearing—for you. He bears them as precious and glorious jewels, for they drew from his pierced heart those eternally-resounding words: "Father, forgive them…"

To forgive is to love. And God is love. Go now to Him. You will know what to say…

❧ Chapter Six:
Exiles From Paradise ❧

We long for Paradise because we long for home. God made us to dwell with Him in peace and joy and untroubled freedom. But our first parents lost our birthright, and we've been searching ever since through the twisting alleyways of time and space, straining for a glimpse of the candle in the window of Eden's gatehouse. We feel it in our bones: we don't belong in the valley of the shadow of death. So we turn our hearts heavenward, watching and waiting...

If I Forget You, Jerusalem

A great and tragic lament arose from the hearts and lips of God's chosen people when they were exiled to Babylon. It was not only a matter of the hardships of physical expatriation, nor of the social and cultural humiliation experienced at the hands of their enemies. Their greatest sorrow was to be banished from the Temple of the Lord and his holy city, along with the knowledge that it had been razed to the ground.

The Temple was the dwelling place of the Lord and hence the only place where sacrifice and true worship could be offered. How could they now expiate their sins? Psalms composed (in whole or in part) during the time of exile expressed the need to find some way to connect with God, to somehow substitute for the Temple worship. "Let *my prayer* rise like incense before You"—for incense could no longer be offered in the Temple—"*the lifting of my hands* like the evening sacrifice"—for there were no more sacrifices in the Temple (Psalm 141). For the same reason: "My sacrifice is a broken spirit, a humble and contrite heart..." (Psalm 51).

But nothing could ever really take the place of Jerusalem and the Temple. Hence we have the deeply poignant Psalm 137: "By the rivers of Babylon we sat and wept, remembering Zion... Our captors asked of us, 'Sing for us the songs of Zion!' How could we sing the song of the Lord in a foreign land? If I forget you, Jerusalem, let my right hand wither... Let my tongue cleave to my mouth...if I consider not Jerusalem the source of my joy."

We too are in exile. We have been banished from Paradise because of our sins. For many it may seem such an ancient and distant memory that they no longer lament its loss (or perhaps they have simply resigned themselves to lives of quiet desperation). Yet Christians still long for Jerusalem, that is, the New Jerusalem, Heaven, of which all believers are citizens (see Philippians 3:20). If we have lost our awareness of being exiles from Paradise, citizens of Heaven, and have thus contented ourselves with life in Babylon, we must at once recover our longing. We must not forget Heaven, for such forgetfulness puts us on the path to sin. *To sin is to forget that Heaven is the source of our joy.* If we do forget "Jerusalem," we end up looking to other, foreign, polluted sources that can never provide true or lasting happiness. Heaven is where we belong, for Heaven we were created, for Heaven God has destined us—if only we choose to leave Babylon (in spirit, for we cannot yet leave the earth) and return to our fatherland.

We are in exile, but not without hope. We are in a foreign land, but not without a passport. We have fallen from grace, but we can be restored. We may still have many years to live far from Paradise, but earthly exile is not forever. Forget not Jerusalem, and the Lord will bring you home.

Where Are You?

Good thing that the heavenly Paradise lasts forever, because anything resembling Paradise on earth seems doomed to be short-lived. After the magnificent introduction to God and his creation of the universe—and of man, the pinnacle of creation, made in God's image—it was only a short time before the first man and woman lost their paradisal privileges and began the sorry history of fallen mankind.

How blissful it must have been in that brief period of sinless peace in Paradise! Effortlessly tilling the soil and reaping bountiful fruits, living in love with God and with each other, the weather always perfect, sleep always peaceful, every experience fulfilling and pleasant, no pain, no sorrow, no taxes, no alarm clocks, no traffic jams, no indigestion, no insurance premiums, no abortionists, *absolutely* no possibility of a same-sex marriage, no

Marilyn Manson, Osama bin Laden, or talking heads on TV— Paradise indeed! But it didn't last, for there was someone who had used his freedom to destroy his own happiness, and he was Hell-bent on getting everyone else to use theirs to destroy theirs.

We know the story of the temptation and fall. Temptation often starts gently enough, with an attempt at misdirection so as to engage the prey in dialogue, which is the beginning of the end. "Did God really say...?" Having made a choice against God and thus against their own happiness, Adam and Eve found themselves naked and ashamed (whereas before they were naked and *un*ashamed—this means that sin had changed for them the meaning of nakedness, which was intended by God as part of their original bliss). So what does one do when one is naked and ashamed? One hides.

Thus came the inevitable and deeply-dreaded words of the Lord God: "Where are you?" Of course, God knew where they were, but that question was for Adam's (and our) own reflection. The question He asked of Eve, once they were found, is more precise: "What have you done?"

These are questions God still asks of us sinners when we try to hide from his face because of our shameful sins, our using of our freedom to serve our passions instead of the will of God. It's rather strange how we, in choosing what looks like freedom enslave ourselves, in choosing what looks like pleasure torment ourselves, in choosing what promises to be Paradise condemn ourselves to Hell. Too bad we don't trust God with our happiness. He's the one who designed Paradise, after all, so He knows what makes for our fulfillment and joy. Alas, we listen to seductive voices and find ourselves running to hide, naked and ashamed, and it's too late to undo the deed—though not too late to find forgiveness.

If there is to be redemption, however, we have to hear that divine voice: Where are you? Why have you run away from the One who loves you? What have you done? Are you ready to come out of hiding, face the truth, and start living in the light? That voice has haunted man since the question was first asked in Eden, for man has ever been fleeing from his God down the passageways of time, having left his innocence far behind him. But God never stops searching for him, calling out to him, inviting him back to Paradise like the father of the prodigal son.

It is time to stop hiding, to stop fleeing the voice of the Lord God. Our consciences hold the record of our infidelities, and the simple question, "Where are you?" brings everything to our conscious awareness. Yes, where are we, vis-à-vis the Lord God and his commandments? What is it that we might still be trying to hide from Him, from ourselves? We've all become sinners due to our lamentable inheritance from the first ones to hide from God. But the restored Paradise to come is for repentant, not fugitive, sinners. We must listen no longer to the lies of the crafty serpent, but to the word of the Lord God.

Come out of hiding. He is calling you. The tree of life is still blooming in Paradise.

Glimpses of Home

We can all use a little encouragement to help survive the time that remains in the land of exile. Even though the psalmist could not sing the song of the Lord on alien soil, we see that Tobit praised God in the land of his exile (Tob. 13:6), so there is still hope.

The blessings that we receive from God in this life are meant as consolations and helps to persevere in this time of trial—not as encouragements to think that this earth is Paradise or our final destination. Once in a while I go to the coast and find peace and blessing in the beauty of the ocean, dazzling me with sunny coruscations, calming me with soothing surf—coupled with the caress of a light and pleasant sea breeze. But I think to myself: this is too much like Paradise; that's why I can only come here once in a while. I can't start thinking that I should have this all the time, as if I could establish some permanent satisfaction in this land of exile. Wanting it all the time is precisely the error we humans make as we turn blessings into addictions. But God's gifts, however temporary, are still glimpses of Home, reminders that the best is yet to come.

While trials and sufferings are inevitable and inescapable, we are still called to be fruitful in the land of exile, to turn to God, seeking his face, his reflection, wherever we can find it. "The commandment to love God with all our strength, to the limits of our individual capacity, does not extend simply to man, but to all nature, which was created for no other reason than to glorify him, to reveal him, to love him...in confession, devotion, and regeneration. And it is up to us, seasoned, stirred, sharpened, and whetted by the breath of the Holy Spirit, to apply to the universe that fiery tongue capable of translating it and transmuting it into splendor, fragrance, song, poetry and praise" (Paul Claudel).

Yet again, nature herself is not Paradise, for she also provides earthquakes, hurricanes, volcanoes, and other destructive manifestations for which we are not likely to compose ecstatic hymns. We are still in exile, but with glimpses of Home. Beyond nature, however, the Lord gives us foretastes of Heaven through the sacraments, especially the Holy Eucharist, and this ought to be our greatest consolation in this Valley of Tears. This is the most profound "connection" we can experience with that Homeland from which we've been banished because of our sins.

The Lord still watches over us. In the Liturgy of St. Basil the Great, we hear that even after Adam and Eve were banished from Paradise, the Lord did not cease to care for mankind, sending angels as guardians, giving the law, speaking through the prophets, until the fullness of time saw the coming of the Son of God in the flesh.

So even though we are still in exile—and will be so until the day we die—we're much better off than many generations of our forebears. We're in exile, yet redeemed. We've been justly banished, but we're still in possession of our passports, which identify us as citizens of Heaven. We can still sing on alien soil, though our songs are not of revelry, but of longing and hope.

Let us, then, accept the human condition of limitation, suffering, and sorrow—and not try to escape from it, deny it, drug it, or put on a phony happy-face while constructing a flimsy sham-paradise to shore up our failing courage. Let's look reality straight in the face, repent of our sins, take our licks, but live with a lively faith and eager hope for the coming of the everlasting Kingdom. And let us give thanks to God for giving us in the meantime, undeservedly, precious blessings and glimpses of Home.

After This our Exile

A faded memory—only a dream?—
returns like a trickling stream
flowing from a distant spring,
trying still to bring
life to the deepest part
of a sorely wounded heart,
sentenced to suffer and grieve.

Exile is dark and cold;
I have need to be told
again and yet again
of that ancient time when
all was light and warm,
and this present storm
one could not even conceive.

Tired to my bones,
and stinging cold stones
bruise my feet. I fear
there are no angels here.
But in darkness shines a light—
perhaps, I sense, this might
be a place for me to rest.

A house on a narrow path;
someone's drawn a bath
for me, with oil to heal
my wounds. I feel
renewed. My clothes—the old—
I leave behind, for behold,
new ones—white—the very best.

As I set out again, it seems
that they weren't merely dreams
of a time, a place, without sorrow.
So with hope for tomorrow
I hasten to I'm-not-sure-where,
yet knowing that only there
will my joy be made complete.

New battles to fight:
my garment of white
enrages ungodly powers
who devise, in their timeless hours,
all manner of malice and plunder,
tearing my robe asunder.
And the serpent hisses at my defeat.

Dazed and wandering again—
have I lost the way?—but then

light once more appears,
calming my dark fears.
And drawing closer I see:
Someone's been expecting me
to arrive and spend the night.

On a table, fresh bread,
and wine, blood-red,
so sweet—and strong!
It won't be long
'til I relax into warm sleep
and so rest in the deep
peace of divine delight.

Arising, I discover a note
my unseen host apparently wrote:
"This is real Food, real Drink.
I am with you, though you think
that I abandon you to strife.
I am the Resurrection and the Life:
I am coming to bring you home."

Strengthened by that bread
I resume the road instead
of staying in that wayside place—
going on to seek the face
of the One who speaks of Paradise,
remaining ever in disguise,
yet ever saying, "Come."

At length—at last!--one more light;
a place in which I think I might
settle down for a while.
A Lady with a lovely smile
shows me a place to rest
as if I were an honored guest.
And those memories again arise.

She writes names in an ancient book;
With pounding heart I beg to look.
She says that even the least
are invited to the Wedding Feast.

With a smile, she bids me sleep,
the divine promise so to keep:
"This day you will be with Me in Paradise."

Till We Have Faces

"The complaint was the answer. To have heard myself
making it was to be answered. Lightly men talk of saying what they
mean... 'to say the very thing you really mean...that's the whole art
and joy of words.' A glib saying. When the time comes to you at
which you will be forced at last to utter the speech which has lain at
the center of your soul for years...you'll not talk about the joy of
words. I saw well why the gods do not speak to us openly, nor let us
answer. Till that word can be dug out of us, why should they hear
the babble that we think we mean? How can they meet us face to
face till we have faces?"

That passage is part of the climax in C.S. Lewis' retelling, in
novel form, of the myth of Cupid and Psyche, entitled *Till We Have
Faces*. I'd like to reflect on that for a moment. The speaker in that
passage was the old Queen Orual, who finally discovered, after
making her complaint to the gods (read: God), that she really had
no grounds for complaint because her life was a lie and she never
really even knew herself, so her perception of gods and other
people was skewed as well. She lost everyone she ever loved,
especially her younger sister Psyche (which is Greek for "soul";
reflect on that), but she discovered in the end that her "love" was
selfish, possessive, bitter, and unforgiving.

When she became queen because of her harsh father's death,
she constantly wore a veil over her face, because she was quite
unattractive, and the veil served to enhance her mystery and
power. But as she hid her lack of physical beauty from the world,
she also hid her true self from her own awareness. Others could see
how she used rather than loved people, but for her this inner truth
was veiled. Finally, in a vision in which she stood before the gods to
be judged, the veil was taken off her face, and her clothes were
removed as well. Standing naked before the multitude, she was
required to speak, and was convicted by her own words, hearing
them almost as if another were speaking. Her inner self was
exposed along with the outer.

People tend to wear masks or veils of one sort or another,
personas or postures they adopt in order to hide what they don't

want to be seen or known, giving the illusion that they are wiser, more powerful, or simply more "together" than they really are. But they end up deceiving themselves as well as others (and perhaps they aren't really even deceiving the others).

We may say what we think we mean, but until we discover and begin to live the profound meaning of our life, our indignant complaints and self-justifications are just so much babble that isn't worth listening to. We might as well be wearing a veil, for our true face is not being shown. Until we arrive at genuine self-knowledge (which is nothing like self-absorbed introspection or other forms of narcissism), we cannot have a genuine dialogue with God: how can we meet him face to face if we don't yet have a face? God sees through all veils, all defenses and self-deceptions, but He cannot do a whole lot for us until we are ready to be unmasked.

Repentance and honest examination of conscience are the beginnings of self-knowledge, of finding our true face, finding the "word" within us that goes deeper than the daily babble and expresses the truth of who we are, i.e., who God has made us to be, and what we have done with his gift.

We had better learn now how to stand naked (figuratively) before God on a daily basis, because we will have to stand naked (literally) before his awesome judgment seat. We also have to learn how to remove the veils with which we cover our faces before other people, because the same veil hides our true self from ourselves. Allow yourself to be unmasked; get more comfortable with being "uncovered." The truth will always come out in the end, so why not begin to live it now? You may discover that you don't want to veil the real you after all. You may discover within you the face of Christ, who alone can refashion all your pain and shame and can speak that defining word of grace and love within you—and thus make you able to live a life of integrity and truth in this world.

God is waiting till we have faces, till we stop hiding behind masks and veils, till it's OK to be naked before Him. Then judgment day will not be the painful stripping of the self-deceived, but rather the homecoming of the free.

You Get What You Want

No one is going to have any reason to complain on Judgment Day. We're going to get just what we want. That doesn't necessarily mean, however, that we're all going to Heaven. Some people are not going to *want* to go there. How can that be? Wouldn't anyone prefer eternal happiness to eternal torment? The answer lies in what we make of ourselves in this life.

In order to want Heaven in the end, you have to live now in such a way that you want Heaven all along. Our souls have to be, as it were, compatible with Heaven. We become that way by loving what God loves, by seeking the truth and following the divine commandments. It's relatively simple (though not very easy), despite the complications our contemporary culture adds.

We know from Scripture that God desires the salvation of all (e.g. 1Timothy 2:3-4). He loves us all and does not thrust people away from Him, even the bad, because He loves them; they are still made in his image. That is why we, who are also made in his image, are called to forgive and pray for even the worst of men. But that does not necessarily mean that they are saved.

If one lives a life of sin and refuses to repent, even at the very end, he will discover that by his many bad choices and his lack of repentance he has turned himself into something that is incompatible with Heaven. Notice in the accounts of Jesus' exorcism of the possessed man (or men) of the Gadarene territory, that it was a *torment* for the demons to be in the presence of Jesus, and they couldn't wait to leave. Evil cannot endure holiness and will flee at the first opportunity. Notice that Jesus didn't even have to *cast out* the demons; they begged Him to let them enter the swine, and He just gave them permission. They got what they wanted, and ended up in Hell.

So what happens on Judgment Day? All people will stand before the Lord of Glory, the Holy One, and all will see themselves in the clear light of truth—no more excuses, no more self-deception, no more blaming others. God is Love, as St. John declares (1John 4:8,16), and those who lived in faith and love, and who followed the Lord as best as they could, repenting of their sins and not dying in a state of estrangement from Him, will hasten to his loving and eternal embrace, for theirs is the Kingdom of Heaven. Those who lived in deep sin and who refused to repent, having destroyed within themselves all connaturality with the things of God and of Heaven, will also stand before the God who is Love. But seeing at last the terrible truth of what they have made of themselves, they *will not be able* to go to God, having destroyed all capacity for goodness and love, no longer having within them anything with which to "hold" the grace or joy of the Lord. Because of what they have done to themselves through the evil of their lives, they will regard coming close to God as a greater torment than being separated from his penetrating truth and love. They will *want* to get as far away from Him as possible. So, like the demons whom they followed in their lives, they will hasten to flee from the presence of the Holy One. God in his compassion will grant them their wish: for a demon or a hardened sinner, Hell is easier to bear than Heaven—though it is still every bit as horrible as we have come to know through divine revelation. They have all eternity to suffer and to hate and curse Him whose gentle love is experienced as torment—a love that they rejected and which could have made them happy forever.

The point for us is this: do not make those choices, do not live in such a way that you will turn yourself into someone who can't help but *prefer* Hell to Heaven, someone who will not be able to endure the loving presence of the Holy One because of a soul steeped in sin. Notice a faint shadow of this truth when even in this life a person may withdraw from another's love and compassion because of fear, spite, or a self-absorbed despair that allows no comfort from another and even takes a kind of perverse pleasure in refusing it.

Satan would like to make us like him, preferring to reign in Hell than to serve in Heaven, refusing to obey, accepting the agony of eternal torment for the pathetic satisfaction of being able to say "no" to God. Make no mistake, we will all get what we want in the end. Therefore it is imperative that we live *now* in such a way that *then* we will find ourselves compatible with Heaven: able to want, and to enter, the Kingdom of love and peace and eternal happiness.

Useless Servants

Jesus' teaching in Luke 17:7-10 used to bother me a bit, though it doesn't anymore. It's about a servant who, after coming in from his day's work, cooked his master's supper and waited on him until he was finished. Jesus said that after all that, the master didn't even thank his servant, yet Jesus did not reproach the master for that. Here is his conclusion, for us: "So you also, when you have done all that is commanded you, say, 'We are useless [or unprofitable, or worthless] servants; we have only done what was our duty.'"

My former reaction was: "Gee, they're not *exactly* useless, after having worked all day and then cooked and served their master. And what's so useless about doing one's duty? Many people don't even do *that*!" Well, that may be true as far as it goes, but it misses the point of the parable.

Our worth does not reside primarily in what we do, in our labors or accomplishments. The Pharisees did good things (and weren't shy about letting others know!), yet they were rejected by God. They did formally keep the commandments, except perhaps the most important ones, the two Great Commandments. However, they were not only useless, but also corrupt and hypocritical. Let's leave them aside for now, though, and see what might be closer to home.

Hopefully we are not as arrogant and as blatantly in contradiction to the Gospel as the Pharisees were. But what about those of us who are trying to do our duty, to do what has been commanded by God, and perhaps even do it well, yet still end up being useless servants? What are we doing wrong? Probably it is not a matter of performing commands but a matter of the heart. Are we bearing the fruit of the Holy Spirit through our duty? Do we manifest love, joy, peace, patience, kindness, etc., in the work we do for the Lord? Or are we perhaps impatient, complaining, irritable, or simply angry that we have to serve at all? The same work gets done, but some of those who do it are useful and profitable in the Lord's sight, and some are not.

Or perhaps we do our duty out of fear or anxiety. Do we do what is commanded merely because we fear the consequences of *not* doing it? Do we serve God only because we're afraid of what will happen to us if we don't? It's not very pleasant to work with a sword over our heads. We may be getting things done, but we're not really bearing fruit.

We are indeed servants, but the Lord has indicated that He would like us to be friends as well. We have tasks to accomplish, but it would go much better for us if we did so with love and with a cheerful acceptance of whatever is required to serve the Lord. If we view our service to the Lord as irksome drudgery, it profits us nothing. I think it was St. John of the Cross who said that all of our efforts and ascetical acts and hardships are as nothing before the Lord; only love is what matters, and that's all He takes into consideration. So that's why the master didn't thank his servant for working and serving. The servant did his duty, but in a loveless manner, perhaps "longing for the shade," as Job said, not concerned with the joy of his master but only with getting the job done, getting the unpleasantness out of the way, and then having a little free time for himself.

So it is with us, says the Lord. If we've put in our time and punched the clock and said good riddance to our service, it doesn't matter if we've done our duty—we are worthless servants or hirelings. But if we make an offering of our labors to the Lord, out of love and gratitude and a desire to please Him, our duty turns into profitable and useful work. Then He says: "Well done, good and faithful servant... enter into the joy of your Lord!" If we put ourselves at the service of his joy, we will share in it. If we do our duty half-heartedly, selfishly or without love, then we receive only the reproach of useless servants. It's not an easy teaching, but life isn't easy, either.

It's up to us. Our duty has to be done, one way or another. We can be worthless servants, or we can serve with love and hear the Lord say: "I no longer call you a servant but a friend."

Meditations on a Dysfunctional Water Heater

The other day I turned on the hot water and cold came out. I have one of those energy-saving propane water heaters that only turns on when you turn the water on. But this time it didn't turn on at all. As I pondered how long it might be before I would have hot water again, and what I might do in the meantime, I thought I'd bring the whole mess into my meditation, since it was distracting me anyway.

I came to the following conclusion: the water heater broke down because it was *supposed* to break down. Now don't think that I'm indulging in fatalism here. The heater was *designed* to cease functioning—not only by unscrupulous manufacturers with their cheap materials, shoddy workmanship, and planned obsolescence, but by God Himself. You see, it was just "going the way of all flesh," which inevitably wears out, breaks down, ceases functioning, decomposes. It is the rule of all bodies, machines, vehicles, and monks. If the water heater had *refused* to malfunction, it would have been *lying* to me about its true nature, and I may have been deceived into thinking I would never need a new one, that I could rely on it forever. But I can't, so I ought to be told the truth. Thank you, [expletive deleted] machine!

Things don't go as we would like them to, because they're not *supposed* to. We're not in Paradise, remember—we're in exile. All things pass because the heavens and the earth themselves are going to pass. Everything here is provisional, temporary, fragile, brittle, and subject to innumerable failures, diseases, and problems. Now, take my computer—please! My septic system is also slowing down fearfully; when that finally backs up, I'll give you a meditation on Hell.

So, my water heater was preaching a homily to me—on the brevity of life, the unreliability of ephemeral material goods, the ultimate decomposition of all living and non-living things—and hence was pointing me in the direction of That Alone which endures forever. Jesus said we would have suffering in this world; He said that unrighteous mammon (and all that it provides) would fail us. It is common wisdom that you can't take it with you—no U-hauls are ever seen hitched to hearses, as they say. So we ought to get more or less used to everything going wrong, for here we have no lasting city. We must, however, take reasonable care of ourselves and our loved ones and whatever God's providence has entrusted to us, but we can't guard anything too jealously, for nothing is ours to keep—nothing except that which survives death. Our outer selves are wasting away, said the Apostle, but our inner selves are being renewed each day. Focus, then, on the renewal of the inner self; don't cling too tightly to outer things or put your trust in them. They're going to break down, because they're meant to. It's one way God teaches us the truth about life, and about what really matters.

In case you're wondering, I tinkered with the heater for a while and got it to work—for now.

First Love, New Name

The risen Lord Jesus communicated messages, through his servant John, to the seven churches in chapters 2-3 of the Book of Revelation. Though we are not first-century Christians in what is now Turkey, the messages are still valid and fresh for us.

The first message is to the Church in Ephesus. Notice that it doesn't say the church *of* Ephesus, but the Church *in* Ephesus, and it's the same to all the others. This is not a minor distinction, for it indicates that the Church is one, even though its particular manifestations are spread over the world. Today's bishops would do well to remember that the Church *in* Los Angeles, for example, is supposed to be the same Church as that in Rome, where the universal leadership resides. It is not the church *of* Los Angeles, as if the local leadership had authority to re-invent Christianity according to contemporary trends.

Anyway, the Church in Ephesus was hardworking, discerning, and patiently enduring for the Lord's sake, but He still had a reproach for them: "You have abandoned the love you had at first. Remember, then, from what you have fallen, repent and do the works you did at first" (2:4-5). This can probably apply to many of us, especially those who have been laboring in the Lord's vineyard for many years. The first fervor, the first love, tends to wear a little thin—"the thrill is gone" as one succumbs to routine or becomes a bit weary under continual burdens, even if they are borne in faith and hope.

I remember a kind of spiritual springtime back around 1980, when I was beginning to discern my vocation. (Come to think of it, it *was* springtime. I was living in Orlando, Florida, and the air was filled with the scent of orange blossoms. And I mean *filled.* You could be driving down Interstate 4 and, despite the freeway traffic and pollution, orange blossoms would still be flying in through your open windows.) During that time, everything was fresh, I was re-discovering the presence of the Lord and my soul was being cleansed and invigorated as I turned from a dead-end way of life toward the boundless horizons of the Kingdom of God, sweeter even than orange blossoms. And my early years in the monastery, though laced with hardships and deprivations, were full of grace and fervor, and at times I even went beyond the call of duty in vigils, penances, and the like.

Well, now I have to go back to the Book and hear the Lord tell me how far I've fallen from my first love! In some ways, though, I think (I hope) I have matured since then, though I must confess that with advancing age and decreasing energy I'm not exactly turning cartwheels for the Lord. Each of us in our own way has to receive the word of the Lord and see where we might have slipped from a level of joy and generosity that He would like us to recover. This is for our sake, because our falling away from fervor can only be harmful to us, and can make us vulnerable to even more destructive failures.

There's something that the Lord promises to the saved (that is, to "him who conquers"), something that has often intrigued me: "I will give him...a new name...which no one knows except him who receives it" (2:17). This is an expression of a very personal intimacy, a secret shared with Jesus. Our founder Fr. Boniface, who was for many years a missionary in Africa, told us that in certain tribes, along with the name the child is known by in the family and public society, the mother gives the child a name known only to her and the child, and by which she will address the child at certain special times. This creates a unique bond between the two, for no one else is allowed into this particular intimacy. So, along with our baptismal or religious names, by which we are known to all, the Lord will give us a special name, known only to Him and to us. It will be something that expresses our inner essence and beauty and perhaps the witness of our life—as only He knows it, so it will fill us with delight to learn of the way He sees and loves us. So many wonderful things await us in the heavenly Jerusalem!

Let us, then, both recover our first love and realize the unique intimacy that Jesus would like to establish with us. Perhaps He will give us a hint of our new name even before we leave this earth. In any case, nothing is lost and everything is gained by our increasing fervor, fidelity, and love for the Lord. Through his grace and mercy, may this prophecy of love and pure intimacy come true for us: "They shall walk with Me in white, for they are worthy" (3:4).

Paradise

"Today you will be with Me in Paradise." So spoke Christ to the good thief on the Cross. Perhaps God spoke similar words to Adam when He first created him. There is a rather rare icon entitled: "The Word Introduces Adam into Paradise." That was the original earthly Paradise: walking with the Lord in naked innocence through a garden of delights, free from suffering, sorrow, and death. It is perhaps an ironic testimony to how far man has fallen that what was once Eden is now war-torn Iraq, wherein flow the Tigris and the Euphrates mentioned in Genesis (2:10-14), though now polluted with human blood. The mark of Cain reappears in our fratricidal madness.

The theme of Paradise is abundant in literature, and I think it dwells in man at a deep and practically inaccessible level, where it is experienced perhaps only as an occasional whisper, a haunting reminder of the original nobility and beauty of the human being in a pristinely pure relationship to God. Elusive and ineffable though it may be, it won't let us alone. Paradise—exile and return—seems to be one of the great themes of my own life, something that hovers around my consciousness and smites my soul with a yearning for the complete and peaceful communion with God that humanity has all but lost: walking with Him in the cool of the day in unhindered freedom, and in joyful, childlike gratitude for the abundance of his love and goodness. I feel deeply both the sense of exile and the longing for home.

We have lost the pure and holy naiveté of the newly-created Adam and Eve. They could walk naked through God's garden with neither lust nor self-consciousness. It was only after the "fall" that the human form became associated with shame instead of innocence (except in little babies). This distortion has been utilized by pornographers and other advertisers to stimulate passion (as well as the economy), while most other people simply continue to harvest fig leaves and hide from God.

We know well the story of the fall; we feel it in our bones, in our wounded and waylaid souls. We may despair of ever recovering what has been lost, for the congenital curse has ravaged our very nature. Perhaps we dream of being re-created, starting all over in a new paradise, getting it right this time. This is essentially not an idle fantasy, for "if any one is in Christ, he is a new creation; the old has passed away, behold, the new has come. All this is from God, who through Christ reconciled us to Himself..." (2Cor. 5:17-18). There is an astonishing exchange that is at the source of this re-creation: God allowed us to exchange our sins for his righteousness (v. 21), by accepting the reconciling sacrifice of his only-begotten Son on the altar of the Cross. Christ, the new Adam, "trampled death by death" and recalled the fiery swordsman from the gate of Paradise. The icon venerated at Easter depicts Christ descending to the netherworld, raising up Adam and Eve by the hand. There is also a legend that the place where Jesus was crucified is the burial place of Adam, and hence it was called the Place of the Skull. Most icons of the crucifixion depict a skull beneath the Cross, sometimes with the redeeming Blood pouring over it.

All these references to Adam bring our thoughts back to Paradise. In both the icon of the original Paradise and the regained Paradise of the resurrection, Christ takes Adam by the hand. (Perhaps the resurrection icon ought to be called "The Word *Re-introduces* Adam into Paradise.") Adam lost and regained Paradise; we've lost it, too, but can also regain it by reaching for the hand of the risen Christ, who lifts us "out of the depths" to seat us with Him next to the Father.

Our nature is still wounded but has been infused with the potential for transfiguration. Christ retained the wounds of his sacrifice, and they serve not to diminish but to enhance his glory. Our problem may simply be that we don't really believe that Christ can make (or already has made, through baptism) a new creation out of us. We become resigned to our intransigent defects and make dutiful but discouraging trips to the confessional. We should rather (while not foregoing the confessional) put our faith in the word of God which reveals the great things He has accomplished for us—and not rest until we have learned to plunge into the bracing current of the River of Life that flows in twin streams from the divine Eden of the pierced Heart of Christ.

We cannot literally return to the original Paradise, but "we await a new heavens and a new earth where righteousness dwells" (2Peter 3:13). We can still walk in renewed innocence through the grace of Christ, while the new creation which He has made out of the wreckage of our former beauty begins to manifest within us. We may be in exile, but we are still citizens of Heaven, and "in our hearts are the roads to [the heavenly] Zion" (Psalm 83/84).

Perhaps Paradise still seems like a dream. But when we at length hear the voice of the Son of God calling us unto Himself, it is the present life that will seem like a dream from which we have finally awakened, and we will find ourselves clothed not in the skins of shame but in the garments of glory.

❧ Chapter Seven:
Fight the Good Fight ❧

Our time in exile is not a time of idle waiting for the appearance of the Heavenly Jerusalem. The place one is exiled to is never as pleasant as the place one is exiled from. As long as we're still on this side of the Pearly Gates, there will be struggles with the classic enemies: the world, the flesh, and the devil. While the battle may at times seem bitter and even hopeless, we have on our side a great spiritual arsenal: the angels and saints, the Mother of God, the victory of Christ through his Cross, and the ever-flowing grace of the Most Holy Trinity. Plus we have the Sacraments, the Scriptures, prayer, and "every spiritual blessing from heaven" (Eph. 1:3). Just choose, and you can't lose!

A War of Worlds

We hear a lot about spiritual warfare, and perhaps we don't understand it very well. It may seem like some mystical conflict between us and satanic powers, full of Book-of-Revelation images of beasts and dragons. On a certain level, it actually *is* that. But our practical daily "warfare" is more subtle, and hence we may not even be aware of the battles we're losing.

One way to look at it is to see it as a "war of worlds." There are a number of "worlds" in which we live, some of which need to be "baptized" into the Gospel, and others need to be entirely severed from us. Some examples may be the business and employment world, the world of leisure and recreation, the world of information and entertainment, and the dark world of satanic evil.

The main world in which we live ought to be the world of God, of prayer and truth and love. This world should influence other worlds we need to have contact with, and must shield us from the evil world. It might seem simple enough for us to embrace whatever is good in them, and reject whatever is evil, but unfortunately it isn't. Why not?

Each "world" has its own logic and rationale, and when you accept its presuppositions, mentality, and psychological "environment," then it will begin to make sense to you, and you will be comfortable living in it. For example, if a certain amount of lying and cheating and "doctoring the books" is part and parcel of the business world, and if it seems to work for you, you may find yourself thinking that it is acceptable. Or if you immerse yourself in the mindset and perspectives of what you find in magazines, TV, and movies, its own peculiar logic might eventually make sense to you, because if you accept faulty premises, you will accept faulty conclusions as well. If you engage in such things as impure fantasies or desires (which can be called "deceitful lusts," Eph. 4:22), you will eventually find that even what is contained in that evil world will make sense to you, because you have placed yourself within its psychological and spiritual framework. Evil thoughts make perfect sense within an evil world, and you may start asking yourself why anyone would think it wrong.

The spiritual warfare consists in not allowing ourselves, in mind and heart, to come near enough to any world that is not God's world (or that cannot be easily integrated into God's world), so that it could draw us in. Once we adopt the mentality of the other worlds, we have lost our strength to fight. The evil world encroaches upon us, much like a virus that approaches a healthy cell: a virus injects its own genetic information into the healthy cell and destroys it from within, reproducing itself as a parasite within the cell.

We must not allow evil to do this to us. Where possible, we must introduce the mind of Christ into the mentality of a world in which we must still function, like the world of commerce and government. When dealing with a world that is nothing but evil (the arena of satanic temptations and deceptions), we must sever all ties to it absolutely. For as soon as we start thinking that there might be something acceptable about what the devil offers us, we have entered his world and will find it very difficult to escape it without sin. We must constantly turn to the Lord, to *his* world, seeking first his kingdom and righteousness—the teachings of the Bible and the Church will make clear what constitutes God's world—and then all evil will be unmasked as such, so that we are not deceived and drawn into a world that will be our downfall.

So you see, spiritual warfare is not dueling Darth Vader with light sabers. The arena is our own heart and mind, and the places we live and work. Our weapons are truth and purity of heart, the Scriptures and the Sacraments. Choose the world in which you want to live. "Resist the devil and he will flee; draw near to God and He will draw near to you" (James 4:7-8).

The Armored Heart

Wouldn't it be wonderful if all people could "walk together in harmony in the house of God" (Psalm 55:15)? Wouldn't it be peaceful and satisfying to stroll in the gardens of a global paradise, free from all manner of evil? We may look with nostalgia upon the original Paradise, or with impatient longing for the establishment of the New Heavens and New Earth, but at the present moment what shall we do? The holy Apostle Paul has some advice: "Put on the whole armor of God that you may be able to stand against…the principalities, against the powers, against the world rulers of this present darkness, against the spiritual hosts of wickedness in high places" (Ephesians 6:10-12). A wake-up call for would-be utopians if I ever heard one!

In describing this spiritual armor, St. Paul speaks of the various virtues that are its components: truth, righteousness, faith, etc. It is interesting to note that "truth" is the armor for the loins. Back then, as today, the liars, relativists, and other distorters of truth commonly hit "below the belt." So we have to be well-protected with knowledge and fidelity to the truth, especially that which is revealed by God and proclaimed and defended by the Church. "Truth" as protection for our loins may also be armor against the "deceitful lusts" that the Apostle mentioned earlier in the same Epistle (4:22).

"Righteousness" is the breastplate, or armor of the heart. The heart, like the loins, is one of the most vulnerable parts of the body (and most essential) and hence needs the strongest protection. Our poor, wounded hearts need strong spiritual support and fortification. The heart is protected by righteousness, for genuine love flows from a right relationship to God. If we are not right with God, then our love is suspect, or even polluted or false. Righteousness is inseparable from truth, and love can only flourish in that environment.

Notice that among the virtues that constitute the armor of God, you will not find love (love may be *amor*, but it's not armor!). That's because love is of the heart, which has to *be* protected, rather than to protect. Be it fiercely faithful and stronger than death, love is still the deep, warm, interior, all-pervading milieu of grace—not a hard outer shell. But it needs that external armor to function and flourish. Our vulnerable inner life, in which love is always struggling to grow and be firmly established, must put on truth and righteousness as armor, carry the shield of faith and the sword of the Spirit, that is, the word of God. For we have to "stand against the wiles of the devil" and "quench all the flaming arrows of the evil one."

To armor your heart spiritually is not to try to insulate it from the sufferings of life, from the pain that the vulnerability of love inevitably brings. It is rather to shield it from wickedness and defilement, to protect it from the cunning counterfeits of love suggested by the evil spirits through the mass media and other organs of deceit.

If you want to claim Paradise at the end of your life, know that it is meant to begin now in your heart. Protect your investment. Put on the armor of God.

Serpents and Scorpions

Some time ago I was rather rudely reminded of my lack of splendid isolation when I perceived on the floor of my cabin, shortly after awakening in the early morning hours, a scorpion positioned perilously close to my bare foot. I did manage—thank God—to carefully remove myself from harm's way and to send the little monster to its forefathers via the impact of a suitably sturdy implement.

I thought of the words of Jesus: "Behold, I have given you authority to tread upon serpents and scorpions, and over all the power of the enemy; and nothing shall hurt you" (Luke 10:19). Being unshod at the time, I deemed it imprudent literally to tread upon the beast, which would undoubtedly have envenomed me with its dying reflex, but the divine dictum lost none of it force thereby—I still had authority over its power, and it did not harm me.

We will probably never be without some intrusion or another of adverse elements in our lives, be they minor natural irritations or actual onslaughts of evil. But the Lord has promised his protection in the midst of it, even if our ultimate deliverance is not quite at hand. "I do not ask that You take them out of the world, but that You should keep them from the evil one" (John 17:15). Since He hasn't decided to take us out of the world, He has granted us protection from and authority over the spiritual serpents and scorpions that would seek to harm or destroy us.

We have to remember that *this* is the arena of our warfare: "we are not contending against flesh and blood, but against...the spiritual hosts of wickedness" (Eph. 6:12). We have not been given authority to tread on *each other*, though we seem to feel obliged to entertain those same hosts of wickedness by engaging in that very folly. We are called by God to be united with each other in order to present a strong and invincible front against the principalities and powers, the serpents and scorpions, who attempt to divide and conquer, to sow fear and suspicion and anger and lust. If we try to go it alone, we walk in the dark and get stung when we least expect it.

The Lord told his disciples to rejoice, not so much over their newfound authority over adverse powers, but in the fact that their names were written in Heaven. That is the chief cause of joy; all other gifts and victories are benefits deriving from our citizenship in Heaven. It's great to see the devil fall from the sky like lightning, but the goal is to end up in that place where you'll never see him again! We're not there yet, but the Lord has given us the means to navigate the treacherous waters of this life and so arrive at Heaven's safe harbor.

So keep your eyes open. Authority to tread on scorpions will not do you much good if your lack of vigilance enables its stealthy approach, and you end up noticing its presence only by the feel of its plunging stinger. How pitiful is the overcoming of an armed man in his sleep! The Lord has not taken us out of the world, but if we're spiritually awake, we will be safe from the evil one. Tread on!

Vultures of Death

Pope John Paul II spoke eloquently and prophetically about the "culture of death" in the Western world, and that expression has become widely accepted as an accurate label for our present society. In such a society, which lives in denial of death and its eternal consequences, there is paradoxically an obsession with death, and many people and organizations feed on it like vultures on a carcass.

These vultures of death feed on the murderous mentality of much of modern mankind: kill human embryos for scientific research, kill unborn babies for convenience or economics, kill *newborn* babies if they have birth defects (yes, this is already being done in some places), kill old or terminally ill people to rid society of useless burdens, and finally, go ahead and kill yourself if you are sick or depressed. They feed on death because it is lucrative (one midwestern abortionist was even charged with literally feeding on the corpses of aborted babies). The promotion of the culture of death (strangely enough) brings academic prestige, media recognition, and political advancement. It also puts people in the company of the demons and the damned, but if they're young and healthy and upwardly mobile, what do they care? Live for today if you have survived the cut.

As a little aside, I read about a very interesting protester at an abortion clinic. There was a man dressed up as the devil, pointing the way to the clinic, and expressing his diabolical "compassion" to the women going in for abortions: "I understand completely how you feel, and I agree that this is the only solution; yes, go right in, I'm with you all the way on this; it's exactly what I'd do if I were you..." If *that* didn't put things in perspective and make them think twice about it, nothing would.

The vultures of death devour their murdered prey in the name of the "quality of life," but it certainly is not the quality of life of their victims. We're already well aware of the grim reapers in the abortion industry, the genetic manipulators, and the advocates of "assisted suicide." Now things are being taken an eerie step further by those who kill for "spiritual" reasons. That was the justification for the killing of Terri Schiavo by the attorney who helped seal her doom.

One day the vultures may find that their own lives will be forcibly taken from them, by law or the will of another, and the culture they created will take its own pitiless vengeance on *them*. Meanwhile, the rest of us must refuse to be driven by the prevailing winds of the culture of death, refuse to jump on the hell-bound bandwagons. We must pray and work for the recognition (in hearts and laws) of the sanctity of life, and of the Creator who makes human life holy.

The buzzards are circling overhead, but it's not too late. The victory still lies with Jesus Christ and the Gospel of Life.

Hell No!

The most well-known retort of the devil to God is the infamous *non serviam* (I will not serve). Hence it follows that all his fellow hell-dwellers scream (though no one hears) an incessant and eternal NO to God. To be damned is to be suffocated in an everlasting negation, not only of all that is good, but of all that simply *is*.

I've quoted the Christian novelist Charles Williams several times already, because he has some very interesting insights into the supernatural world, both the bright side and the dark side. In *War in Heaven*, the villains are a few satanists: one a mere dabbler, another an experienced practitioner, and the other a soft-spoken fellow who is completely possessed. We can learn a few things about the nature of the devil from this novel, and hence why we ought to stay as far away from that horror as possible.

First, and this is nothing more than a point of traditional theology, it is asserted that evil is not a "thing" in itself, but an absence of good, as darkness is an absence of light. If evil were something that substantially exists, then we would have to assert that the all-good God created it, for He created all that exists. What of the devil, then? He was created as one of the most glorious and powerful of the angels. The name "Lucifer" means "light-bearer". But as the saying goes, the corruption of the best is the worst. When the light-bearer forsook the Light through pride and disobedience, the absence of Light became total, and there was nothing but darkness left. Angels, with their superior intelligence, do not have the ignorance and other limitations humans do, which make us eligible for another chance, through repentance, after we sin. They *know* what they do, and therefore they are eternally confirmed in their choice for or against God. The fallen angels are not substantial evil, but absence of good to the fullest extent possible in an existing being. This "absence" is not passive or inert, however. It is manifested in every form of malice, blasphemy, and degradation known to man (and then some).

The devil incites moral evil in the hearts of men, but is himself beyond all that. He is even beyond hate, even though it is the air he breathes (into people). The devil simply is utter and total negation, absolute rejection of God, of all that God is and does. Satan tries to negate good with evil, truth with lies, love with hate, and, perhaps most insidiously, reality with illusion (this is the essence of temptation). He is "NO" personified and as such is the adversary of Christ, because "the Son of God, Jesus Christ...was not Yes and No; but in him it is always Yes. For all the promises of God find their Yes in him" (2Cor. 1:19-20). Christ is wholly Yes; the devil is wholly No. His only objective is to destroy—everything, totally (see John 10:10). And, as one of the satanists in the novel ominously says about his infernal master: "He is the last mystery, and all destruction is his own destroying of himself." This total negation would not stop even if he could destroy the whole universe. If it were possible, he would ultimately annihilate himself, for he is compelled to utterly reject and negate all that is.

Why does he want to destroy not only what is good but all that simply *is*? This is the reason: being as such is good in itself, and here lies the intolerable, eternal conflict within the devil himself. The fact that he was created by God indicates the good of being. His insatiable lust for negation must destroy all good, and if the fact of his existence is a good (originally, at least), then he has to destroy himself as well. But he *can't*, because he was created to be immortal, and this is part of his hell. Goodness and light may be wholly and irrevocably absent from him, but he still exists. Satan is a black hole of evil, sucking itself into itself unto an eternally frustrated act of self-destruction in a maniacal, suicidal cosmic frenzy—and he'd like nothing better than to take you with him.

Why have I been going on about such dark things? Well, think about it. This applies to each of us. Every sin is a No to God. The more you say No to God, the more you are confirmed in rejection of what is holy, good, true, and beautiful. The more you reject God and disobey his commandments, the more you share in the total darkness, the total negation that is the activity of the evil demons. Do you want to share forever in that raging (but impotent) hatred that can never spend or satisfy itself on the object of its hate? Do you want to endure the torment of endless self-destruction that never quite attains annihilation?

There will be no surprises on Judgment Day. That Day simply will reveal what we are, what we have made of ourselves. If our habitual response to God has been No (without final repentance), then we will in the end be consumed with that horrible spirit of negation, and we will flee as far as possible from the Light, from the Love that is all Yes. The only place to go then is hell. Human life is a high-stakes adventure, and it is imperative that we say Yes to all that God is and has given for our salvation. The only thing we should say No to is the "negator" himself, to all the evil he incites in the world, and to all temptations to negate the will of God in our own lives.

Hell? No! I won't go. I will be a Yes to God in Jesus Christ, through fidelity to his will, "for faith says Yes to every truth of God, seen or unseen" (Hans Urs von Balthasar). In gratitude for the Lord's merciful love, I *will* serve. How about you?

More Fundamental Difficulties?

I read a book not long ago which was a reasonable attempt to examine what are known as the "seven deadly sins" and some related ones. But that's just the problem. In his attempt to be reasonable, balanced, inoffensive and acceptable to the general Christian public, the book lacks fire. It doesn't get you to jump up with the desire to change your life. His most impassioned exhortations begin with something like, "perhaps we should ponder..."

But all that isn't the point. The point is that this bland approach also leads to some errors which people can easily adopt if they don't want to rock the boat. In one place he says this: "Alarm bells should be ringing in our churches over real family values, but instead, we watch liberals and conservatives bicker over issues like homosexuality and abortion, which affect only a small segment of our population, while ignoring more fundamental difficulties." More fundamental difficulties? Is there anything more fundamental to a human being than the right to life? And is not the nature of human love and sexuality one of the most fundamental dimensions of life? He writes them off as only affecting a small segment of our population. If serial killers murdered over a million people a year in our country (like the abortion rate), would we dismiss this issue and go on to "more fundamental" ones, since such a small segment of our population was killed by them?

In trying to discover what he thought the more fundamental difficulties were, I discovered divorce, teen pregnancies, rape, and incest. The problem with the problem pregnancies, he says, is that they are "likely to disrupt the mother's education and lessen her chances for advancement." If the young mother had a bit of *abstinence* education, perhaps then she could have continued and advanced! Well, not to worry; since she went and got pregnant, the minor difficulty of abortion can still pave the way for her advancement.

Amazingly enough, the very sentence before he dismisses abortion as a non-fundamental difficulty, he writes: "Contemporary society, so sharply focused on the happiness of the parent, sadly neglects the best interests of the child." But that's precisely the reason that abortion has become such a major issue! Abortion is offered by our society as a solution that preserves the freedom and "happiness" of the selfish parent—by *destroying* the child. The author laments the neglect of the best interests of the child, but among these interests, *life* doesn't seem to be an important one! Yet he wants us to be concerned with *real* family values.

The reason I bring all this up is simply that support for things like abortion and homosexuality are no longer just the sick chant of the lunatic fringe. They are finding their way into the writings of otherwise intelligent Christians who have chosen to blow with the prevailing winds of the current society and do not have the courage to stand up for God's truth. Perhaps it's the "if you can't beat 'em, join 'em" approach. But I say, if you can't beat 'em, keep fighting, and God will take care of the rest!

If we're not going to take a courageous stand, God will shame us by those who do. Some time ago I read this in a letter to the editor of a Catholic magazine: "My disillusionment with Archbishop Levada began in 1996 when...he caved in to San Francisco Mayor Willie Brown by paying for health premiums for the same-sex and live-in partners of Catholic Charities employees. This was in order to keep the pipeline of secular, city tax money flowing into the Church. On the other hand, the Salvation Army stood up for Jesus Christ before men and told Brown to keep his public tax money. The Salvation Army was not for sale." Shamed by the Salvation Army! Well, God bless them!

We ought not to let people get away with dismissing the serious moral issues of our day as mere political bickering. Nor should we tolerate the mainstream acceptance of things like abortion and homosexual militancy. We have to make sure that we aren't lulled into the same "reasonable" and "tolerant" positions of those who seek the praise of men rather than the glory of God. If we're to be but a few voices crying in the wilderness, so be it. We'll also be the ones crying "Hosanna!" in the Kingdom of Heaven—while in Hell there will be some rather fundamental difficulties to be pondered...

Dynamics of Temptation, Part One

This is a rather serious and important topic, and I'm going to treat it at some length, although it's such a complex one that I'm only going to give you a few basics. First, we'll look at the situation we find ourselves in. It will be easier to understand what to do if we first see clearly what has been going on. The following description is from Fr. Basil Maturin's *Christian Self-Mastery*:

"There are many who have fallen from a childhood and early youth of spotless purity into a life of sin. There are men of business who have never diverged from the path of honesty until after middle life. There are men who knew nothing of intemperance until long after their characters and habits were formed and their position seemed well secured.

"To such persons the memory must still be clear of the first approach of the temptation that was later to take so firm a hold upon them, of the recoil of the mind from it, with terror and repulsion, and yet with a kind of horrible fascination. It came again and again and stood at the door of the soul, awaiting its admission with a kind of insolent assurance that if it waited long enough, it would have its way. By degrees, the mind was seized with a kind of tremulous excitement at its approach, and bid it begone in tones of less confidence. It gradually became habituated to its presence outside the soul, feeling its influence, although never yet allowed deliberately to cross the threshold. Then it seemed to gain a certain strange influence over the various faculties, exciting an unaccountable curiosity and forcing them, as it were, to look at it, if only so that they might realize how hateful it was. At last it pushed open the door in a moment when conscience was off its guard and entered, and in an instant demoralized the whole household of the soul, loosened the passions, won over the imagination, and hypnotized the will. And although it was driven out and the doors barred against it, in that moment of its entry, it had made allies for itself, and now the passions and the imagination would loosen the bolts and the will itself would open the door for it. So it entered without hindrance, with an ever-weakening protest from conscience, until at last it gained possession..."

Do you see yourself anywhere in there? The author must have been a man of experience, for he articulated it very well! One thing I've noticed, however, in a number of spiritual books, is that the authors quite accurately and even eloquently present the problem, but the solution is not so clearly proclaimed, and often is rather vague or perhaps clichéd. In this book I find a similar situation (though it is quite detailed and practical in other areas). His main solution to dealing with temptations is that we have to crowd out the bad thoughts with good ones. It is not enough merely to try to empty our minds of evil. Remember what Jesus said about seven spirits returning after one is cast out (Luke 11:24-26). We have to overcome evil with good. This is true, but certainly not sufficient for the struggle. One way of augmenting this teaching may be to enter directly into dialogue with Jesus, reiterating that you love Him more than you love whatever you are being tempted with (thus also reminding yourself of your own noblest aspirations), and that you belong to Him and are committed to doing his will. At least this way you open the door to grace—an objective help in your need—rather than trying to summon a subjective "good thought" that you hope will in some way be more attractive than the bad ones.

Another thing Fr. Maturin suggests is self-discipline in small things, apparently unrelated to that by which you are tempted. Learning to say "no" in one area can strengthen you to say it in another, because it is the *person* who is being strengthened. Does the Church ask us to fast because food is not good for us? Of course not. But the discipline of self-denial will aid us when we are called to renounce something that *is* bad for us, something for which we may hunger as for food. Success in any endeavor begins with training, and the training for success in overcoming temptations is largely the practice of self-denial and daily faithfulness to the commandments of the One who loves you.

One thing to learn (and take warning) from the above passage is the way our thoughts and even our conscience can become habituated to what is bad for us, simply by small concessions, a bit of curiosity, or some specious reason for investigating the nature of the temptation. You could find yourself eventually in the quite unpleasant and spiritually dangerous situation of realizing that your conscience is losing its power to object to evil and is learning how to rationalize and compromise—if you realize it at all and aren't completely blind to your falling from grace!

Next we'll see more of how the tempter works and how to cut him off.

Dynamics of Temptation, Part Two

To see how subtly the devil works on us, we'll take a little look at the process as it is dramatized in C.S. Lewis' novel *Perelandra*. It is a kind of retelling of the story of Paradise and the temptation of the first woman, but it all happens on another planet—and unlike Eve, this one does not fall for the temptation!

If the devil can easily tempt us with coarse and base lusts and heinous evils, he will, but most of us probably can successfully ward off temptations to the worst of crimes—in fact, if there's no real attraction, it can't rightly be called a temptation at all. So he has to appeal to something other than a raw lust for evil if he is going to succeed. And for this he has many tricks up his sleeve. The first hook is that there is almost always a bit of truth mixed with the devil's lies. That's where we begin to get interested in the bait, because whatever he shows us or suggests is presented as something good. He's especially successful when he presents an indisputably good end (like the material sustenance of your family) and offers a bad means toward it (like embezzling from your company—just small amounts that will never be missed, of course, and besides, they hardly pay a living wage, etc., etc.).

The matter is often simple enough. God gives certain commandments which we are to obey if we are to please Him and to find the deep and lasting fulfillment that comes from loving fidelity to his will. But God sometimes seems far away, and the demon tries to get us to complicate what ought to be simple matters, so that he can get us to think that disobedience is somehow nobler than obedience. He will make appeals to freedom, to a creative, pioneering spirit, even to love (his own distorted version of it). The more we reflect on all that, the wiser it seems, and God's wisdom seems a bit simplistic and even selfishly authoritarian (keeping the secrets of "being like God" for himself and forbidding us to explore). The heroes and heroines of independent conviction, who suffer for taking a "courageous" stand against restrictive rules are offered as the ones to emulate.

The devil (who appeared not in the form of a serpent, but in that of a man) said to the woman on the paradisal planet Perelandra, concerning something God had forbidden her to do:

"But He has never forbidden you to *think* about it. Might not that be one of the reasons why you are forbidden to do it—so that you may have a Might Be to think about... If you refused to learn things from me and kept on saying you would wait for the King, would that not be like turning away from the fruit you had found... He is making you a full woman, for up to now you were only half made... This time, when you meet the King again, it is *you* who will have things to tell *him*... You could become more like the women of my world [i.e., the fallen ones of Earth]... They are of a great spirit. They always reach out their hands for the new and unexpected good... Their minds run ahead of what [God] has told them. They do not need to wait for Him to tell them what is good, but know it for themselves as He does. They are, as it were, little [gods]. And because of their wisdom, their beauty is much greater than yours..."

According to the devil, God's secret desire is that we exercise our free will, even in our "no" to the divine command: "He longs...to see his creature become fully itself, to stand up in its own reason and its own courage even against Him. But how can He *tell* it to do this? That would spoil all... Do you think He is not weary of seeing nothing but Himself in all that He has made? If that contented Him, why should He create at all? To find the other—the thing whose will is no longer His—that is [God's] desire... But He cannot tell you. The nearest He can come to telling you is to let some other creature tell it for Him. And behold, He has done so. Is it for nothing, or without His will, that I have journeyed through Deep Heaven [i.e., outer space] to teach you what He would have you know but must not teach you Himself?"

Pretty slick, huh? Observe for yourself the same type of reasoning in any situation in which there is a clear command of God, out of which the tempter is trying to help you rationalize your way. His lies are subtle, his reasoning attractive. How did that first Perelandrian woman defeat satan? She clung to the word of God. After all his trickery and subtle appeals, her conclusion was, in effect: "Your offer seems interesting, but I can't follow it, because that would mean doing what God doesn't want me to do. And I want to do what He wants me to do." Her simplicity and her love for her Creator were stronger than the attractive complexities of the devil's seduction.

Thus there is only one defense against all appeals to your independent and adventurous nature (which is really your slavish and self-serving weakness): simple obedience to the simple command. God says "Thou shalt not"; therefore do not. Don't second-guess God's motives or intentions; don't think He doesn't understand the complexities of situations or the labyrinth of your own inner reasonings. Don't think He's going to reward you for "courageously" stepping over that precipice. You know what is right and what is wrong. You know the commandments, the Gospel, the teachings of the Church (you ought to by now, anyway).

Stand firm against all specious reasoning. It is all seduction. The devil can even quote Scripture if it will serve the purpose of his deception. You should know Scripture better than the devil so you know what really applies to your situation and what is a demonic misuse of it. Don't give the devil the opportunity to work you over. My elementary school religion teacher used to say, "Don't dilly-dally with the devil," and that advice is as good today as it ever was. If you have a desire for what you know is wrong, you may wish there were some convincing justification for it. The devil is always ready to provide one, to your ruin.

So don't even get interested in any other way but the Lord's, or in any interpretation of what He has said that is in effect a pandering to your sinful desires. Simple and steadfast obedience to God is the best defense and security against the encroachment of the father of lies. In the following section I'll share more about fighting the good fight and recognizing the devil's tactics.

Dynamics of Temptation, Part Three

Here I will work with the fine book of Fr. Livio Fanzaga entitled, *The Deceiver*, which I recommend for more careful and detailed study. I can only hit a few highlights here.

The title of the book really says it all, for temptation is about deception. That's something that seems hard to sink into our souls, even though we may give intellectual assent to it. Realizing clearly, however, that those suggestions to sin, which make it seem good or desirable, are deceptive, false, misleading, and even destructive, anyone with an ounce of common sense simply wouldn't follow them. But all too often we do anyway, to our subsequent shame and dismay.

The devil deceived Eve by presenting something evil in the guise of good, but rather than obeying the simple and clear command of God, she chose to do things the devil's way and brought disaster on herself and on all subsequent human generations. After she went for the bait, and her husband followed suit, Scripture says that "their eyes were opened," and they realized that they were naked, that is, they felt shame, which they had never felt before, and they were compelled to hide from the Lord. This is what happens (if our conscience still works) when we sin. We fall for the deception, and then our eyes are opened, that is, we realize the guilt of our sin and we feel it. Illusion is followed by disillusion, says Fr. Fanzaga. It is imperative that we learn from our mistakes, recognize the strategies of the demons, and thus successfully ward off future attacks, unmask future deceptions. Pray to see things as they truly are.

We have to realize something about the one who is suggesting to us things contrary to God's will, but which seem good or beneficial to us: he hates us. Stop and think—if someone who hates you furiously and is bent on your eternal suffering offers you something and says it's good, the overwhelming odds are he's lying through his fangs and you will experience quite the opposite of what he promises. He laughs us to scorn as we fall for his lies and think that a sinful life will bring us happiness. "Behind the false light of an immoral life is hidden the sarcastic smile of the [devil]. Evil promises but does not fulfill." Once we fall into sin, there are two, and only two, options: repentance or punishment. Either we turn back to God and are restored to his grace, or we remain turned away and receive just retribution for our sins.

Our spiritual fortitude must come from prayer, the sacraments, and the "sword of the Spirit, which is the word of God" (Ephesians 6:17). The best defense against temptation is a holy life. Demons study us and discover our weaknesses, chinks in the armor, and Achilles' heels. Through the spiritual means the Church supplies we need to close every access point so that evil finds no welcome within us, no unguarded portal. We also need to practice what Fr. Fanzaga calls the "exorcism of mortification." To do penance is not a literal exorcism of the devil, but it is part of our arsenal in the spiritual warfare. Sometimes people would prefer a more dramatic encounter with evil, and to cast it out by rituals and manifestations of power. On the other hand, some might flee the very idea of spiritual warfare for that same reason. But Fr. Fanzaga is trying to tell us that the spiritual battleground is our daily life, and hence the little things count. Our self-denial and penance strengthen us and keep us well-disciplined; therefore we don't *need* to cast the devil out—because he can't enter in the first place! The point is, the practice of penance keeps the devil from making any inroads that could weaken us in the heat of battle. In that sense, mortification fights the devil. Yet we don't practice penance only for the "negative" purpose of fighting evil, but primarily as an expression of obedience to the Lord, who calls us to deny ourselves, take up our crosses and follow Him. The power of our obedience to God is really what chases the demons away.

If it is true that self-discipline and mortification help keep the devil away, it is also true that a lack of these will invite the devil in. Attachments, obsessive anxieties, complaining, immodesty, white lies, gossip, little infidelities, unchaste thoughts, words, or looks, etc., all create fertile ground for temptation to end in sin. The bloated, drunk, or lazy soldier is easy meat for the unsleeping enemy warrior, who overcomes him with little resistance.

In the final analysis, if your fervent desire is to please God in all things, and you make use of the means He offers for that purpose, you will be well-protected against the wiles of the devil. It doesn't mean that you'll never have a weak or wavering moment, or that you'll never commit even a small sin again, but it does mean that you will be walking in the Spirit—you will not be a slave to sin and you will be able to recognize and reject the lies of the deceiver. Never forget that Jesus Christ has definitively disarmed the devil and sealed his fate by dying on the Cross and rising from the dead. He surrounds us with grace as with a shield. The risen Lord has given us his Spirit to continue his work of preaching the Gospel, casting out demons, and leading souls to Paradise. In Him we have the victory, and He does not forsake those who trust in Him.

Not Beyond Your Strength

I'd like to tie up a couple loose ends on the theme of overcoming temptation. I will use the following text, which many find to be a source of consolation, and which some simply refuse to believe: "No temptation has overtaken you that is not common to man. God is faithful, and he will not let you be tempted beyond your strength, but with the temptation will also provide the way of escape, that you may be able to endure it" (1Cor. 10:13).

When you experience some severe temptation, you may be tempted to think that it is beyond your strength to overcome, so you end up giving in. The old joke is that the best way to remove temptation is to give in to it. Well, if that's the case, the joke's on you. Giving in only assures that it will return, more frequently and powerfully than ever before, because you have secured its place in your mind and soul. It's a lot harder to get yourself free from habits than random temptations. A habit is not merely the product of a psychological or emotional attachment (though that's part of it). It also has a biological component, for the brain tends to "re-wire" itself according to what we desire. If a certain thought or act gives you some kind of satisfaction, your brain will habituate itself to that thought or act by linking neurons to form a pathway for impulses to follow which will produce or increase that sense of satisfaction (see Dr. Gerald May's fascinating study, *Addiction and Grace*). Now you have a biological as well as a psycho-emotional vulnerability to temptation, and by this time you may indeed be starting to think that resistance is beyond your strength—especially if you are lax in your spiritual life and have thus abandoned all lines of defense.

But God is faithful, says the Apostle, and will not let you be tempted beyond your strength. This presupposes that you've not already allowed yourself to become completely addicted to some sin, but even then all is not lost. One's guilt is somewhat mitigated if the act is a result of a compulsion that vitiates freedom, but one is still guilty for freely paving the way for that compulsion to take root. As St. John Climacus said, you can hardly blame a drunken man for stumbling—after all, he's drunk! But you *can* blame him for choosing to get drunk in the first place. On the relatively level field of spiritual warfare, however, we all have an assurance of victory if we employ the means I've mentioned in the sections on the dynamics of temptation.

Anyway, back to God's faithfulness. He will provide a way to escape or to endure the temptation without committing sin—if you are willing to co-operate with his grace. The Apostle uses both those words: escape and endure. Each has its place in the fight against temptation. The best means is to escape, for we can't ordinarily trust that we have what it takes to outsmart the devil. He still does possess angelic nature, which is essentially superior to ours, though the devil's is perverse and corrupt beyond repair. So the first thing to do is to ask God for the way of escape when temptations become severe. But it may be that, try as we might, and even pray as we ought, we cannot escape whatever is hammering us or relentlessly clamoring for our attention. In that case, God is probably asking us not to escape but to endure. He will ensure that it will not be stronger than we are, for we can do all things in Him who strengthens us (Phil. 4:13). We may simply have to ride the storm out, determined unto death not to give in, while raising our eyes to heaven in confident (if urgent) supplication.

Mostly we give in because at some level of our being we simply *want* to give in. We want to be overpowered so we can have an excuse for relaxing our vigilance. It's a kind of relief to succumb. But as I mentioned above, the relief is short-lived, and before long we find ourselves in the same battle all over again, so much the worse for having relented, and needing even more strength this time around. But if we do endure (and endurance will lead to escape, if we can't escape immediately), we will find ourselves with renewed strength and courage. If every defeat makes us weaker, then every victory makes us stronger.

God's faithfulness isn't necessarily manifested in protecting us from all temptation. Sometimes he allows such attacks so that we can prove our love for Him through fidelity in trying circumstances. This will add to our everlasting glory and joy. Trust that He knows what He's doing. The Russian saint Nil Sorsky says that if a potter knows just how much heat to apply to a particular vessel so that it becomes strong yet does not crack, and if a man knows how much weight he can load on his donkey so that it is not overburdened, then surely God knows how much temptation or trial we can take—to strengthen, not to break us. We're all in this together. Even if we aren't all susceptible to the same temptations, we all have our weaknesses; we all struggle with desires that are not of God; we all have to fight the good fight, against evil and for righteousness. "Be strong, let your heart take courage, and hope in the Lord" (Psalm 31:25).

❧ Chapter Eight:
With God in Your World ❧

The Lord said that He would be with us always, but what does it mean to be with us? Is it only his omnipresence as Creator? It is that, but much more. He is with us in all the nitty-gritty details of daily life: teaching us, helping us to deal with our fears and struggles, blessing us, showing us how to live his Gospel in a damaged yet redeemed world. God is not just in the world as some sort of impersonal guiding force of the universe—He's a Father, a Friend; He's in your world, and in mine.

In the Beginning

Recently I re-read the Book of Genesis, which I must confess I haven't done for a few years (outside of listening to the readings prescribed in our liturgical tradition during Lenten Vespers). I tend to keep re-reading the New Testament most of the time, with occasional forays into the prophets, the wisdom books, and other interesting stuff. The Book of Genesis, however, is quite important for understanding some essential elements of our faith.

The book opens: "In the beginning, God created the heavens and the earth." Such grandeur surely befits the first page of the word of God. It's something that almost takes your breath away for its sheer magnitude and depth of meaning. There was a time (hard to get around using that word) when everything was not. God was, but everything else wasn't. Genesis tantalizes us with omissions of equal magnitude to its proclamations. What was it like when nothing was? What was God doing with no universe to do it in? Did He create the angels before He created the heavens and earth? Why did He create anything at all? Who is God, anyway?

It seems that the author of the book couldn't quite conceive of absolute nothingness, so he gives us an image of a kind of primordial chaos, a watery, formless void—over which hovered the creative Spirit of God. Good thing there wasn't some cranky atheistic scientist writing the book of Genesis, for he would have ruined it with some brilliant theory, like one I recently read, summarized as follows: in the beginning there was nothing; then nothing exploded and became everything. Somehow, "God created the heavens and the earth" has a much deeper ring of truth (and beauty) to it.

God created. We simply can't imagine what that was like. How did God create something out of nothing? Nothing doesn't become something all by itself; non-being can't evolve into being. The "be-ing" had to come from God. This is how He created: "Let there be..." And so it was. And God saw that it was good. To say that God made everything out of nothing is not like saying a man makes a table out of wood. A man can build a table, but he cannot *create* one. For God, his will and his word are sufficient to make things be.

I've no inclination to get into disputes about the "days" of creation, young earth, old earth, and all that. Just knowing that God said, "let there be," and it was so, should be enough to fire our contemplation. Then we can ponder the depths of what it means that God made man, male and female, in *his own image.* The psalmist says: "When I look at the moon and the stars, I think: what is man that you care for him?" But if we, not the stars, are made in the image of God, then it is the moon and stars that should say: "When we look at man, we think: what are we...?"

We don't get the answers to the several questions I listed above, though St. John gives us some insight into the last one. He must have realized that he was writing a new Bible, as it were. For something incredibly new had happened in the world, something totally astounding and utterly inconceivable had been created: the human nature of God—that is, the humanity of the Word made flesh. To try to help us understand the incomprehensible, John begins the new Bible: "In the beginning was the Word." He takes us back to a beginning before the beginning, not just the creation of the universe, but the eternal inner life of God. "The Word was with God; the Word was God; through Him all things were made."

So we know a little more about this God who created the heavens and the earth, and why God could say, "Let *us* make man in *our* image..." God is not only an "I" but a "We," for God is one in nature and three in person.

Let us not lose our contemplative vision of the world. God created, God creates. He breathes an immortal soul into the microscopic beginnings of every human life. In the beginning of each of our lives, God was there, creating, loving us into being as his images, his children. The Creator of worlds is also the creator of souls, and He wants us forever to rejoice in the "very good" of all He has made.

I AM

After his extraordinary encounter with God in the burning bush, Moses asked God his name, for God was sending Moses to Pharaoh to liberate his people. "Say this to the people of Israel," God told him, "I AM has sent me to you" (Exodus 3:14). This divine name has been used by Jesus on several occasions in the Gospels. He has not only been sent by God to save his people, but is the eternal Son of God Himself, and as such bears the divine name. This name is inscribed in Greek letters in the halo of icons of Christ. Therefore in the Byzantine Offices, Christ is sometimes called "He who is." (The literal translation of the name of God is more dynamic: "the-being-one")

The very fact that God *is* should be a great consolation to us in all our struggles, fears, and needs. For if God *is*, if God is God, then He has to be all that He says He is, and we can trust Him completely. This is the same assurance that Christ gave to his disciples when they were panicking in the midst of a storm on the sea. He came walking to them across the water—He whose Spirit hovered over the waters of the primordial chaos, and through whom all things were made (Genesis 1:2; John 1:3).

What did Jesus say to calm their fears? "Take heart; I AM; have no fear" (Matthew 14:27). Most translations render the Greek *ego eimi* as "It is I." Even though that can work here, it is not a literal translation and loses the force of the divine name. He might well have used another of his names at this time, Emmanuel ("God with us"), for in the person of Christ, God was with them on the raging waters.

Peter, still not over his fear, boldly attempted a test and asked Jesus to prove Himself by enabling Peter also to walk on the water. Humble as always, Jesus simply invited him, and Peter began to walk on the water. Quite a marvelous feat, yet his old fears returned. He took his eyes off Jesus and looked at the wind and the waves (and probably reproached himself: Who do you think you are? *You can't walk on water!*). Thus he lost courage and began to sink. Jesus proved Himself once again by saving Peter from the waves. "Jesus" means "the Lord is Savior," so his divine "I AM" was vindicated.

We are going to find ourselves (as we surely already have) in times of turmoil, fear, doubt, and pain. It is important that we hear the voice of Christ calling to us over the troubled waters. "I AM," He says to us, "It is I; I am here." Therefore we can take heart and have no fear. He may not immediately calm the storm, and we may even find ourselves sinking because of our feeble faith, but He will always be the Savior—He will not let us drown in the sea of our sorrows and tribulations. But we have to keep our eyes fixed on Him, keep our hope and trust in Him. It is so easy to look at the wind and waves and be afraid, and so hard to set aside our own reasoning and calculations in order to trust the Lord in spite of adverse conditions and the fears they generate. But this is what He-who-is asks of us, because He knows how he plans to help and save us.

As the world seems to move farther from belief and trust in God the Creator and Savior, and puts its confidence in technology and other human achievements and plans, we have to reaffirm that there is salvation in no one else but Jesus (Acts 4:12). We are all finite, contingent beings who can't even row our way out of a little squall. God is "The-Being-One," the everlasting Lord who holds us in the palm of his hand. As He says "I AM" to declare his divinity, we can only say "I am not" to declare our radical dependence upon Him for our very existence. Yet this is our joy and hope, for I AM wishes to take us where He is, so that we can share the glory of God that was before the foundation of the world (John 17:24).

Take heart, then; do not fear. God is with you and loves you and is preparing eternal joy for you. I know, because I AM has sent me to tell you...

The True Vine

I have a rather interesting little plant in my monastic cell. When it is watered, it drinks up the precious liquid very quickly and draws it through its stems and leaves with such vigor that it ends up with little drops of water suspended on the tips of its leaves—almost as if there were too much for it to hold. (I don't over-water it, really!) And if a leaf is freshly cut or damaged, the water appears around the wound.

That got me to think about Jesus' image of the Vine and the branches. We have no life except in Him, but in Him we have such abundant life that we can scarcely hold it all in without overflowing. And if we are wounded, his grace flows to the place of pain to soothe and refresh it.

We are called not only to drink the Living Water of the Spirit that nourishes the branches of the Vine, but to overflow for others. "Abide in Me and I in you," Jesus said (John 15:4), but to show that this mutual abiding is not a closed circle, He also said, "Love one another as I have loved you" (15:12). So as we drink, we overflow; as we receive his love we share it with others.

We have to be sure, however, that we are always drinking from the true Vine, because the world has its own bitter waters, which do not nourish but poison. What if I were to water my plant with salt water? It would soon wither up and die. Neither could I give it fresh water sometimes and salt water sometimes if I want it to live and be healthy. Divine grace comes from only one Source: the Heart of God, through his Church, the bearer and distributor of his word and sacraments. If we're getting anything other than the love of God poured into our hearts or the wisdom of God into our minds, it's coming from some other source. "Does a spring pour forth from the same opening fresh water and salt water?" (James 3:11). We become what we feed ourselves (or allow ourselves to be fed). We can either become the body of Christ and bearers of his wisdom, or we can become products of a superficial, licentious, violent, and unbelieving world.

In which vine would you like to abide, of which would you be a branch? The "vine of Sodom" (Deut. 32:32), from which springs all manner of bitterness, vice, and warfare? Or the "true vine" (John 15:1), which provides the spiritual nourishment for bearing fruit unto eternal life? The correct option may look obvious, but it is the way we actually live our lives, the choices we make every day, that proves which vine we truly belong to. To sin is to suck polluted water from the bitter soil in which "worldly" plants live. But remember, "Every plant which My heavenly Father has not planted will be uprooted" (Mt. 15:13).

Abide in Jesus, the True Vine, and learn to love and forgive, and to walk in the light, as He is in the light. The Living Water of his grace will fill you to overflowing.

Be Sun, Be Rain

The Lord makes a rather startling revelation in speaking about the Father's mercy and providence: "He makes his sun rise on the evil and on the good, and sends rain on the just and on the unjust" (Matthew 5:45). God doesn't withhold the benefits of sun and rain from people just because they are wicked or unjust. He would like them to recognize and acknowledge his magnanimity and turn to Him with gratitude and a resolution to change. Yet He wants to manifest to the world that his love is not conditioned by our lack of response. We can condemn *ourselves* by not responding to his love, but that doesn't mean He loves us any less.

Did Jesus tell us this just to show us how wonderful the Father is? Yes, but more than that. The whole point of it is that *we* are to become children of our heavenly Father through imitation of his boundless love, and thus to "be perfect, as your heavenly Father is perfect" (5:48). From most perspectives on the meaning of "perfection," this would be impossible. As humans, the countless perfections that belong to the divine nature are for us wholly out of reach. But the Greek word from which "perfection" stems is *telos*, which connotes completeness, a goal or end. When Jesus died, St. John tells us that He said, *Tetelestai*—it is finished, completed, the goal of his incarnation and sacrifice has been attained. So in one sense, what Jesus is saying is that we have to have the same goals as the Father, striving until we reach the fullness or completion of all that is possible to us with the help of divine grace.

To be able to achieve the goals of the Father for his children in this world, we have to love as He loves. When Jesus said we have to be children of the Father, it was in the context of loving and praying for our enemies or persecutors. God shines the sun (literally, *his* sun) on them, gives them rain when it is needed. We have to realize that those whom we have reason to call our enemies, those who hurt or malign us, are living in darkness and are like parched and arid earth. When Jesus says love them and pray for them, He is saying: Be sun for them, be rain for them, give them light in their darkness, pray that they will be open to the transforming refreshment of grace. "For if you love only those who love you," He goes on, "what reward is there in that?" Anybody, even evildoers, can do that. You, however, are called to be children of the Father who gives sun and rain to all, deserving or undeserving. The final judgment is in his hands, and no one pulls the wool over his eyes—but this is the time for mercy, for generosity, for being the Father's hands and heart as He seeks to achieve his goal of salvation for all.

Be sun, then, and be rain, for the sake of those for whom Christ died. Be a child of your heavenly Father. Love and pray and go forth in peace, in the name of the Lord.

Be Presence Where There Is Absence

Here is another way of being "sun and rain" for others. I mentioned Jean Vanier in chapter five. He has a rather specialized vocation—caring for the severely disabled, both mentally and physically—but perhaps for that very reason his proclamation of the Gospel is all the more clear and pure. His work with these "little ones" enables him to see and be the face of Christ in the world. The following is what he understands, in general terms, as the mission of the Christian in the world. It is taken from his book, *Drawn Into the Mystery of Jesus through the Gospel of John.*

"This is what Jesus is leading up to: his disciples will continue his mission and his works. But what is his mission? It is to give life, eternal life, and to reveal the face and heart of God to people. It is to be a presence of God in the world where there is an absence of God. God's works are not big miracles, which some heroic disciples may be called to do, but all those works of simple kindness and goodness which give people life and lead them to trust in themselves and in God...

"Something will have to happen to change and transform them, so that they will be able to do the works of Jesus, and even greater ones! Jesus tells them how this will be: 'If you love me, you will keep my commandments. And I will ask the Father and he will give you another Paraclete to be with you forever. This is the Spirit of truth whom the world cannot receive because it neither sees him nor knows him. You know him because he abides with you and he will be in you' (John 14:15-17). That is the answer: the disciples are going to receive another Paraclete, the Spirit of truth, who will live in them and transform them. They will no longer be caught up in a lot of very human queries and needs flowing from their fears, culture and education; they will be separated from the emptiness of the world and brought into the place of God. Jesus reveals to them that they are not first of all going to do things, but God is going to live in them. Later we will see that because the Spirit is in them, they will do the works of God."

The task of manifesting the face of God in the world, which is the continuation of Jesus' mission, is to be God's presence where there is a perceived absence. It reminds me of the prayer of St. Francis: put love where there is hatred, light where there is darkness, joy where there is sadness, etc. Remember that story about the man who complained to God about the various needs and sufferings he experienced all around him, and he asked God why He didn't do anything about it. God answered: "I *did* do something about it. I made *you*."

In order to be God's presence where this is needed, it is not enough simply to will it, or to go about trying to do good things solely with our own ingenuity or effort. We must be *filled with God* if we are to manifest God. No one gives what he doesn't have. This is the primary thing: being filled with the Spirit of truth and love. Once God lives in us, then we can do the works of God; then we can be Presence where there is absence.

The urgent needs of the world may seem to push us to get busy right away, to throw ourselves willy-nilly into damage control, putting our fingers in the holes of the dyke. But it is a sterile activism that does not first draw wisdom, peace, and strength from the Source, in whose hand alone lies the healing, renewal, and salvation of mankind. Pray, worship, be silent, receive the Holy Eucharist, discover the life of God in yourself—and then begin to communicate it to others. When Christ is the Presence in your own interior emptiness, then you can fill the emptiness around you with that same Presence.

So, be presence where there is absence. People need to see the face of Jesus in this world, in which satan rears his ugly head all too often, sometimes thinly disguised, but easily unmasked by the Spirit of Truth. Abide in Christ and He will abide in you. Fill one absence at a time—and start renewing the face of the earth.

All This and Heaven Too

St. Paul warned us about accepting a different gospel than the one he preached, and it seems that there *are* different gospels out there, and here I'm not referring to the far-out ones of the several quasi-Christian sects. One of the different gospels, which is both pernicious and ubiquitous, might be termed the "gospel of prosperity," or the "All-this-and-Heaven-too gospel."

Such a reading of Christianity could only flourish in wealthy countries like America. Tune into any feel-good televangelist worth his Rolex and you'll discover that God wants to give you not only the Kingdom of Heaven, but also health, wealth, and all manner of earthly happiness. When I check the true Gospel, though, I find that Jesus says that it's *really hard* for someone to try to hold onto all that and receive Heaven too. Wealth as a sign of divine favor was an Old Testament belief (they mostly weren't aware that there was even such a thing as "Heaven, too," so they can be forgiven), but Jesus was at pains to make it clear that such was not the case for those who would follow Him into Paradise.

I read about one Christian seeker who was getting fed up with the quality of the Christianity that was within his experience. He recounted hearing a man at a prayer meeting asking God to give him a new Toyota SUV, and he even told God what engine size he wanted, and the color and pinstriping, hastening to add "in Jesus' name" so as to be sure his prayer would be heard. Is that what Christ came to teach us? Another fed-up person, when told that America was one of the most religious countries of the world, shot back: "I'm talking about *actual* religion, not these rich Pharisees...rotting inside painted tombs, hypocrites...praying for washing machines."

Sometimes I'll read something by one of the saints (canonized or not)—who really had a grasp of what the Gospel is all about, who actually lived it at great personal cost, and deep joy as well—and it is refreshing to the point of being startling. Hey, that's right, I say, slapping my forehead, *that's* the Gospel of Jesus! But if it is startling to hear a real Christian speaking of Christianity, how far have we fallen? How much have I myself been influenced by the bourgeois decency of bland, mainstream, toothless, superficial California Christianity? O Lord, give me a new computer (160GB hard drive, 3.2GHz processor, DVD/CD-RW drive) before the warranty on my old one runs out!

Seek first the Kingdom of God and his righteousness, said the Lord, and everything else you need will be given you. We have to go back to the real Gospel and make sure we're asking for the right things, make sure we know what being a Christian really entails before we blithely present ourselves as such. We don't want to be a scandal for those in search of the real thing. Jesus never preached a gospel of prosperity; He preached a Gospel of cross and resurrection, a Gospel of faith and love, a Gospel of mercy and truth.

Jesus ought to take us on a tour of the world, *his* world. He would show us sinners repenting, people serving the poor, sick, and elderly, others prostrate in heartfelt adoration and supplication, people trusting God despite poverty and hardship, others making difficult renunciations in the midst of the seductions of this world, people comforting the bereaved and the hurting, others spreading truth and beauty through art, literature, and music, people standing up for the truth of the Faith in the face of malicious opposition, etc. "All this," He says with a smile, "and Heaven, too!"

The Poverty of Prosperity

In some of my readings and conversations, a certain theme surfaces from time to time, one that I think we need to look at if we expect to grow in our life in Christ. It can perhaps be summarized by saying that material prosperity generally produces spiritual poverty. By spiritual poverty here I'm not referring to the "poor in spirit" whom the Lord blessed, but a spiritual poverty that is the opposite of being rich in divine grace and holiness.

What it comes down to is that we too often take our faith and God's gifts for granted, or we include them somewhere among the various benefits of our affluent lives. But because our relationship to God isn't *everything* to us, we tend to give it insufficient attention or regard. Abraham Heschel once said: "God is of no importance if He is not of utmost importance." If God is not of utmost significance in your life, you will eventually regard Him as more or less insignificant. God can't be someone we can either take or leave, or, to quote an old song: "He's not the kind you have to wind up on Sundays."

I wrote in chapter one about the price that many Christians have had to pay for their faith, like Fr. Arseny in the Siberian concentration camp. I once read a book about a Muslim woman who had a vision of Christ and converted to Christianity, and then was hunted down by the Egyptian police and had to flee the country with a phony passport to save her life. All those who in any way assisted her were arrested and beaten. We don't live in countries ruled by Communists or Muslims, as millions of Christians do, where it can be a capital crime to profess or share the faith. Sure, as Christians (if we admit it in public) we may have to endure the comments or sneers of the "evolved" secularists of our day, but that is little enough. Neither do we live in abject poverty as millions of other Christians do, yet they give thanks to God for the slightest bit of food or shelter, while we complain and get angry at God over trifles.

There's something about prosperity, material comfort and security—or merely preoccupation with worldly things—that dulls the mind and heart to spiritual awareness and the appreciation of God's gifts, and that puts out the inner fire. Affluence breeds lukewarmness. Those who are rich in possessions are often poor in grace; those who are rich in activities and pursuits are usually poor in interior life and communion with God. If we find that our other responsibilities or interests leave us no time for prayer, worship, and the contemplation of the mysteries of God, then for us God has become insignificant, and connection with Him is no longer a lifeline, a matter of supreme importance. But if our souls thirst for God, we will become quite creative in making time for Him, and we will easily put other things lower on our list of priorities. God must be the hidden treasure, the priceless pearl for which we are willing to give up everything to obtain. Yet even a cursory internet search will reveal that material prosperity and abundance are the goals not only for worldly unbelievers, but also for various new-age "spiritual" people and even some who call themselves Christians.

Faith flourishes among the martyrs, confessors, the persecuted and the disadvantaged; it languishes among the well-to-do, the "Sunday Catholics," the nominal Christians. We need to understand that faith in God is not an optional feature of human life, not something that we'd like to get around to someday, not something to delay until old age, not something that can be set aside in the clamor of our daily activities. We don't know what we've got till it's gone, as another old song reminds us. Perhaps if Christianity were outlawed in this country we would discover how precious it really is (or is not) to us. Are we willing to suffer for Jesus, to be persecuted, to lose our jobs or social status or even our lives for Him? That is the Christian life for millions all over the world. As for us, we think it is a hardship to get out of bed on Sunday morning and go to church, or to discipline our wayward desires in accordance with the Gospel.

Someday God is going to ask us what He means to us, what the sacrifice of his Son means to us, what our profession of faith means to us. We must seek Him with our whole heart, as if our eternal destiny depends on it, for it does. We must beg Him for the same fire in our hearts that the saints had, because those who really know God cannot get enough of Him, cannot live without Him—

and they never set Him aside for the trinkets of this world and all its passing fancies and seductions. One of the reasons we fast and give up certain pleasures or activities in Lent is so that our eyes can be opened, that we can live more like the poor for a while, not satisfying our every craving, but learning to live with that emptiness that God alone can fill, discovering that we *need* God if we are not to end up as a hollow shell of humanity. We need to shed the illusions of self-sufficiency, self-satisfaction and security, which impoverish our souls. It is time to stop trusting in material abundance and to rediscover the infinite value of what God gives to those who love Him.

Let us pray for our brothers and sisters for whom faith in Christ is daily a life-and-death matter. And may they pray all the more for us, for whom it is not! We need the same zeal and fervor and courage and trust in God that is proper to those who "have seen the true light and received the heavenly Spirit and found the true faith," those for whom God is of utmost importance. Let our abundance be that of divine grace, that we may understand the meaning of life and set the right priorities, serve Him who loved us unto death, and make our relationship to God the *sine qua non* of our fulfillment and happiness in this life and the life to come. Let not the soul-numbing affluence and the myriad distractions of our pleasure-loving society take their toll on your faith. "Let your manner of life," urges the Apostle, "be worthy of the gospel of Christ" (Phil. 1:27).

I Forgot

I tried to access a certain account on the internet. I couldn't because I evidently forgot my password. I didn't think I had forgotten it, but I guess I forgot that I had forgotten it. I have forgotten appointments, forgotten something I was supposed to do on a certain day, forgotten something that had popped into my mind about what had to be done right away—it popped back out of my mind too quickly. I have nutritional supplements that are supposed to help with brain function and memory, but sometimes I forget to take them. I write reminders on a pocket note pad, on little post-it notes, and even on the back of my hand, but sometimes I still forget.

Why all this talk about forgetfulness? ....oh, yes! I almost forgot—it's because it has an application to the spiritual life. Even if people are not forgetful about daily responsibilities, many seem to be quite forgetful about spiritual matters and what the Lord has been trying to teach us all these years.

It seems to me that most of the sins of people who are actually trying to be good Christians don't stem from raw malice or premeditated evil. More often than not they are the fruit of a kind of spiritual forgetfulness, an inattention or lack of vigilance, or perhaps a rather thoughtless self-centeredness. I wrote in Chapter Six that to sin is to forget that Heaven is the source of our joy. Remember?

In the parable of the sower of seeds, Jesus speaks about those from whom the devil snatches the word of God before it can take root. This can be understood as an image of spiritual forgetfulness. If the seed doesn't find rich, moist, fertile soil in which to quickly sink and germinate, it lies exposed on the hard ground where it is easy prey for anything that comes by. Likewise, when we hear the word of God and don't provide a place in our souls wherein it can help deepen our spiritual understanding, other concerns will seem more compelling (or interesting) and we end up forgetting what we heard, and it does us no good. It is as if the devil has come by and snatched it out of our consciousness.

Sometimes, in our prayer or meditation, we do actually open ourselves to receive the word of the Lord and gain some precious insight or awareness. Then, at a later time, some opportunity arises in which that insight has a practical application, but we act in our ordinary, unenlightened way. Why? Because we forgot what we had learned in the quiet moments of prayer! Such things happen to me more often than I care to admit.

St. James says that we must become "doers of the word." Certainly we have to begin by hearing the word, but that is not enough. He says: "If anyone is a hearer of the word and not a doer, he is like a man who observes his face in a mirror… and goes away and at once forgets what he looked like" (1:22-24). So how do we remember not to forget? If I had the answer to that one, I'd be much farther along the path to sanctity. But it seems to me that the answer must somehow lie in creating good habits of "doing the word." It's easier to remember to do things that we do habitually. We ordinarily don't forget to put on clothing before we go out somewhere, nor do we forget the way to a place we go to every day. Perhaps this is at least partly because if we didn't we'd soon be forced to realize that something has gone terribly wrong. But our spiritual senses may not be as alert as our bodily ones. We may go on for way too long before we realize that we're overdue for confession, or that we've been missing our daily prayers, or that we're supposed to be fasting on fast days, or whatever.

We have to start training ourselves and forming good, healthy, holy habits, so that we won't forget that human life is supposed to be about loving and serving the Lord wholeheartedly. Pray that you will retain whatever the Lord gives you in your meditation or spiritual reading, and that you learn the lessons that He teaches through the events of your life.

We cannot afford to forget, for life is demanding, the stakes are high, and judgment cannot be forestalled forever. Where our treasure is, there will our hearts (and minds) be. If it's really important to us, chances are we'll remember. Just don't forget to pray for that enlightenment by which we will be able to see things clearly, in their proper relations and priorities, so that God's will is always primary. "I will never forget your precepts, for with them You give me life" (Ps. 119:93).

System Restore

I've recently (this could be written at almost any time) endured a harrowing, frustrating, irritating, time-consuming, and generally maddening series of minor and major computer problems, ranging from losing a few downloaded programs to witnessing the dreaded blue-screen announcement: "Fatal System Error."

After praying that the ordeal would end quickly and favorably, I also prayed that I might learn whatever lesson the Lord wished me to learn through all this (also praying that I could learn lessons some other way!). I'm not sure I got whatever He was trying to tell me, but I did make applications of some of the technical terms to the spiritual life.

Two things that computers need, if they're going to access the Internet, are a "firewall" and an anti-virus program. There are "hackers" constantly trying to break into your computer through its various open "ports," so that they can steal confidential information from you (like credit card numbers when you shop online). And viruses are mostly created by demented computer geeks who have nothing better to do than create programs that will enter and jam up or destroy your computer. The devil is like a hacker, intent on stealing our virtue, with a bag full of spiritual viruses meant to ruin our spiritual lives and even destroy our souls. He looks for any open port in our spiritual defenses, any vulnerability he has observed, so that he can enter and do his dirty work. So we need the holy-fire-wall of the Spirit of God, and the sacraments which "disinfect" us from the demonic viruses and from the results of our own errors and sins.

There's an ingenious device on today's computers called "System Restore." It's sort of a time machine, which only travels backwards. When you do something really stupid, or some program has malfunctioned and your computer is in its death throes, you can, if you're able to sneak back in through "safe mode," go back in time. You set the system restore to, say, yesterday's date, *before* the disaster happened, and it will reset your computer to whatever its configurations were at that time. Then, if all goes well, all the disasters of today will disappear, for the computer has been restored to its former good functionality. It's like the crash never happened.

Oh, would that we could perform a "system restore" on our souls! Set it back to the time before your last (or first) grievous sin! Configure your soul as if all that stuff never happened! Well, we *do* have something like that. It's called absolution. We also have Holy Communion, which itself is a great system restore. Actually, the perfect one would be an adult baptism—that clears every error your computer (soul) has ever made, and restores the image of God perfectly! On psychological and emotional levels, however, it still won't be as if nothing ever happened, for we will still carry some scars and memories. But the point is, our souls don't have to "crash," we don't have to be stuck with a "fatal system error" that makes it impossible for us to function as children and servants of God.

I was so stressed after all those problems and hours spent on the phone with tech support (hey, your confessor or spiritual father can be your soul's tech support!), that I actually prayed as I received Communion that it would be a "system restore" for me. Wash away all the aggravation in that Precious Blood! Let me start fresh and at peace.

You don't have to (and I don't recommend it) express your spiritual life in terms of computer technology. But we ought to be able to see the hand of God and learn some spiritual lessons in *whatever* we do. It's important that we "maximize the performance" of our souls through continual spiritual growth (upgrades?). For there is a time on God's "scheduler," the very last event on it, called Judgment Day, when there will be only two functions left for the Master Programmer and Operator to perform: "save" or "delete." So don't delay your system restore!

Bless

"We bless you in the name of the Lord!" (Psalm 129:8). You know what is sorely missing in this world? Blessings. Not God's blessings bestowed upon us, for they are innumerable. At the root of many of the woes of the human condition is *our* failure to bless. We are often told in Holy Scripture to bless those who curse us, to return a blessing when reviled, to overcome evil with good. But somehow we seem not to think of those passages in the heat of the battle, at the moment of our being insulted or cursed or offended in some way. Not thinking of it doesn't let us off the hook, however. We have to *train* ourselves to respond with blessings—and not to wait until we must give a blessing only in response to something else, but to freely and spontaneously bless people and all creation, to have an attitude of readiness to bless.

Here are a few practical examples. Whenever you hear someone take the name of the Lord in vain, just quietly say: "Blessed be the name of the Lord!" There, you have effectively made reparation by honoring God, having "canceled out" the dishonor someone else has just showed Him. When someone is rude or unkind to you, steps ahead of you in line, cuts you off in traffic (lots of curses to overcome here!), or in any way offends you, bless them in the name of the Lord. When someone sneezes, really *mean* it when you say: God bless you! With your spouse or with friends who may have some irritating fault, rather than (first) praying that God change them, ask that He bless them and give them joy and peace. When driving by or flying over some place or city that is known for its sin, call down upon that place the blessing of the Lord. Demons cannot stand God's blessing, so they will have to leave.

In general, just *be* a blessing for others and for the creation. It is true that priests can bless in certain ways that others cannot, because of the grace given and ministry entrusted to them—and priests therefore have a great responsibility to bring God's blessing upon the world. (I once read an account of a mystic—I leave this to your discernment—who said she had a vision of a certain priest in purgatory whose right hand was shriveled, discolored, and very painful, because he did not use it to bless as he should have.) In the Byzantine tradition, when a priest blesses, he forms his hand into the letters which make up the abbreviation of the (Greek/Slavonic) name of Jesus Christ—IC XC, which inscription is found on all icons of Christ. So when a priest blesses, he blesses with the sign of the Cross and in the name of our Lord Jesus Christ—without having to say a word!

But all the baptized can in their own way bless in the name of the Lord. Parents should bless their children; "saying grace" is invoking God's blessing on our food, as well as giving thanks for it. To bless another is literally to "speak well" (*bene dicere,* whence comes "benediction") of another, especially to speak well of them to God. (In Greek a blessing is a *eu logia*, same meaning, whence comes "eulogy," speaking well of, or blessing, the deceased.)

Let us decide to bless the world, every day, in the various ways we find opportunity. If the 1.5 billion Christians in the world would simply invoke the blessing of the Lord daily, we would see things change significantly and soon. Be a blessing for others as you "speak well" of them and draw them into the Lord's blessing by your prayer. The blessed life begins here and now.

Kindled by Hell

Now we look at the flip side of blessing. St. James gives us a quite unambiguous treatment of the matter of sins of the tongue. Meditation on the third chapter of his Epistle is a penance I sometimes give to people who confess gossiping, lying, or any other sort of harm done with words.

Let's get right to the point: "The tongue is a fire. The tongue is an unrighteous world among our members, staining the whole body...and kindled by Hell...a restless evil, full of deadly poison" (3:6-8). He also likens it to a tiny rudder that steers a large ship. Such a small thing, the tongue, but such great pretensions! Such potential for both good and evil! You probably don't have to think too hard to remember times when you've said things you've later regretted, things that hurt other people. Or times when you have used profane language, taken the name of God in vain, ridiculed others, or perhaps started or continued some rumor or gossip that ended up doing far more damage than you bargained for. We all have, and St. James is the first to admit it: "We all make many mistakes, and if anyone makes no mistakes in what he says, he is perfect..." (v 2). But the Apostle is trying to get us to reduce such mistakes to an absolute minimum.

For this he invites us to see things a little more clearly, to see the gravity of what we are doing, and its contradictory nature: "With [the tongue] we bless the Lord and Father, and with it we curse men, who are made in the likeness of God. From the same mouth come blessing and cursing. My brethren, this ought not to be so" (vv 9-10). We bless God and we curse the images of God. Put that way, it is clear how wrong and self-contradictory it is (that's *why* he put it that way). In this we see the slippery nature of the tongue, and why he says it is kindled by Hell and full of poison. The devil is called the "father of lies," so our misuse of the tongue puts us in his camp. To use the tongue to bless God and condemn others is like using a chalice for both sacred and profane purposes.

But we don't literally have to curse or condemn someone to be doing the opposite of blessing. Whatever hurts, whatever cuts, whatever denigrates, whatever spreads falsehood—these are all part of that "restless evil." The correction of all this is an important ascetical work. Now it is clear that sometimes love demands the use of stern words, to correct, to discipline, but ultimately to enlighten and heal. Some words that "hurt" another can actually be therapeutic, if they serve that person's growth and/or conversion. But we usually know darn well what is the intention of our words, whether they are aimed to hurt or to heal, to tear down or to build up, or simply to get the last one in.

One antidote to all the evils of the tongue is simply to bless, as I said above. If we *choose* to bless instead of curse or revile, and make a habit of it, we will notice that we are using our tongues less for evil and more for good. Of course, this is not just a matter of the tongue but of the heart. We will not be able to habitually bless if we have not yet learned to love—or at least to act in loving ways toward others. From a heart that loves, blessing will naturally pour forth, and likewise cursing from a heart that is cold and hard. "Out of the abundance of the heart the mouth speaks" (Matthew 12:34). Lift up your heart, then, to the Lord, and pray that He make it a source of blessing, so that your tongue will be a tongue of fire-- kindled not by Hell, but by the Holy Spirit. Then begin to bless God and all his images.

But I Don't...

Have you ever had the following kind of experience? Let's say you read from Ezekiel 36 and hear the Lord say: "you shall be clean from all your uncleannesses... A new heart I will give you, and a new spirit I will put within you..." Then you pause and reflect for a moment and exclaim: "But I'm *not* clean from uncleanness, I *don't* have a new heart, I *don't* have a new spirit! I'm exactly as I always was, despite my urgent and sincere prayers!" Or what if you read from John 14 and hear Jesus say: "he who believes in me will do the works that I do, and greater works than these he will do... Whatever you ask in my name, I will do it..." After a bit more reflection you shout: "But I *don't* do the works He did, let alone *greater* ones! And I *don't* receive whatever I ask in his name!" Or suppose you just read here and there throughout the Scriptures and finally begin to scream: "But I *don't* have peace with God, I'm *not* filled with all the fullness of God, I'm *not* strong, I have *not* overcome the evil one, I'm *not* the salt of the earth, I'm *not* the light of the world, the truth has *not* set me free, I *don't* 'rejoice with unutterable and exalted joy,' I *don't* have wisdom—I'm constantly failing, messing things up, and I'm full of doubt and confusion despite my best efforts and prayers!"

Well, don't expect *me* to solve your problems—I've got enough of my own! But there are a few things to look at here. Most of the promises in Scripture are conditional in some way. You'll notice that most are also in the future tense, so perhaps their time simply has not yet come. Some things require faith, some require love, as conditions for the manifestation of what God has promised. We are perhaps coming up short in these areas, and though God would like to give us what He promised, He sees we haven't yet the capacity to receive or even to recognize his gifts. It could be that we haven't matured to the level at which we could bear fruit from what we ask for, or that we are simply asking for the wrong things, or the right things at the wrong time, or the right things for the wrong reasons. God has to keep track of all these variables, and we ought to give Him credit for being rather good at it, so we're going to have to do one or more of the following: 1) stop bellyaching; 2) repent; 3) grow up; 4) be patient; 5) redouble our efforts; 6) trust; 7) trust some more; 8) be content with slow progress; 9) get help; 10) persevere anyway.

St. Bernard of Clairvaux wrote something that will perhaps be of no small assistance in the matter: "Every time I speak about prayer, it seems to me that I hear in your heart certain human reflections that I have often heard, even in my own heart. Since we never stop praying, how come we so rarely seem to experience the fruit of prayer? We have the impression that we come out of prayer like we entered into it; no one answers us with even one word, gives us anything at all; we have the impression that we have labored in vain. But what does the Lord say in the gospel? 'Stop judging by appearances and make a just judgment' (Jn. 7 :24). What is a just judgment other than a judgment of faith? For 'the just man shall live by faith' (Gal. 3:11). So follow the judgment of faith rather than your experience, for faith does not deceive, whereas experience can lead into error.

"And what is the truth of faith other than that the Son of God himself promised: 'If you are ready to believe that you will receive whatever you ask for in prayer, it shall be done for you' (Mk. 11:24). Thus, may no one among you, Brothers, consider prayer to be a small thing. For I assure you, the one to whom it is addressed does not consider it a small thing; even before it has left our mouth, he has had it written down in his book. Without the slightest doubt, we can be sure that God will either give us what we are asking him or he will give us something that he knows to be better. For 'we do not know how to pray as we ought' (Rom. 8:26), but God has compassion on our ignorance and he receives our prayer with kindness... So 'take delight in the Lord, and he will grant you your heart's requests'"(Ps. 37:4). [*Sermons for Lent*, no. 5, 5]

Perhaps we should just accept that "we do not know how to pray as we ought," and then put our trust in the providence of God, who knows how to grant what *He* ought, and who knows what is best for our spiritual growth and salvation. So let us take heart. At a recent audience in Rome, the Pope assured us that Jesus "adapts Himself to our weakness," knowing that we aren't what we should be, that we don't know how to pray as we ought, and that we haven't yet born much fruit from his grace. Benedict XVI said: "From the ingenuous enthusiasm of the initial adherence, passing through the painful experience of denial and the tears of conversion, Peter came to entrust himself to Jesus, who adapted Himself to his poor capacity to love. And He also shows us the way, despite all our weakness. We know that Jesus adapts Himself to our weakness. We follow Him, with our poor capacity to love, and we know that Jesus is good and he accepts us."

Courage, then. Look not at your defeats but at Christ's victory, not at your inner chaos, but at Him who makes all things new. If you pray but one prayer earnestly and from the heart—"Thy will be done!"—you can be sure it will be answered.

Reflections on My Reflections on St. Bernard's Reflections

Perhaps I ought to clarify or further reflect on a few things I wrote above. While we can always expect to receive edifying insights from the writings of the saints, we (thankfully) don't have to expect warmed-over hackneyed piety. In his sermon I just quoted, St. Bernard makes the unvarnished statement that the rest of us recognize as true but are afraid to come right out and say: "We have the impression that we come out of prayer like we entered into it; no one answers us with even one word, gives us anything at all; we have the impression that we have labored in vain." But of course he doesn't just leave us hanging there with our disappointed hopes. He offers a profound insight.

Now, the Fathers and Doctors of the Church are criticized (sometimes justly) for interpreting issues or answering questions with their (sometimes ingenious) concatenations of wholly unrelated biblical passages. But I like St. Bernard's answer here: "What does the Lord say in the gospel? 'Stop judging by appearances and make a just judgment' (Jn. 7 :24). What is a just judgment other than a judgment of faith? For 'the just man shall live by faith' (Gal. 3:11). So follow the judgment of faith rather than your experience, for faith does not deceive, whereas experience can lead into error."

A just judgment of the issue of apparently unanswered prayer is a judgment of faith, for if you are just you live by faith. If you live by faith, that means you assess and interpret the events and experiences of your life according to the content and dynamics of Christian faith, and not merely by what you see, hear, feel, etc. So if you live by faith, you trust that God hears your prayer and will answer in the way that is best for your spiritual progress and salvation. This "judgment of faith" is more reliable than your subjective experience, says St. Bernard, and we ought to have discovered by now that indeed "faith does not deceive, whereas experience can lead into error." For we seldom know how to interpret our own experience, bound up as it often is with emotional excess, perceptual defect, and the coloration of our own desires and expectations.

This "judgment of faith" can apply to the other issues treated above, which are matters of experience—or rather, of *not* experiencing the joy, the peace, the inner transformation and renewal that the Gospel promises. Therefore experience, or the lack thereof, cannot be the ultimate measure of our life in Christ. Living by faith must be the bottom line. That's why the last of the 10 suggestions is probably the most important: Persevere Anyway. For if the just one is to live by faith, such a one must learn how to persevere through the vicissitudes of various experiences and through the uncharted waters of "unknowing." We may simply have to humble ourselves in the awareness that we still have a long way to go before we are even capable of immersion in the mysteries of God. The Elder Macarius of Optina said: "Do not look for any remarkable gift of prayer in your heart. You are not worthy of it. Rather, let the empty, cold dryness of your prayer be food for your humility..." You won't find *that* passage quoted in any modern spiritual self-help book!

Finally, as to what I quoted from the Pope. His gentle teaching about Christ adapting Himself to our weakness should not be interpreted as Christ condoning or tolerating our sin, permitting us to remain in it and promising forgiveness in the end. No, Christ hates sin and does not tolerate any sort of evil at all. But He adapts Himself to our weakness by accepting our inadequate (though sincere) response to his love and his call to holiness. He meets us at our low level, but this is for the sake of raising us up to his exalted level. He accepts our meager offerings—if that's all we're able to offer at this moment—while He tries to teach us the meaning of a complete and unreserved self-gift. He doesn't hold us to a standard impossible for us to meet—but He still grants us the grace to continually meet higher standards than before. He will not stop at anything short of our perfection, for nothing defiled can enter the Kingdom of Heaven, as the Good Book says.

So continue to pray, continue to struggle, continue to seek the face of Him who calls you—in short, continue to live by faith. Make the judgment of faith upon the events of your life, and not merely that of experience. Then someday you'll have the opportunity to talk things over with St. Bernard in that place where you don't even need faith anymore—only love.

Rush Hour

A man wedged in traffic
has no patience for poetry.
Don't tell him that the clouds
look like angels today,
as he laments the long trail of snails
that delays access to his next
arena of frustration.

He fumes, like the massive metal beast
whose black, poison exhaust mingles with
his own exhausted soul.
His horn cries unnoticed by that
mountainous machine
beyond which he can see
nothing.

On with the A/C, the CD,
or the DJ's traffic update—oh,
an accident a mile ahead will
detain him another hour!
Coffee's cold; out of smokes;
vacation's still three months away.

Was it an accident? Or was it designed
by some sadistic mind,
this daily round of hurrying toward
dead-end streets,
always looking for his exit
yet never breaking free?

He's entered the twilight zone.
It's the spite of the gods
(he made for himself)
that sends him on this endless trek
only to realize that it's
Monday morning, once again...

Me, I crunch my way down leaf-strewn paths
as the choirs in the trees
herald with gentle melodies

the peaceful sun of the morning,
enraptured, as if today's a new creation.
And I'm given patience for poetry.

But I don't dare "thank God
I'm not like other men,"
condemned to impotent rage.
True, I do prefer our rustic trails
to those highway snails, by far—
but harried, hurried hearts
can also lodge in sacred temples.

And I know that there are still souls
who drive those relentless roads,
who have received their Christ-key
to open the gate to the Other World.
They see the cloud-angels
and they've learned the secret of blessing.

The God of mountain-top ecstasies
and inaccessible Light
will speak his own poetry
of wordless, pure refreshment
to anyone who's not yet sold his soul,
who longs for eyes to see
His omnipresent artistry.

❧ Chapter Nine:
My Prayer is My Prayer ❧

Some people, who don't pray much, like to say things like, "My work is my prayer," or "My nature walks are my prayer." Those assertions can be true, but only if there is an actual prayer-life fueling the work and the walks. Your work can be your prayer only if there are times when your prayer is your work. Prayer— real, focused, serious, extended, explicit—is essential to any deep and genuine relationship with God, for it is our primary "contact" with Heaven. Let your prayer be your prayer; then everything else you do will share in its blessings.

What is Prayer? Speaking, Listening, Living

Many volumes can be (and have been) written on prayer, so I won't go into whole lot of detail here. I would, however, like to begin with a little refresher course on three very general dimensions: prayer as speaking, listening, and living.

We're probably mostly familiar with prayer as speaking, talking to God—though sometimes it degenerates into "instructing" Him about how things ought to be, or yelling or complaining. Liturgical prayer is full of words, though these are better sung than spoken. Most of our various devotions are full of words, too, and this is OK, as long as it isn't the sum total of our prayer.

We really must speak to God, because we need to unburden our hearts, to know that there is Someone there who will listen to us and who understands both our inner and outer situations, as well as our stumbling attempts to express ourselves. We don't have to walk on eggshells around God or polish our grammar. He wants us to be ourselves, because He has no use for phony piety or a veneer of righteousness, if that's what we're going to present to Him. All He really wants to do is heal our broken or defiled hearts.

So the first thing is to be honest. Once you've offered some formal or traditional prayers, just sit down and open your heart and tell the Lord about your day. Sometimes the above-mentioned yelling and complaining might enter here, but even that is not so bad, as long as it isn't mean-spirited or self-indulgent. After all, even the psalmists, whose prayers are part of the Bible, yelled and complained. One of my favorite introductions is from Psalm 64: "Hear me, O God, as I complain..." No pious façade there! But your prayer must not *end* with your complaint. Shortly I'll discuss quietly waiting for God's answer.

Words can be helpful for expressing what we wish to offer to God in prayer, be it adoration, thanksgiving, supplication, or repentance. We have to be a little careful, though, especially if we happen to be rather good with words, that we don't end up offering prayers that have a satisfying sound for us, when they may not be so satisfying to God! Yet we were created as the only earthbound beings that can think and communicate with words, so it's of our very nature to want to speak to God, to praise and thank Him, to enter into a dialogue of love with Him. The mouth speaks from the abundance of the heart, and the Lord is waiting to hear from us.

Probably the bulk of most people's prayers are prayers of petition. In fact, the word "prayer" literally means a request or entreaty. This kind of prayer is often considered the lowest form of prayer, unless your entreaty is an act of intercession for others. But it's clear in the Scriptures that God knows we'll be praying for our own needs as well, and He welcomes such prayer. Pope John Paul II, one of the great men of prayer of recent decades, said that when he was young, he didn't use this kind of prayer much. "A prayer of supplication seemed to be something unworthy," he told one of his biographers. Asking for things seemed too small. But as he grew older, he changed his mind. "Today I ask very much," he then said.

The Lord told us to ask and we shall receive—perhaps not exactly what and when our prayers specify, but we shall receive good things from the hand of the Father, as He does everything for our spiritual growth and salvation. But it is still important to ask. Once a man was healed from a certain affliction, and he gave the credit to God. A friend taunted him a bit: "How do you know it was *God* who healed you?" "Simple," he replied, "He was the only one I asked!"

Then let's open our hearts and our mouths to bless the Lord and pray to Him. So much evil is done with words, so many mouths need a good washing out with soap! Let us use ours to adore the

Lord and give him thanks, to make reparation for those who blaspheme or sin with words, to repent of our own sins and to seek his assistance in our needs and those of others. For even if speaking to God isn't the highest form of prayer, it is one He cherishes and expects from us, his children. But let us ask the Holy Spirit to inspire our words, for we know not how to pray as we ought, yet the Spirit can give us words that will find their way to the Heart of God. "Hear my prayer, O Lord, and let my cry come unto You... Incline your ear to me; answer me speedily in the day when I call!" (Ps. 102).

Though speaking to God is legitimate prayer, it is often, and rightly, said that prayer is a *dialogue* with God. I don't think it has ever been said that prayer is a *monologue* directed towards God. But that's what it often becomes if we don't become quiet after we've said our piece and give God a chance to say his.
For a while those "Question Authority" bumper stickers were popular, until someone came out with one that read: "Question Authority: Then Listen for the Answer."

An essential part of prayer is listening, though that may be the part we're somewhat uncomfortable with. We may get a little fidgety, anxious, or discouraged, if we don't "hear" anything while we're trying to listen in prayer. Even so, it ought to be clear to us that listening is still more important than speaking, when it comes to prayer (and most anything else). We already know what *we* have to say; wouldn't it be much more beneficial to listen to what Eternal Wisdom and Love has to say?

But what can you expect God to say, anyway? Is He going to give you tips on how to manage your day, or will He point out your faults, or will He speak words of blessing and comfort, or will He just give a sermon? I don't know. *Ask* Him! Then listen.

The first thing to do is to try to get a little outer, then inner, silence. You can't expect to hear the whispers of the Holy Spirit with the stereo on, or with a lot of commotion going on around you. Go find a quiet place and do your best to set aside all your cares and worries for just a little while. Remind yourself that you're not going to solve your problems in the next 20 minutes anyway, so just put them on hold. Now, if you want to hear what God has to say to you, where's the first place you'd go? To his word, of course! The Bible is full of God's dialogues with man, and many people have found that God really answers the cries of their hearts (and even their specific questions) through the words of the Scriptures. So open the Book, read until something moves you, then put it down and let the word sink into you, let the Holy Spirit enlighten you and show you how the word of God is living and active, penetrating your very soul, making clear the way of salvation. You may wish to pray the Jesus Prayer or some other short, repetitive prayer in case your attention wanders, but even that prayer is meant to turn into silence while you just rest (not sleep!) in the presence of the Lord, who loves you and wants to engage in an ongoing dialogue with you. Focus on a holy icon of Christ or the Mother of God if that helps keep your attention and sense of communication with God.

You may find (or not) that your mind clears, your body and spirit relax, that the truths of revelation become more lucid, more meaningful to you, and that you become aware of the presence of the Lord. Actually, the various possible "effects" of prayer are not all that important at any given time. The Lord, not you, will choose when the moments of grace and clarity and revelation and peace will come. What you are doing when you try to listen in prayer is at the root of all contemplative prayer: you are creating an inner "space" for God; you are cultivating an interior disposition of readiness, surrender, openness, and loving docility to the movements of the Holy Spirit. Your prayer may seem dry and even boring sometimes, but as long as you are opening that interior "place of the heart" for God, He will respond. Perhaps not during your time of prayer; perhaps when you least expect it. But leave it up to Him. When you make a place for God, He will fill it.

Though I'm offering a few short reflections here, you shouldn't really expect anyone to be able to *tell* you how to pray. Does anyone have to tell you how to appreciate a sunset or a starry sky, or how to enjoy the company of someone you love? It just happens—though you have to put yourself in the place where the sun or stars or your beloved are, and pay a little attention. (If you're so burdened that you don't even look up, you won't see the stars— but that doesn't mean they're not there, waiting to fill you with wonder and delight.) Someone once said that you learn to pray by praying, and you pray well by praying much.

So, be still and know that the Lord is God. Give Him some time, let go of your diversions and ceaseless activities for a while. Make the effort to listen during times of prayer, and you'll end up being able to listen to Him all the time, and in all different circumstances. Then you're ready for the dialogue of love.

Speaking and listening bear fruit in the "prayer of living." This is in some ways both the easiest and most difficult way of prayer. It's easy because virtually everything you do can be transformed into prayer, and difficult because you need to be conscious of it and also to avoid that which really *can't* be turned into prayer.

If prayer is a dialogue with God, then it shouldn't be limited to short periods of actually sitting down and speaking or listening, but it ought to be ongoing. People often tend not to want to pray a whole lot because they compartmentalize their lives in such a way as to set aside "religious" activities for a certain time and place— and those activities aren't the most "fun." But, you know, God isn't "religious." To be in frequent or constant contact with or awareness of God is not being religious, it is being *real*. God is the Ultimate Reality, the Creator and Destiny of all that is real, and without his ever-present sustaining power and love, we would instantly vanish into nothingness! So prayer is life, connection with the Source of life without whom we cannot even exist, let alone plan our lives as we see fit.

All we do can be an offering to God, a prayer. But daily activities can only be transformed into prayer if the deep relationship with God that this requires is cultivated through sufficient time devoted to nothing else but speaking and listening to God. What kind of relationship would parents have with their children if, for example, they said: "I work all day to provide for them," but *never spent any time* with them? But if sufficient time is spent with them to build up a personal and loving relationship, then your time at work which provides for them will also be a fruitful part of the relationship. So it is with God. Don't say that you serve Him if you don't spend any time with Him cultivating a loving relationship. When you do that, however, then your other activities can contribute to fostering this relationship, and all will bear fruit.

We ought to start the day with some sort of dedication of it to God (see an example below), so that his providence and presence will be manifest throughout, and so that you can *be* a living prayer, even when your duties are so absorbing that you can't explicitly say the words of prayer or take time to be silent. Then try to "connect" with God regularly throughout the day. This is not that hard, if only you can leave yourself some sort of reminder. Every now and then, take one minute—sixty seconds—to stop whatever you are doing and re-invite God into your day, your heart, thoughts, and work. This may not seem like much in the way of prayer, but it is quite significant. You are breaking through the wall of your unawareness that makes it seem like God is far away. You are piercing the insulating bubble of the world with all its demands and seductions, and you are letting God in to bring his peace and holiness and divine refreshment. Try it and see if it doesn't make a difference in your day and in your spiritual life. Then when you return to your time of more explicit prayer, you won't feel as if you've been away from God since your last prayer time.

We have to keep recalling ourselves to the meaning of our lives, to our reason of being, to the awareness of where we came from and where we are going. The meaning of life isn't mere biological survival, emotional satisfaction, or the pursuit of anything that can only bring ephemeral pleasure or security. We were created by and for God, who has revealed to us that He wants us to have everlasting happiness with Him.

So let prayer be life and life be prayer. When you learn how to stop during the day to give thanks and praise to God, the next step will be to develop the ability to use the Jesus Prayer or something similar frequently throughout the day, so that it eventually becomes a constant, quiet, murmuring stream in your heart, in your conscious and unconscious mind. Then you can even take prayer into your sleep!

Speak to God, listen to God, live for and in God. This is the life of prayer. It's so much different (and better) than merely "saying your prayers." It's *being your* prayers!

Morning Prayer

There's a beautiful (yet sober) morning prayer which is worth remembering and praying. I find it quite helpful for facing each new day. It is called the Morning Prayer of the Optina Elders (Optina is a famous Russian monastery).

> *"O Lord, grant that I may greet with your
> peace all that this day is to bring. Grant me the
> grace to surrender myself completely to your
> holy will. In every hour of this day, instruct
> and guide me in all things. Whatever tidings I
> may receive during this day, teach me to
> accept them tranquilly in the firm belief that
> your holy will governs all. Govern my thoughts
> and feelings in all I do and say. When*

*unforeseen things occur, let me not forget that
all is sent by You. Teach me to behave sincerely
and reasonably toward everyone, that I may
bring confusion and sorrow to no one. Bestow
on me, O Lord, the strength to endure the
fatigue of the day and to bear my part in its
events. Guide my will and teach me to pray, to
believe, to hope, to suffer, to forgive, and to
love.”*

Unlike some other prayers I have said in the past, this one
seems to be sticking with me and coming to mind during the day. I
think that is because I tend to view unpleasant circumstances or
unexpected trials as rude and unacceptable intrusions into the
order of my day. So I have to start out by asking to be able to “greet
with [God’s] peace” all these things, and whatever the day will
bring, surrendering myself to God’s will. Since I don’t often know
precisely what this will is to which I’m surrendering myself, I need
to be instructed and guided, “every hour of this day,” and “in all
things.”

The passage that keeps coming to me, because of the “tidings
I may receive this day,” is the governance of God’s will. When I get
sick or injured or just have a million little things go wrong, I have
to keep saying: “Your holy will governs all.” Therefore my thoughts
and emotions also have to be governed by that same will. One of
the hardest ones is: “let me not forget that all is sent by You.”
Perhaps we could say that even if not everything, especially the bad
stuff, is directly *sent* by God, it has been *permitted* (which is still a
divine act), and therefore it retains a place in his plan for my
growth and salvation. If evil suggestions or morally-compromising
situations come into our lives, however, we ought to assume that
God has permitted them not that we might *accept* them, but that
we might *fight* them. To accept his will doesn’t mean to roll over
and play dead, but to *do what his will requires* in any given
situation, trusting that everything is in his hands. God is the Lord—
of the galaxies and of the details of my daily life, and nothing
escapes his loving attention and faithful application of his divine
decrees and remedies.

Thus the prayer has us look at what *we* have to do. It’s not
only for us passively to accept what the day brings, but we are
required to “behave sincerely and reasonably toward everyone,”
bringing “confusion and sorrow to no one.” Finally we ask for

strength to bear the burdens of the day and to be able to cooperate with God's designs therein. And if only we can do this: "to pray, to believe, to hope, to suffer, to forgive, and to love," then we are surely allowing God's will to govern all.

Try this prayer out. See if it doesn't remind you of the active presence of God's will in the events of your day and help you surrender thereto. If we can accept all things tranquilly in the firm belief that God's will governs all, we've come a long way into the life of blessed peace and trust to which He calls us.

Intercession: The Love of Christ Impels Us

What does it mean when we "intercede" for someone, offer "intercessory" prayer? Is it something other than just "saying a prayer" for them? As you have probably just guessed, it is. The word "intercede" literally means to "go between." If I offer intercessory prayer for you, I stand between you and God, "connecting" the two of you, as it were. I bring your needs before the face of God, and if it pleases Him, He will hear my prayer and grant what you need.

Why is it, though, that I don't merely pray for my own needs and you pray for yours? Do we need each other as "go-betweens" with God? The answer lies not in any metaphysical necessity, but in the will and love of God. God is personal and He works through persons, be they angels or men, and not simply by almighty divine *fiat*. God is love, and what He does in and through us is love. Jean Lafrance, after reading the writings of St. Silouan of Mt. Athos, remarked: "He especially showed me how much *God's love impels us to intercede* for our brothers" (emphasis in the original).

In her book, *Secret of the Heart: Spiritual Being*, Jean-Marie Howe, OCSO, writes: "In the second letter to the Corinthians, Saint Paul makes a remark about people who believe that Jesus died for all in order that all might live in him. He says that the love of God 'controls' or 'compels' them; some translations use the words 'forces,' 'constrains,' or 'pushes.' These are strong words; Saint Paul is speaking of an intense interior movement rather than of some vague influence."

She continues: "What is this love of which he speaks? It is the love that 'impelled' Christ to die in order for all to be reconciled with God... The love of Christ that inspires Christians is a love that seeks the salvation of all humanity. Ultimately, Christians are motivated, perhaps even 'compelled,' not by their love *for* Christ, but by the very love *of* Christ burning within their hearts...

Allow me to let her do the talking: "If one pursues this passage of Scripture a bit further, one finds that the Greek word which is translated as 'constrains' or 'compels' is used elsewhere with the additional connotation of 'anguish' (Lk. 12:50; 2Cor. 2:4). This love of Christ is an anguished love; perhaps this is what Pascal meant when he said that Christ would be in agony until the end of the world. The love that compels Christ can know no respite until *all* creation is reconciled with God. To the degree that one can say, 'I live now not with my own life but with the life of Christ who lives in me' (Gal. 2:20), one will be compelled by this consuming love which gives itself for the salvation of the world. This *anguished love* is the heart of Christian prayer... In speaking this way, we realize that Christian intercession is intimately associated with the primordial intercession of Christ, identified both with the sin of the world and the loving will of the Father, even to the point of holocaust."

Finally, she quotes a passage from Dom Andre Louf, who wrote the following after visiting a hermit on Mt. Athos: "Suddenly, I was very, very touched by a deep impression that in this private chapel before a primitive iconostasis, in the sanctuary of this hermit I was really at the heart of the world and of the Church. There was nothing more important than to be there and pray. The only important thing in the world was to be there before the face of Christ."

Mother Jean-Marie concludes that monks especially ought to have this attitude in response to all those who seek our intercession, who need us to stand for them before the face of God—He who alone can soothe the wounds of bodies and souls that ache with their need for the Savior. For monks, she says, "The only thing that matters is to *be* there, in the monastery, at the heart of the world, at the heart of the Church, and pray."

Monks may have a special charism for intercession, but as members of the Body of Christ we are all called to stand before the face of God for those who entrust their needs to us, those who perhaps have lost all strength and hope and confidence to go to the Throne of Grace alone. We bear the burdens of our brothers and sisters and thus fulfill the law of Christ (Gal. 6:2). We don't just say prayers. We intercede, we "go between," for the love of Christ impels us.

Heschel on Prayer

I began reading Abraham Heschel a few years ago, and I still go back to him once in a while for some spiritual refreshment. His insights into the mystery of God are profound and his articulation is eloquent. Even though his works need the completion which only the revelation of Christ can bring, what I quote from him can benefit the spiritual life of any Christian. The following passages on prayer are from *Man's Quest for God.*

"How good it is to wrap oneself in prayer, spinning a deep softness of gratitude to God around all thoughts, enveloping oneself in the silken veil of song... [Prayer's] drive enables us to delve into what is beneath our beliefs and desires, and emerge with a renewed taste for the infinite simplicity of the good. On the globe of the microcosm, the flow of prayer is like the Gulf Stream, imparting warmth to all that is cold, melting all that is hard in our life. For even loyalties may freeze to indifference if detached from the stream which carries the strength to be loyal... Prayer revives and keeps alive the rare greatness of some past experience in which things glowed with meaning and blessing. It remains important, even when we ignore it for a while, like a candlestick set aside for the day. Night will come, and we shall again gather round its tiny flame...

"It is the spiritual power of the praying man that makes manifest what is dormant in the text [of the prayer]... The service of prayer, the worship of the heart, fulfills itself not in the employment of words as a human expression, but in the celebration of words as a holy reality... Praying means to take hold of a word, the end, so to speak, of a line that leads to God... But praying also means that the echo of the word falls like a plummet into the depth of the soul...

"Whose ear has ever heard how all the trees sing to God? Has our reason ever thought of calling upon the sun to praise the Lord? And yet, what the ear fails to perceive, what reason fails to conceive, our prayer makes clear to our souls. It is a higher truth, to be grasped by the spirit: 'All Thy works praise Thee' (Ps. 145:10). We are not alone in our acts of praise. Wherever there is life, there is silent worship. The world is always on the verge of becoming one in adoration. It is man who is the cantor of the universe, and in whose life the secret of cosmic prayer is disclosed."

Makes you want to start praying right away, doesn't it? I think we often need to acquire a more profound vision of prayer and of our relationship to God, lest we succumb to lassitude, boredom, or frustration. Merely "saying our prayers" in a routine or inattentive manner will not plunge us into the heart of the Mystery. We have to breathe prayer, be prayer, and let it flow through us like a river of life. It's your turn now—be the cantor of the universe.

Believe and Receive?

There are some texts in the Bible that make it seem like getting what you ask for in prayer is a pretty simple thing. Just believe and receive: "Whatever you ask in prayer, believe that you receive it, and you will" (Mark 11:24). If I prayed for a Mercedes, or a 20-pound bar of gold, and believed that I would receive it, would I? St. James says I wouldn't: "You ask and do not receive, because you ask wrongly, to spend it on your passions" (4:3). So, there's more to it than simply believing and asking! The point is, you can't isolate one passage of Scripture from the rest, and then try to make it work to your advantage. The "believe and receive, name it and claim it" approach is not valid or authentic, and it certainly doesn't do justice to the dynamic and loving relationship with God that He desires from us.

Jesus has said many things about prayer, and what He said must be taken as a whole to understand what his teaching really is, and thus to be able to expect the true fruits of prayer. He did say in one place, "Ask and you shall receive," but He qualified it in another place: *If you abide in me, and my words abide in you*, ask whatever you will, and it shall be done for you" (John 15:7). This is an important condition. Jesus is not a vending machine for miracles. If we are to receive what we ask for in prayer, we must be in a living, personal relationship with Him (abiding in Him), and we must live fully in accord with his teaching (his words abide in us). Only then can we expect to receive what we ask for. But there is another, even more fundamental condition.

St. John gives it to us in his First Epistle: "If we ask anything *according to his will*, he hears us" (5:14). This is the bottom line of all prayer of petition. It follows from the previous condition: if we abide in Christ and his words abide in us, then we will *know* what to ask for, we will have the knowledge and awareness to ask for what He wills. Certainly, then, we will receive it, since He wants his will to be done, for our well-being and salvation. This union with Christ and his words, however, may be a long process, and therefore it may take time, and perhaps some trial and error, before his will becomes clear to us. That is why we have to trust Him enough so that if we *don't* receive what we asked for, we can accept that we were asking for something that was not his will, at least not at that time.

Our faith is not in the power of faith or of prayer; our faith is in God. Period. Therefore we don't try to use biblical passages as foolproof formulas for getting what we want. We submit ourselves to the will of God because we believe in Him and love Him, and because "we know and believe the love God has for us" (1John 4:16). We don't ask for anything "so that we can spend it on our passions." We pray that God will "grant our petitions which are unto salvation" (from the Byzantine Liturgy). Surely if a human father will give his children not stones but bread, the Heavenly Father will give all that is good from the treasury of the Holy Spirit to those who ask in faith and trust.

So it's not just "believe and receive." It's believe—abide, let his words abide, ask according to his will, trust in his wise providence—and receive, as it pleases God to give. That alone will ensure our spiritual well-being and eternal happiness, and it will keep us in peace and free from frustration in the meantime. We're in good hands, and we don't have to attempt to wrest anything out of them by "working" the Bible to our advantage.

All right, so I won't get the gold or the Mercedes. But those are mere trinkets compared to what God has prepared for those who love Him.

Martha, Martha

The story of Jesus' visit to his friends Martha and Mary (Luke 10:38-42) is well-known, as is its standard spiritual interpretation: Martha represents the "active" life and Mary the "contemplative" life, the latter being understood to have higher value because of its more direct relation to God and because of Jesus' words about Mary choosing the "better part" (literally, the "good portion"). But the story deserves another look. We ought to notice that it is not the "active life" as such, i.e., the labors of active service to God and one's neighbor, that is somehow of inferior value. Martha was not criticized, either by Luke or by Jesus, for serving (indeed, to serve is of the essence of Christian life, and Jesus Himself said that He came to serve). Luke says, however, that Martha was "distracted" because of her service, and this is the beginning of the difficulties. Jesus does not offer his gentle reproach because she is serving, but because she is "anxious and troubled about many things." It is her anxiety, not her serving, that places her, on the scale of values, a step below Mary's quiet listening to Jesus' words.

One can listen to the word of God even while serving, if one is free from anxiety, distraction, and other such troubles. Listening to the words of Jesus is always the "good portion" in comparison to anxious and unrecollected busyness. But service is essential to the Christian vocation, so we have to learn how to listen while serving, in addition to making adequate time for quiet listening alone. For if we do not set aside sufficient "quality time" for contemplative prayer, which is basically listening to the word of God and responding in faith and love, we will not be able to listen well during our times of more active service.

As I mentioned above, God will fill whatever interior space we open to Him, and our silent prayer time is meant precisely to create "space" within our hearts for his indwelling. It doesn't matter if we do not experience his presence during the times we explicitly invite Him to abide in us. As long as we faithfully do so, He will come, perhaps in a way and at an hour we least expect. God is sovereign and free, and the fact that we give Him a certain amount of time each day doesn't bind Him to manifest Himself during those particular times. But be sure that if you open your heart to Him in prayer, He will come to you, sooner or later, with his blessing and grace.

So be like Martha in your zeal to serve, but do not be like her in her anxiety and distraction. Be like Mary in your quiet, focused listening to the Lord, both in the solitude of your contemplative prayer time and in the activity of your serving. No one will take from you this good portion.

What do You Need?

Only you can answer that question. Or can you? Maybe you don't know what you really need, or maybe you *think* you know, but in fact you've got it all wrong. Maybe you know what you'd like, but maybe that isn't good for you, or for your salvation. There is someone who knows what you need. You may not think so, or you may not confidently entrust your needs to Him, but Jesus says clearly that your heavenly Father does know what you need, even before you ask Him.

Consider the lilies of the field, the Lord says, how God clothes them with beauty—plants that bloom and die within a few weeks. What about us who have been created and destined for eternal life? Not only does He know our needs better than we do, He tries to enlighten us to understand that, so we can trust Him enough to wait for the fulfillment of his providence in our lives.

God's very presence ought to be enough for us. Now that doesn't mean that the spiritual awareness of his presence will replace food and clothing and the means to acquire other material needs. But it means that our prayer can be a simple entering into his presence, without a list of anxious or urgent petitions that we're trying to get Him to act upon now, alerting Him to our needs. To pray is to become aware that He already knows, already has our best interests at heart.

"This entrusting to God the judgment of my real needs, therefore, is the heart of the prayer of request. For a Christian, asking God for specific things is optional; what is not optional is entering in silence and solitude of heart into his presence... Prayer, far from being an effort to inform God of anything He does not yet know, is the crucial entering of the Christian into the lived reality of his trust in God, his passing from a condition of incertitude, anxiety, and distrust to a firm state of soul in which all his tendency to calculate and to insure his own welfare gradually yields to the encompassing presence of God's providence" (Erasmo Leiva-Merikakis).

So before you *tell* God what you need, *ask* God what you need. We try desperately to convince God, to demonstrate that what we're asking for is the only sensible solution, to remind Him that it is really the best thing for us, and basically to bring Him around to our way of seeing things and assessing our situation (since, being somewhat far away in Heaven and not being burdened with the exigencies of earthly life, He might not quite understand). But all that is unnecessary and fruitless, and can even get in the way of our receiving what we *really* need. God knows what you need. Repeat after me: "God knows what I need." Enter into his presence with trust. As the saying goes, God gives the best to those who leave the choice to Him.

Let Down Your Nets

Sometimes praying is like fishing. You go to the ocean or lake (the environment you create for prayer), bring your gear (Bible, prayer beads, etc), get comfortably situated—and wait. It may be, however, that you work hard at it and apparently come up with nothing. But perhaps you are still fishing in shallow water.

Jesus got into Peter's boat to do a little preaching, which was actually fishing, in his own way. Afterwards, He said to Peter: "Put out into deep water and let down your nets for a catch" (Luke 5:4). Peter responded as we might, with just a touch of exasperation, if someone told us how to do our own job: "We have (already) worked hard all night and have caught nothing." Though he didn't really expect anything, Peter's saving grace was in the next words he spoke: "But *at your word*, I will lower the nets."

At the word of Jesus, everything changes, for even the wind and the sea and the fish obey Him. Peter knew his profession; he knew the logic of the time and the tide; he knew there wouldn't be any fish there. But at Jesus' word he let down the nets and suddenly he knew that God had visited his boat. He cried out a confession of personal unworthiness, as we also might do in the presence of the *Mysterium Tremendum*. Thus began a great, lifelong adventure for Peter and the other fishermen.

The experience of prayer, especially contemplative prayer, is like letting down your nets into the deep water. The surface may have its own charms, but the real treasures are discovered in the depths. You have to go to the place of the heart, the place of the divine indwelling, to discover the mystery of God. In the Eastern Christian tradition, contemplative prayer is sometimes described as "descending with the mind into the heart." The goal is union of mind and heart, the two becoming one, and this "one" becoming one with God. In one sense, the mind is the net that is let down into the deep waters of the heart, so that our souls can be filled with the richness of grace, of communion with God.

Contemplative prayer is not something that you "do," but the creation of an interior disposition and openness to let *God* do what He wills in and through you. Our efforts to make something happen in prayer are like Peter's working hard and catching nothing. Our own notions about prayer and life in God are woefully inadequate. But if, by quietly listening to the word of the Lord, we let down our nets into the deep, descend with the mind into the heart—the place of stillness and presence—we will meet the Mystery; we will stand in awe of the undreamed-of wonder. There still may be long nights of waiting, but it will not be useless toil, for the Lord is near.

So let down your nets. Begin by letting down your defenses, your rationalizations, your ego-props, your fantasies of who you think you'd like to be. Then humbly listen—in your soul's unaccustomed solitude, in the nakedness of your lack of self-defense—to the gentle call of the Master: put out into the deep. When you set aside human logic to obey the divine Logos, the deep waters will begin to yield their treasures.

❧ Chapter Ten:
A Mystery to Me ❧

I've used the term "mystery" in the preceding chapters, and in the following ones as well, though I haven't really defined a "mystery." That's because by its very nature a mystery resists definition. But I can at least say that a mystery (and here I mean a divine mystery) points to some attribute of God, or something that He has accomplished through Christ and his Spirit in the world, or something that happens to us as a result. A mystery is partly revealed (enough for the "content" of faith and hence for salvation) and partly concealed (in the unsearchable depths of God). But divine mysteries are always, for us, points of contact, avenues to communion with the triune God. You'll notice I've included a series of meditations below on the Holy Eucharist, for that is one of the most profound mysteries in which it is our privilege to partake.

Beyond the Questions

"Jesus knew that they wanted to ask Him..." (John 16:19). The disciples' heads were full of questions. They had heard some quite extraordinary things: Jesus was returning to the Father, the world was going to hate them, the Spirit of Truth was coming to enlighten them, etc. They had way too much to process, and I'm sure they were in complete agreement with Jesus when He said: "I have yet many things to say to you, but you cannot bear them now" (16:12).

They did ask Jesus one question, which He answered in his own mysterious way, Himself admitting that He spoke "in figures." Then, still not quite understanding, but with a bit of false bravado, they exclaimed: "Now we know that you know all things, and there is no need for anyone to question you!" That they didn't get it was clear from Jesus' immediate prediction that in his hour of need they would all desert Him.

But the disciples were right about one thing: He does know all things and there is no need to question Him. Not that it's *wrong* to question God; He's quite understanding and indulgent with our gropings and perplexities. But if we do decide to question God, there are two other things that need to be done: 1) Wait long enough to receive an answer, and/or 2) Realize that even though He has much to tell us, we cannot bear it now. The latter is the one we'll most often have to accept.

In C.S. Lewis' marvelous paradisal novel, *Perelandra*, the embattled hero asks a question of a great Angel about some deep mystery, only to receive the reply that there was no "holding-place" in his limited mind for the answer. He did eventually receive a flash of insight concerning the "Great Dance," that intricately interwoven tapestry—or fabulously, minutely interconnected glorious grid—of God's providential design for all times, places, persons, and things, from galaxies to grains of dust, but it was so overwhelmingly brilliant, wondrous, and mind-exploding that he could barely grasp enough even to begin to adequately articulate it. But the thing to hold on to for now is that there *is* a plan (or countless interdependent ones), there *are* answers, and God *is* the Master of the universe and of our own individual destinies.

We have to realize that we're simply not ready or able to receive all there is to know about the divine mysteries, or even those of the material cosmos and our own souls. There will always be questions, and sometimes we frustrate ourselves needlessly. We have to get beyond the questions, or beyond the need to constantly ask questions, especially if we do it in an over-curious, impatient, or arrogant manner. But to go beyond the questions is not necessarily to go to the place of answers—it is to go to the place of confidence in Christ, "in whom are hidden all the treasures of wisdom and knowledge" (Colossians 2:3). Just knowing that there *is* a design, a plan, worked out from time immemorial by a loving God, should ease our anxious uncertainties about all the vicissitudes of life and the threats to our fragile security. We're not cut adrift, we're not accidental, we're not unknown or forgotten, we're not random chunks of evolved protoplasm milling about a spinning orb of rock and water, hurtling towards an ultimate and meaningless dissolution.

Jesus said that the Spirit of Truth would teach us all things. He said that so that in Him we might have peace (John 16:33). Trust in Him; wait for the Promise of the Father. Move beyond the questions. Don't fret over what you don't understand. After all, we're in the hands of Angels, those bright and glorious "ministering spirits sent forth…for the sake of those who are to obtain salvation" (Hebrews 1:14). If we don't have holding-places in our minds for all the mysteries, let's at least hold in our hearts some trust in that ineffably transcendent yet intimately personal God, who loved us enough to give us a unique place in his marvelous design.

Awareness of the Ineffable

A great philosopher of Judaism, Abraham Heschel, said that our first intimations of God come from an "awareness of the ineffable," that which is profoundly real but which eludes our concepts and formulations. In a pithy phrase, he says, "in moments of insight, the ineffable is a metaphor in a forgotten mother tongue." It's as if the voice of God in us is like a half-remembered dream, which we know was quite vivid in the night but which now hangs about us like an intangible mist, a disappearing image. But it calls us to return.

"We…leave the shore of the known…because our mind is like a fantastic seashell, and when applying our ear to its lips we hear a perpetual murmur from the waves beyond the shore. Citizens of two realms, we must all sustain a dual allegiance: we sense the ineffable in one realm, we name and exploit reality in another. Between the two we set up a system of references, but we can never fill the gap. They are as far and as close to each other as time and calendar, as violin and melody, as life and what lies beyond the last breath."

The awareness of the ineffable creates a sense of awe, for the Lord is near. "Awe is a sense for the transcendence, for the reference everywhere to mystery beyond all things. It enables us to perceive in the world intimations of the divine… to feel in the rush of the passing the stillness of the eternal. What we cannot comprehend by analysis, we become aware of in awe."

One pitfall in our own spiritual lives may be to try to contain the Ineffable in a conceptual box in order to gain a sense of knowledge and control. But God will always resist that, and He will withdraw until we let Him be who He is on his own terms. When I begin to have some experience of the Ineffable, I tend to try to articulate or analyze it (so as to remember it, or even to write an article about it!), and thus I either dissipate it or send it back into hiding. Some people can sense the mystery underlying all things and are filled with wonder and awe, but the majority walk around like blind, deaf, stumbling clods who would rather "wield the definitions of the superficial" than "be overwhelmed by the symbols of the inconceivable." It's time to quietly listen and let God be God, even if his essential incomprehensibility is daunting to our fragile spirits.

"We ring the hollow bell of selfishness rather than absorb the stillness that surrounds the world, hovering over all the restlessness and fear of life... Is not listening to the pulse of wonder worth silence and abstinence from self-assertion?... We dwell on the edge of mystery and ignore it, wasting our souls, risking our stake in God. We constantly pour our inner light away from Him, setting up the thick screen of self between Him and us, adding more shadows to the darkness that already hovers between Him and our wayward reason..."

Take some time to enter into the stillness—of a quiet dawn, of the depth of your own soul. The Lord is near. Don't try to figure Him out; you can't anyway, and that's not why He's here. Be there for Him who is there for you. Begin to realize that God is your origin and your destiny and ultimately all that matters. "God is of no importance unless He is of supreme importance." We may have relativized his importance in our daily lives, but in the end we will behold the full truth. Pray for open eyes.

Hidden Kingdom

Through his parables, Jesus has revealed much about the Kingdom of God. Often the parables concern The End, when there will be a final separation of the righteous and the wicked. Those that do not directly concern The End often tell us about the hidden nature of the Kingdom. The Kingdom of everlasting glory and triumphant joy is not yet manifest; the final separation has not yet occurred. The weeds still grow along with the wheat, and if one is to find the Kingdom one must diligently seek.

The Kingdom is like a mustard seed, almost invisible; it is like yeast mixed into dough; it is like a seed planted by a man, which "sprouts and grows, he knows not how" (Mark 4:27). The Kingdom does not have an address, a location you can visit; it is not visible "with signs to be observed; nor will they say, 'Lo, here it is!' or 'There!'" (Luke 17:20-21).

But according to these parables, the Kingdom will be known by its effects, as yeast raises dough, and seeds sprout and grow. The Kingdom will be manifest where Christ is allowed to work, within and among us. The common liturgical greeting in our tradition is "Christ is in our midst." We have to remind each other of that, and seek the indications that this is truly so, allowing Him to grow in us, even if we know not how.

There's a hidden aspect of the Kingdom in the Incarnation of the Son of God. The King decided not to show up with a noisy entourage, with fanfare, with the pride of a conqueror. He decided to be hidden, like a mustard seed, like a baby in a manger. Yet the Lord was not hiding *from* us; He was hiding *for* us. He knew that He could not make his entrance as the eschatological Judge, as the King of Glory. We would all disintegrate in the blazing brilliance of the light of his face, and his infinite holiness would send us scattering like guilty cockroaches into the caves and crevices of the earth.

So He came, a baby. Someone you could pick up and hold to your cheek; someone who is defenseless, vulnerable, trusting. He was not intimidating at all (and He mercifully didn't let us see the Seraphim covering their faces in trembling awe). In fact, He sent a few other angels to tell us some Good News: the Savior had come at last.

This is something that many people do not understand, or at least not rightly. The Son of God came into the world not to judge it, but to save it. Oh, He will judge it all right, at the Last Day, and He won't be a cuddly baby then, but now is the moment of his mercy, now is the day of salvation. Some people don't think they need to be saved, so they don't understand or turn to the Savior. But they obviously don't understand themselves, either, for if they did they'd be running to Him. Others think the Savior won't be the end-time Judge, so they treat Him as a sort of milquetoast messiah, good for some sagacious sayings but not calling us to account for our actions.

Christianity is full of paradoxes, and we must allow them their full value and power, and not try to whittle down its frightening/consoling mysteries to the size of our own comfort zones. God is *both* the Theophanic Thunder of Sinai and the Baby of Bethlehem, the merciful Savior and the just Judge, the universal King whose kingdom is both hidden and manifest. God is both frightening and consoling because that's how love is, and God is love. He loves us so much that He must hate evil, and He hates evil so much (especially what it does to us) that He must reduce Himself to our size and bear it all in Himself—because He loves us so much. He must hide Himself so that we can discover Him without fear, and He must reveal Himself so that we can know the truth and be set free.

We have to come to terms with all this—his terms. The salvation of our souls must be his way or no way, for we are wholly unable to put the lid back on Pandora's Box, to disarm the demons we've unleashed, to cross the threshold of death with confidence. We need the Savior. When we fully entrust ourselves to Him who made it easy to come to Him, we will be free to let go of our sins, to give ourselves wholly to Him who gave Himself wholly to us. Then, like a mustard seed, we will sprout and grow, though we know not how. Behold, your King—and his hidden Kingdom.

Deified Creation

Now don't let that heading make you think I'm a pantheist. Actually, the very use of the term "creation" should make that clear, since creation implies a Creator. But I think we have to realize that God is very much involved with his creation. God has not simply *made* things; He gives the things He has made the capacity to reflect his glory, speak of his presence, and even to communicate his grace, as in the elements used for the sacraments.

But his greatest project is man. You see, man isn't some *thing*, like a rock or a tree or a spider. Nowhere in the Scriptures do we hear God say: "Let us make trees in our image." Man is some *one*, a rational, spiritual/material being whom Scripture does say was created in the image of God. Therefore, of all that God has created, man has the greatest capacity for growth and transformation, for the perfection of the image in which he was created—in a word, for deification.

The Eastern Fathers understand deification, or *theosis*, as the goal of human life and being. They make a distinction between the "image" and "likeness" of God. They say that we are created in God's image, something that cannot be changed or destroyed, but we can (and must) grow in his likeness, by grace and virtue. This growth in divine likeness is the process of *theosis*, which is aided by the sacraments, prayer, and self-renunciation for the sake of the Kingdom. The image of God within us was not destroyed by the Fall of Man or even by our own personal sins, but it has been obscured or disfigured. The grace of God works an actual transformation within us, not merely a forensic acquittal that does not affect our very being. If we persevere in sin, however, the divine image can be *eternally* obscured, and in Hell the inner image of God irrevocably stamped into our immortal souls will be our torment, not our joy, for we will forever be unable to escape the fact that we have rejected that which was most precious and holy within us.

We see in a dramatic and profound way what God can do with what He has made when we reflect upon the mystery of the Holy Eucharist. That is deified creation in its fullest realization. Bread and wine become the Body and Blood of Christ, and when that bit of Deified Creation unites with our souls and bodies, the work of *theosis* is happening in us in the depths of our being. Atheist materialists coined the phrase, "you are what you eat," in order to deny the reality of the Supernatural, but we can use the same phrase to *affirm* it, because we are, as Scripture says, the Body of Christ. When we eat Jesus' flesh and drink his blood, as He commanded us to do, He abides in us and we in Him—this is the mystical union for which Jesus prayed to his Father before his Passion.

We ought to be aware that God is making out of the universe an immense tabernacle, in which dwell the members of the Body of Christ: transformed, deified, made "partakers of the divine nature" (2Peter 1:4). Christ is not merely gathering his disciples to Himself as a loose collection of individuals. He is fashioning his Body out of many members, for the Church is his Body—not something extraneous to Him, but rather "the fullness of Him who fills all in all" (Eph. 1:23).

The Food that Endures

"Do not labor for the food that perishes," said the Lord Jesus, "but for the food that endures to eternal life, which the Son of Man will give you" (John 6:27). This enduring food the Lord called Bread from Heaven and Bread of Life. What precisely did He mean by that? "The bread which I shall give is my flesh, for the life of the world" (6:51). Thus we know that the Holy Eucharist is the Food that endures unto eternal life: "My flesh is real food, and my blood is real drink. He who eats my flesh and drinks my blood abides in me, and I in him" (6:55-56).

Since the Holy Eucharist has been given to us as spiritual food, there ought to be some analogy with material food: the food that endures with the food that perishes. We ought to expect that we will be spiritually nourished, strengthened, and invigorated, as ordinary good food would do for the body. We probably ought to expect also that the spiritual food will *not* necessarily do for the soul what material food does *not* do for the body.

If you have a serious physical illness, for example, a good meal (however nourishing or well-balanced) is not going to cure you. It will certainly help sustain your bodily functions, and in general will be a welcome support. In the big picture, eating properly all the time will contribute greatly to good health and well-being and longevity. Some may think that the Holy Eucharist, being the very Body and Blood of the Son of God, must instantly cure all spiritual maladies, even severe and deep-rooted ones. It is certainly possible for miracles like that to be worked, and they have, but that is not the ordinary purpose of the Food that endures. Experience has probably already taught you that receiving the Holy Eucharist, even devoutly and frequently, is not a magic eraser for all your faults, wounds, quirks, or bad habits. It is like healthy food for the body: over a whole lifetime it produces beneficial results, and sustains you all along the way, but it's not a panacea for every disease. Perhaps you've wondered about someone: he must have received Jesus in the Holy Eucharist 10,000 times in his life; why is he still such a self-centered, obnoxious crank? There may be many answers for this, but two immediately present themselves. First, it may be his own darn fault for being the hard, rocky, or weed-filled soil that receives the good seed yet bears no fruit (see Mark 4:1-20). But it may also be that the inner work sustained by the Eucharist is actually being done, gradually, even imperceptibly, and that we won't see the fruit until the Last Day draws near.

The Holy Eucharist is food for the journey, for the long haul, a medicine for the sin-sick soul, but we may not experience the full healing or deliverance for which we've prayed and longed for years—until at the Final Examination we discover that we've been given a clean bill of health, for we have persevered in eating the Food that endures to eternal life. Don't lose faith if you haven't received a sought-after miracle from the Eucharistic chalice; thank God that He sustains you with the Sacrament even in the midst of your afflictions. After all, it is not some *thing* you receive, but some *One*. The answers to your prayers spring from the mutual abiding, Christ in you and you in Him, that the Holy Eucharist effects.

The Food endures; we have to endure. We have to endure the painfully slow growth, the disappointments and the struggles. We have to realize, too, that sin is a great setback to our spiritual health and progress. The benefits of our spiritual food are perhaps being expended to repair all the damage that sin does to our souls. We may lament that we are not progressing, but how much would our sins make us *regress* if we did not consistently apply the healing remedy of the Body and Blood of Christ? The sooner we shake off our besetting sins, the faster our spiritual food will enable us to advance on the way of holiness.

The Son of Man will give the Food that endures to those who ask Him, who become members of his Body, the Church, wherein this heavenly banquet is available. Don't approach only for quick fixes or extraordinary manifestations, but realize that this Bread is the Staff of Life Eternal.

Bread From Heaven

Jesus had a discussion with a group of the people whom He had miraculously fed with loaves and fish—one that is profoundly enlightening for all who would follow Him, but that scandalized many, so much so that they closed their hearts and forsook their allegiance to Him altogether.

The people asked for a further sign, reminding him of one God worked for their ancestors in the desert: "it is written, 'He gave them bread from heaven to eat.'" That was but a foreshadowing of the full revelation, for "My Father gives you the true bread from heaven. For the bread of God is that which comes down from heaven and gives life to the world" (vv. 32-33). At this point the people were still "with" Him, so they said: "Give us this bread always."

Yet when Jesus offered it to them, they rejected it, because, as He said in another place, they could not bear to hear his word. They started to reason according to mere human perceptions and possibilities. "Is not this Jesus, the son of Joseph, whose father and mother we know? How does he now say, 'I have come down from heaven'?" But rather than try to accommodate their ignorance and their growing hostility, Jesus presses on to the profound point: "I am the living bread which came down from heaven; if anyone eats of this bread he will live forever; and the bread that I shall give is my flesh, for the life of the world" (v. 51).

Being still confined to the narrowness of their own concepts, they asked, incredulously: "How can this man give us his flesh to eat?" How indeed. It is only possible if He really is who He says He is: the Son of God, the Bread from Heaven. Undaunted by their unbelief, and unwilling to compromise the whole truth for the sake of making it easier for them to accept, the Lord drives the point home: "Amen, amen, I say to you [that is how He introduces his most solemn statements], unless you eat the flesh of the Son of Man and drink his blood, you have no life in you. He who eats my flesh and drinks my blood has eternal life, and I will raise him up at the last day. For my flesh is food indeed, and my blood is drink indeed. He who eats my flesh and drinks my blood abides in me and I in him" (vv. 53-56).

The people's reaction was one that many people have today: "This is a hard saying; who can listen to it?" The Gospel tells us that many no longer followed Jesus after hearing those words. If He were speaking in mere symbols or metaphors, which they had wrongly taken literally and hence withdrew from Him, He would have made the effort to gather them back, to explain it to them, for He did not come to drive people away but to gather them to Himself. But He *was* speaking the literal truth, and on that He could not compromise, for He *is* the truth—so He had to let them go. Either they believed or they didn't; the choice to follow Him was theirs.

His words are clear: his flesh and blood are not symbolic food, metaphorical food, but real, true (*alithis*) food. It's rather odd how some people can believe that the Son of God made the universe, healed the sick, raised the dead, walked on water—and yet vigorously deny the possibility of his giving us his body and blood as food and drink unto eternal life, *even though He explicitly said just that*. Moreover, the Lord said that eating and drinking his body and blood is for the sake of the two most important things there are: abiding in Christ and attaining eternal life.

Through the ministry of the Church, in which Christ is ever present to communicate the fullness of his grace and to assure the fulfillment of his words for our salvation, we can eat and drink the flesh and blood of the Son of God, the Bread from Heaven who came to give life to the world. He gives life by giving Himself, the Bread of Life, the Holy Eucharist, as food for our pilgrimage to Heaven, as a precious means by which He abides in us and we in Him. Really, we must be aware that the Holy Eucharist is actually a gift straight from Heaven, which "connects" us to Heaven. It is a miracle in our midst, a Light shining in the darkness of this life, a ray of hope, life, truth, and love that secures us in the Heart of our Savior. To have Jesus' body and blood within us is like a branch of the Vine receiving the nourishment it needs to live and be fruitful.

After many had left Jesus, refusing to believe his words, He turned to his closest friends: "Will you also go away?" He asks us the same question. Will we go away from Him because we can't believe that his flesh is real food and his blood real drink? Many even in the Church today, having fallen away from true faith, and choosing to believe only the testimony of their senses or the modern, rationalistic, politically-correct (and woefully inadequate) approaches to God, in effect walk away from Him by removing the "spirit and life" from his words, diminishing their power, taming them to their tastes, and thus refusing to open themselves to the profound mystery of his inexpressible gift. But let us be among those who follow Jesus, even when He says things that make others refuse to believe. Let us eat the Bread from Heaven; it is given for the life of the world—given so that He can raise us up on the last day.

The Mystical Supper

I draw heavily here on Pope Benedict XVI's reflection on the Eucharist as the "Sacrament of Transformations." At the Last Supper (and at every Divine Liturgy and Mass) bread is transformed into Christ's body, wine into his blood. God nourishes us with this transformed Bread and Wine in a way that transcends earthly life, which prepares the Resurrection and even initiates it. The Lord could have turned stones into bread to satisfy his physical hunger, but He turned bread into his body to satisfy the spiritual hunger of the whole world.

To transform the bread into his body, there is more to say than "this is my body"; He has also to say, "which is broken, given up for you." The same with the wine: not only "this is my blood," but also "which is poured out for you." Thus the transformation of bread and wine into Jesus' body and blood is inseparable from his sacrificial death, which itself is a transformation.

What happens to Him during his passion is a series of acts of violence and hatred which result in his suffering and death. But Christ transforms, from within, men's acts of violence against Him into an act of self-giving, an act of love. He does not counter violence with violence but puts an end to violence by transforming it into love; violence is conquered by love. By Christ's loving acceptance of the Father's will, forgiving those who killed Him, Jesus showed that love is stronger than death. This is soon manifested when death is transformed into resurrection.

At the Last Supper Jesus anticipates and interiorly accomplishes the essence of the Calvary event. He accepts suffering and death, and by this acceptance transforms it into self-giving love. For the inner core of his sacrifice is his "yes" to the Father; its external manifestation we see on the Cross. The mystery of the Cross is accepted and interiorly transformed at the table with his disciples.

Because the essence of his bloody sacrifice is a transformation—transforming evil into good, the murder of the Son of God into the redemption of mankind—and because the essence of this sacrifice is *interiorly* accomplished at the Last Supper, another transformation that is necessarily related to this is also mystically present at the Last Supper: mortal body into glorified body, with the power that makes possible the transformation of bread into body given, wine into blood poured out. So when Jesus says of bread, "this is my body," and of wine, "this is my blood," He makes of them an external manifestation of the interior essence of his redeeming sacrifice.

What is happening, then, at every altar where the Holy Mysteries are offered? Christ is present through those He commanded to do what He did, in memory of Him. Not just anyone can do this, but only those whom He has chosen as instruments of that same transforming power. The essence of the same sacrifice that Christ interiorly accepted and accomplished at the Last Supper, and then finally accomplished in a bloody manner on Calvary—the essence of that same sacrifice is manifested here; his act of self-giving is perpetuated till the end of time. He doesn't just give Himself to us once. Of course, He doesn't have to suffer the bloody immolation of the Cross repeatedly, as Hebrews says, for that dimension of his sacrifice happened at a certain time and place and was once for all.

But the *essence* of his sacrifice, the redeeming power of his total self-offering, is perpetual; it stands before the face of the Father forever, and hence is always fruitful, always available, and that is what we ritually and mystically make present on our altars. He never ceases to love us, to give Himself to us, so the transforming power of his sacrifice is available to us as it was to the first apostles, when Jesus said: take, eat, this is my body; drink, this is my blood, shed for the forgiveness of sins.

So when the priests say his words, this is my body broken, this is my blood poured out, and when the Holy Spirit is invoked upon the gifts, Jesus is giving Himself to us, here and now, with the very same power of transforming love by which He reconciled the world to his Father from the Cross. That power is so great that it transforms the bread and wine *we* offer into the body and blood *He* offered on the Cross. Everything is transformed in the gift of Himself for our salvation. What Jesus gives is Himself; He cannot do otherwise. It is of the very essence of the Trinity that each divine Person exists in the gift of himself to the others, and in receiving the self-gift of the others. So when Jesus wants to give Himself to us and says, eat and drink—the bread and wine are transformed *because* He is giving Himself; the bread and wine *become* Himself in the very act of His giving them to us. We offer them to Him in the liturgy as humble gifts; He returns them to us as Himself, because at his command we have lifted them up into the sphere of his transforming sacrifice, the love that is stronger than sin and death, the power of his Cross and Resurrection. The inner divine energy of that sacrifice changes bread and wine into his body and blood, takes away the sin of the world, and will raise us up on the last day.

All this shows that the consecration of the Eucharist is not a kind of magic act, a display of sheer divine power to work a miracle simply because He *can*. The Eucharist is not a *thing* that is invested with a certain power to achieve a specific effect, like a drug that one takes, which infallibly produces some effect through chemical reactions. That is why some people benefit from Holy Communion and some don't. It is *Someone* who is giving Himself to us, and we have to be open to receive Him. We have a part to play; it depends to a great extent on *us* whether or not the Eucharist will bear the fruit of sanctity within us. Perhaps we're not sufficiently aware that we are being drawn into a momentous encounter with the living God, who wants us to be caught up in the great heavenward movement of worship and thanksgiving, who wants us to enter the divine mystery of his everlasting love. Like the wise virgins we have to go out with joy to meet the Bridegroom, for He comes! He is here!

We have to have faith and love and a commitment to do His will. Only then will the *next* transformation take place. *We* are transformed by Holy Communion. When we receive the Holy

Eucharist, we are meeting Christ in the act of his self-giving, we are sharing in the mystery of the love that neutralizes the power of evil, that makes all things new. If we come as repentant sinners He sanctifies us—his divine grace meets our weakness and suffering and He transforms it, gives it meaning, invests it with the power to transform the lives of others, to conquer *their* evil with love, for we are now members of the Body of Christ, called to love as Jesus loves.

Let us then be more aware of the incredible gift God has given us, and never take the Holy Eucharist for granted. It is Jesus Himself giving Himself, that the fruit of his Cross and Resurrection be borne in us: reconciliation with the Father, the forgiveness of sins, the sanctification of our souls and bodies—unto life everlasting.

A Paradox of Beauty

In the chapter entitled "Wounded by the Arrow of Beauty" in his book *On the Way to Jesus Christ*, Pope Benedict XVI makes a couple of points that I'd like to reflect upon here.

He notes that in the Divine Office for the Latin Church, Psalm 45 is used with two different antiphons that seem to be contradictory. One is taken from the psalm itself—"You are the fairest of the children of men"—and the other is taken from the prophet Isaiah: "He had neither beauty nor majesty." So Christ is the most beautiful of human beings, yet at the climax of his life He had neither beauty nor majesty. Through such a paradox, the Pope says that the Holy Spirit "sets before us the totality of true beauty, of truth itself."

"Whoever believes in God," he goes on, "knows that beauty is truth and truth beauty; but in the suffering Christ he also learns that the beauty of truth also involves wounds, pain, and even the obscure mystery of death... Beauty wounds, but that is precisely how it awakens man to his ultimate destiny." Beauty in its fullness is the "glory of God on the face of Christ" (2Cor. 4:6), be it the face of the newborn King in Bethlehem's manger or that of the bleeding Man of Sorrows on Golgotha's cross. To be wounded by beauty is to be called to transcend the merely aesthetic and to enter the heart of truth, of reality.

Beauty gives us access to a kind of knowledge that is beyond rational inquiry or scientific experimentation. Through beauty we intuitively recognize the truth of God shining through his creation. Some people have become convinced of the existence of God simply by hearing a certain symphony or being moved by a certain icon. The highest forms of beauty communicate something that goes beyond the experience of the senses. We hear music with our ears and see an icon with our eyes, but whatever is truly beautiful in them seizes our whole being and reveals horizons that open up to God.

The beauty on the face of Him who "had neither beauty nor majesty"—as the eyes would perceive it—was the beauty of truth and love. It is a beauty experienced in one's heart and spirit. This beauty is a counter-argument to that which declares beauty an illusion, which sees the violence, horror, and degradation of this fallen world the only actual truth and reality. A certain one-sided view of human history may seem to confirm that. But this is precisely why the "fairest of men" accepted the loss of his external beauty: to manifest that the enduring, profound beauty of divine truth and love can shine through the darkest night, the deepest horror, the most excruciating pain. The fact that there is ugliness and absurdity in the world should not make us think that these are the ultimate realities, but should urge us to seek the hidden beauty, the deeper truth about what God has made. It is man who has disfigured the face of the earth and then proclaimed this distortion to be the fundamental truth. But Christ came to dispel the lie and to manifest redemption and transfiguration in this fallen world. There is yet another attack on true beauty from the father of lies: not the contention that ugliness and horror are the last word, but the offering of a deceptive, superficial, and hence false beauty. "Such beauty does not awaken a longing for the ineffable...but instead stirs up desire, the will for power, possession, and pleasure." Here is a criterion, then, for true beauty: if what is called beautiful opens us up to transcendent knowledge and experience, that is, if it leads us (even implicitly) toward the face of God shining in this world, it is true beauty. If it stirs up a desire for power, possession, and pleasure it is a deception. The superficial beauty, if sought for the sake of any form of self-gratification, ultimately becomes anti-beauty, anti-truth.

The "world" offers us, then, nihilism and life's harshness as the only truth, or an illusory beauty, the indulgence in which brings only surfeit and disgust. We can perhaps see in certain forms of sexual perversion, for example, the devil's one-two punch of the exaltation of degradation and the sham beauty of deceptive seductions: experiencing attraction and pleasure in that which is foul and degrading.

But that is not the beauty of truth that Christ came to reveal and to give, and which we must embrace if we are to live genuine human lives. I will let the Pope conclude. He says that the Christian "must oppose the cult of the ugly, which says that everything else, anything beautiful, is a deception and that only the depiction of what is cruel, base, and vulgar is the truth and true enlightenment [witness some forms of modern "art"]. And it must withstand the deceptive beauty that diminishes man instead of making him great and that, for that very reason, is false... If we...are struck by the arrow of Christ's paradoxical beauty, then we will truly come to know him... Then we will have encountered the beauty of truth, of redeeming truth."

God Is Not Pink

G.K. Chesterton's intellectual and spiritual pilgrimage took some interesting turns, as we read in his famous book, *Orthodoxy*. One of the things he found attractive about Christianity and the Church is the paradoxical way in which some apparent opposites could be held together: mercy and justice, humility and dignity, marriage and celibacy, losing one's life to save it, etc. But in order to hold these things together, the Church does not emphasize one over the other, nor seek some compromise that is neither one nor the other. She holds each in its full strength.

> "We want not an amalgam or compromise, but both things at the top of their energy: love and wrath both burning... I need not remind the reader that the idea of this combination is indeed central in orthodox theology. For orthodox theology has specially insisted that Christ was not a being apart from God and man, like an elf, nor yet a being half human and half not, like a centaur, but both things at once and both things thoroughly, very man and very God...
>
> "It is true that the historic Church has at once emphasized celibacy and emphasized the family; has at once (if one may put it so) been fiercely for having children and fiercely for not having children. It has kept them side by side like two strong colors, red and white,

like the red and white on the shield of St. George. It has always had a healthy hatred of pink. It hates that combination of two colors which is the feeble expedient of the philosophers. It hates that evolution of black into white which is tantamount to a dirty gray... Christianity sought in most of these cases to keep two colors coexistent but pure."

In this the Church is the image of Christ, who is God and man, merciful and just, forgiving and chastising, generous and demanding—each in full measure, and not some compromised version in between. A famous icon of Christ from Mt. Sinai gives an image of this fullness, written right into the face of Christ. If you cover one half of the face of Christ, you will see a very stern face, that of the Righteous and Uncompromising Judge. Cover the other half and you will see the face of the Gentle and Compassionate Savior. The same person is both in full—not partly just and partly merciful, but wholly just and wholly merciful, as Christ is true God and true man. To use Chesterton's colors, God is not pink, but is red and white in full strength and purity. This is not a logical presentation; it is a divine mystery.

When washed in the crimson Blood of the Lamb, our robes become white. In the Book of Revelation, those saints who are given special mention are the martyrs and virgins, the red of bloodshed and the white of purity. They stand as one body before God—not made pink but still one, united but distinct, both red and white. The Holy Trinity is one and three; not mixture of the three blended into one, but the full distinctness of three in the full unity of one.

Chesterton continues on the paradoxes of Christianity:

"...this explains what is so inexplicable to all the modern critics of the history of Christianity. I mean the monstrous wars about small points of theology, the earthquakes of emotion about a gesture or a word. It was only a matter of an inch; but an inch is everything when you are balancing. The Church could not afford to swerve a hair's breadth on some things if she was to continue her great and daring experiment of the irregular equilibrium. Once let one idea become less powerful and some other idea would become too powerful. It was not a flock of sheep the Christian shepherd was leading, but a herd of bulls and tigers, of terrible ideals and devouring doctrines, each one of them strong enough to turn to a false religion and lay waste the world. Remember that the Church went in specifically for dangerous ideas... the idea of birth through a Holy Spirit, of the death of a divine being, of the forgiveness of sins, of the fulfillment of prophecies, are ideas which, anyone can see, need but a touch to turn them into something blasphemous or ferocious...

"This is the thrilling romance of orthodoxy. People have fallen into a foolish habit of speaking of orthodoxy as something heavy, humdrum, and safe. There was never anything so perilous or exciting as orthodoxy. It was sanity: and to be sane is more dramatic than to be mad. It was the equilibrium of a man behind madly rushing horses, seeming to stoop this way and to sway that, yet in every attitude having the grace of statuary and the accuracy of arithmetic... The orthodox Church never took the tame course or accepted the conventions; the orthodox Church was never respectable. It would have been easier to have accepted the earthly power of the Arians. It would have been easy, in the Calvinistic seventeenth century, to fall into the bottomless pit of predestination. It is easy to be a madman; it is easy to be a heretic... It is always easy to be a modernist, as it is easy to be a snob... It is always simple to fall; there are an infinity of angles at which one falls, only one at which one stands. To have fallen into any of the fads from Gnosticism to Christian Science would indeed have been obvious and tame. But to have avoided them all has been one whirling adventure; and in my vision the heavenly chariot flies thundering through the ages, the dull heresies sprawling and prostrate, the wild truth reeling but erect."

We do not want a pink God or a pink Church. We want the whole truth, the full power of divine revelation, the exhilarating, terrifying, consoling, pure coexistence of the red and the white. In short, we want God as He is and the Church as He established her, so we can be who we are really created to be. Only thus will we be able to celebrate the truth and love and glory of God forever.

The Violent Refresher

I don't put much stock in dreams—either as messages from God or as sources of information about persons or events—though I think that dreams can express something of our own inner states, and I can't deny that God has at times spoken to people in dreams. But I am rather fascinated by the fact that we dream at all, and that we unconsciously produce nightly "movies" that may be entertaining, bizarrely convoluted, or even horrifying. Having said all that, I venture to share here something that came to me in a dream (though I don't remember the dream at all). It was odd enough to make me reflect on it to see if there was something of God in it, since it was a name or title for Him. As you've already guessed, I woke up with the words "The Violent Refresher" stuck in my mind. I've never heard those two words put together, and I wouldn't have consciously tried to do so, but God is full of paradoxes, so who knows?

Now I'm not proposing the following as a new section for the Catechism, and you can put it in other terms if you wish, but since God is infinite and therefore can be approached from innumerable perspectives, I'd like to offer one here that's perhaps a bit out of the ordinary, yet which may stimulate a little beneficial reflection.

First, the violent part. Obviously, this cannot mean the violence that is the result of unrestrained human anger, frustration, or malice. We (and the monastic fathers) speak sometimes of "doing violence" to ourselves when we have to break a bad habit or remain faithful to a difficult discipline. The violence of God is like something we would do to yank back a person who is about to step over a precipice, or to arouse a sleeping person whose house is on fire around him. To such, a gentle whisper would achieve nothing but abandonment to certain death. Similarly, a therapeutic slap across the face, rather than soft-spoken reasoning, is more beneficial to someone who is hysterically babbling. Sometimes God has to be "violent" with us in order to give us a wake-up call, when all his gentle whispers and pleasant invitations have gone unnoticed or unheeded—because He desires at all costs to save our souls from the "second death" (see Rev. 20:14-15).

God is all life, strength, vigor, dynamism, decisiveness, wisdom, overflowing energy—in short, Love that is stronger than death. He wants to be in personal, life-giving, bracing communion with all He has made. There is nothing mushy, maudlin, timid, half-hearted, impotent, or wishy-washy about Him. He acts powerfully in the world, though He exercises sufficient restraint to leave room for the free decision of faith, lest He overwhelm us with his blinding glory and endless miracles. He is called a "jealous God" in Scripture, and it is clear what severe measures He often took to try to keep his beloved people from destroying themselves or the covenant they made with Him.

But God is the Refresher also. He does not merely enforce his laws that are necessary for our salvation. He also is lavish in bestowing blessing, grace, encouragement, and mercy upon us, as Scripture repeatedly testifies. We also say in one of our liturgical texts that He is the One "whose delight it is to bestow gifts upon us." Jesus invites us burdened ones to come to Him, saying, "I will refresh you" (Matthew 11:28). In several of the prayers of the priest at Matins, we thank God for having refreshed us during the night. Divine refreshment is not, however, mere pleasure or relaxation, but torrents of grace and spiritual enlightenment that carry us off into the world of God. He wants us to stand under his waterfall. The Lord would rather refresh, revitalize, and renew us all the time, but He must resort to "violence" when we've strayed so far that only a stern jolt will bring us back to reality, that is, to the path of salvation.

Yet there is another way that violence and refreshment come from God, though perhaps this is reserved chiefly for the saints. I mentioned twice already the book about a Russian Orthodox priest-monk named Fr. Arseny, who suffered for many years in Soviet concentration camps (perhaps his experience is something that my mind fashioned into a dream to produce those strange words). God allowed him to suffer terribly for years, and even when he finally died from illness and exhaustion, God told him it wasn't his time and sent him back for more years of service in suffering! (This means that his sufferings were part of God's plan and were not merely the product of random human or demonic malice.) He was frequently beaten, and often was nearly starved or frozen to death. This is the "violence" of God upon the saints, his specially chosen ones. He tries them, tests them, pushes them to their limits, in order to perfect them. "God tested them and found them worthy of Himself; like gold in the furnace He tried them, and like a sacrificial burnt offering He accepted them" (Wisdom 3:5-6). He takes them to the Cross and seems to abandon them there (ask Jesus what that was like), making them endure more than what is ordinarily humanly endurable. Yet they love Him so much, and their faith and trust are so strong that they do not complain, but rather grow in holiness as they persevere in prayer and patient endurance. They know that Heaven is worth it.

God also refreshes these saints in extraordinary ways. Fr. Arseny received graces and spiritual experiences in his captivity and suffering that literally took him to Heaven and temporarily made his squalid surroundings and intolerable pains recede out of conscious awareness. He was with God and that was all that mattered, and God was pleased to lavish gifts and miracles upon his beloved, faithful son and servant, while at the same time requiring him to endure still more suffering. This is the paradox of the Violent Refresher, who takes people to the Cross and to Heaven, and back to the Cross again, until Heaven will be the only and eternal reality and happiness. God's love and call to intimacy are all-demanding, and no half-measures or lukewarmness are acceptable to Him. With God it is all or nothing, and whoever is not with Him is against Him. Those who die not wholly matured in love and fidelity must undergo a further purgatorial purification after death. All this is so that He can take us into his perfect love and joy for all eternity. To those who are willing to bear his "violent" purification, his "jealousy" that proceeds from an irrepressible and blazing love, He will grant refreshment and peace beyond all measure, beyond all imagination and hope, in this age and in the eternal age to come. "The sufferings of the present time are not worth comparing to the glory that is to be revealed..." (Romans 8:18).

When your faith and love are so strong that you see and accept God's will in everything, even the worst of sufferings, and love Him above all, holding nothing more precious in life than the salvation of your soul (and the souls of others), then He takes you into his most breathtaking, crucifying, marvelous, ecstatic intimacy, and you know what He means when he says: The Kingdom of Heaven is at hand.

For HIM

I once experienced in the Divine Liturgy for the feast of Pentecost an awareness that the whole universe was created to sing blessings to Christ. Now, being in a somewhat less exalted state of mind and spirit—I simply have to reaffirm it all the more! If it were not so, then Christ isn't who He, the Scriptures, and the Church say He is.

Let's decide once and for all to do away with all lowest-common-denominator-comparative-religion versions of Jesus. If we don't have a thoroughly Christian one, with all its scandalously absolute and unique claims, we have a false one, or at least a distorted or inadequate one.

St. Paul (whom no one can accuse of not being thoroughly Christian) has this to say about Christ and the universe: "...all things were created through him and for him. He is before all things, and in him all things hold together" (Colossians 1:16-17). I want to focus here on the "for Him." Think about it: *all* things—that is, the whole universe—were created *for Christ*. An earthly papa might build a little swing-set or backyard playground for his son, but God the Father created the whole universe for his!

We can read in the Book of Revelation how all creation, heaven, earth, sea, etc., joins in a chorus of praise and adoration of Him who sits on the throne and the Lamb (5:11-14). This is simply an expression of *what is*, that is, what is the mind of God and what the final restoration of all things will look like. It's what the angels and saints are doing as you read this. It's a vision of what everything, if unfallen and hence unblinded, would always spontaneously do. St. Cyril of Jerusalem says that one of the gifts of the Holy Spirit is to be able to see things we've never seen before, that is, to recognize hitherto hidden mysteries of God, the reality of which has always been there but opaque to our spiritual perception.

Perhaps few people today believe that the Son of God is the center of the universe—the beginning of it, the sustainer of it, the meaning of it, the destiny of it. Perhaps many do not *want* to believe it. Why? Because then the whole phony edifice of selfish, materialistic, hedonistic, avaricious, lustful, godless pursuits that they call "life" will have to come crashing down, *that's* why! They try to save this life only to lose it, while refusing to take up their crosses and follow Jesus—by which they could lose that worthless life in order to find true life, joyous and eternal. When you finally see the truth, you can no longer live a lie, unless you *choose* to do so, in violation of conscience and right reason.

When you have "once been enlightened, have tasted the heavenly gift, and have partaken of the Holy Spirit, and have tasted the goodness of the word of God and the powers of the age to come" (Hebrews 6:4-5), all that the world and its vulgar media have to offer looks base and tawdry and unworthy of even passing attention. Yet for all this, the vision of Christ-All-in-all remains a vision of faith. It will not force itself on us, and it may even seem to hide from us. What we have seen and heard in the moments of clarity and light that God occasionally grants us must be sustained by prayer and sacraments and meditation on the word of God, and thus we attain the higher ground where the flood of filth and deception cannot easily reach us.

Know then, that the glory of God is all around you. The heavens tell it, as the psalmist says, and the birds sing it (did you ever notice that songbirds never sing off-key, that even if fifty species are singing their different notes all at once, they are always in harmony?—no accident!). Everything was made for Christ; to deny Him is to deny reality. He holds the universe in existence, and his joy reaches from one end of it to the other. When we receive the Holy Eucharist, we feel the Heartbeat of Heaven, and his precious blood pulses through our bodies as our own. It's all for Him, and He would like nothing better than to share it all with us!

Pray, then, to the Holy Spirit, that you may be granted to see things you haven't seen before, that the veil may be lifted—at least a little, at least for a while, so that you can be assured that everything exists *for* Him, that everything is designed to point and move *toward* Him, and that it is a horrible aberration and departure from what is and what is meant to be, if we set out upon a path in any other direction. So find Christ everywhere; you won't be seeing what's not there; rather, you'll be seeing reflections of Him Who Is.

❧ Chapter Eleven:
Every Word that Proceeds… ❧

We are to live by every word that proceeds from the mouth of God, for his commandments mean eternal life (John 12:50). This life comes through personal communion with the eternal Word made flesh. Yet God sometimes puts words in our mouths, too (see Jeremiah 1:9). This is so that the divine words can be preached and shared by every generation in every place. The ways that the Lord speaks to us are many: words, works, wisdom—just be attentive and you'll hear the voice of the Beloved.

Words, Words, Words

I've written hundreds of thousands of words over the years, and it isn't likely I'll quit anytime soon. What is the value of all these words? Is a word only worth 1/1000 of a picture? Talk is cheap, and words can be mere lip-service, chatter, blather, garrulity, superfluity, or fluff. But I'd still like to say a few words about words, the two sides of the coin.

On the negative side, we know that "actions speak louder than words," and that words can often be meaningless, mendacious, or hurtful. "When words are many, sin is not lacking," says the author of Proverbs (10:19). Therefore great caution is advised concerning the use of words. Indeed, the Lord Himself said, "On the day of judgment, men will render account for every careless word they utter" (Matthew 12:36). Woe is me! I'll have a lot to account for on that day!

Abraham Heschel explains what happens when our words become disconnected from the depths of our own souls, wherein the word of God ought to dwell: "Estranged from the soil of our soul, our words do not grow as fruits of insights, but are found as sapless clichés, refuse in the backyard of intelligence… We all live in them, feel in them, think in them, but failing to uphold their independent dignity, to respect their power and weight, they turn waif, elusive—a mouthful of dust..." (*Man's Quest for God*).

On the other hand, words have great potential to express noble ideas and even divine truths, and to do so in a beautiful, moving manner. Words can be vehicles of enlightenment, healing, revelation, and reconciliation. Words are a manner of self-expression. God's own definitive Self-expression, his only-begotten Son, is called the Word in the writings of the evangelist St. John. In the beginning was the Word, and as it was in the beginning, it shall ever be, for "the word of the Lord endures forever" (1Peter 1:25). I call my internet web-log "Word Incarnate" not only in honor of my Lord, but as an acknowledgement that words have the ability to "take flesh" in people's lives, to make a difference, to help lead them, by the grace of the Holy Spirit, to the whole truth. I pray that this will in fact happen, that my words will not be mere dust in the wind, but seeds of the Spirit.

Words have power. They have changed lives and altered the course of history. When taken up into the sphere of prayer, they realize their highest potential.

> "To begin to pray is to confront the word, to face its dignity, its singularity, and to sense its potential might... The words must not fall off our lips like dead leaves in the autumn. They must rise like birds out of the heart into the vast expanse of eternity... In our own civilization, in which so much is being done for the cause of the liquidation of language, the realm of prayer is like an arsenal for the spirit, where words are kept clean, holy, full of power to inspire and to keep us spiritually alive... In crisis, in moments of despair, a word of prayer is like a strap we take hold of when tottering in a rushing street car which seems to be turning over..." (Heschel).

In order to be able to speak words of truth, love, beauty, and healing, we have to be immersed in the word of God, first to be purified of our false and empty words by that divine word: "Thus says the Lord: Is not my word like fire?" (Jer. 23:29). Once we are purified in the fire of the word of God, it becomes for us sustenance and joy: "I found your words and I ate them, and your words became to me a joy and the delight of my heart" (Jer. 15:16).

Let us remember Jesus' warning about the judgment upon careless words, but also that this is a call to wisdom, not to an intimidated silence. For "a wise man advances himself by his words" (Sirach 20:26), using them to bless and instruct, to build up and not to tear down. We ought to realize what a great gift we have been given in the ability to express ourselves in words, to communicate something of our inaccessible interior to others.

Words must be chosen wisely, both those we speak and those we read or listen to. There are plenty of words available that are deceptive, seductive, lascivious, mean-spirited, degrading, trite, or just plain stupid. We are offered so much of that "junk food" through the TV, magazines, internet, etc. Yet there are beautiful, holy, uplifting, profound, instructive, motivating, edifying, encouraging words available as well (you may even find a few in this very book!). By our words we will be justified and by our words we will be condemned (Mt 12:37). It always comes down to a choice, doesn't it?

Hear the word of the Lord. Let it define you, delight you, and lead you to wisdom. Let it purify you, nourish you, and enable you to share it with others—so that your words will have the weight and the power to bring more beauty and wisdom into this world, to raise hearts to a vision of the good things to come. Then return your words to God in hymns of adoration and thanksgiving, as our liturgy says: "weaving a melody of words for the Word."

All the Words of God

When we read Holy Scripture, we have to make sure that we do not take a selective approach. Taking a passage out of context, or in isolation from other texts on the same subject, can easily lead to error and to the strange irony that one can use the infallible word of God to go astray.

For example, you may think that Christ abides in us only through faith after reading "that Christ may dwell in your hearts through faith" (Ephesians 3:17). But Jesus Himself said, "He who eats my flesh and drinks my blood abides in Me and I in him" (John 6:56). You can't hold one (honestly, that is) without holding the other as well, for it is all the word of God. Perhaps you think you have the secret to answered prayer when you see that Jesus has said: "If you ask anything in my name, I will do it" (John 14:14). Just think, whatever you want, simply tack "in Jesus' name" at the end of your petition and it is yours! But notice that He also said: "If you abide in Me, and my words abide in you, ask whatever you will, and it will be done for you" (John 15:7). Those are two very important conditions He gives, but the ultimate one is found in First John: "if we ask anything *according to his will*, He hears us" (5:14). So, abide in Him, let his words abide in you, and if what you ask is in keeping with his will, you will receive it. That is the teaching of Scripture.

A rather startling example of what I'm saying is found in the following texts: "Everyone who calls upon the name of the Lord will be saved" (Romans 10:13), and "Not everyone who says to Me, 'Lord, Lord,'" shall enter the kingdom of heaven" (Matthew 7:21). This shows that the first text is incomplete without the second, and the Lord gives the reason why in the second half of the verse: "but only the one who does the will of my Father in heaven." Calling on the name of the Lord must be coupled with doing his will, or it will be an empty prayer and certainly will not save you. This is one example (among many in the Scriptures) that shows how it is impossible to be saved by anything *alone*, not faith alone, not works alone, not dogged determination alone. If St. Paul says we are saved by *believing* in Christ, and Jesus says we are saved by *doing* the will of the Father, then we are saved by faith *and* by doing the will of the Father! Scripture must be taken as a whole, as a unity, for it ultimately derives from the same Source.

So, hear the words of the Lord—*all* of them! Call on the name of the Lord, but make sure you also do the will of the Father. Ask in Jesus' name, but make sure you're abiding in Him and asking according to his will. We will ultimately be judged not by our fidelity to the few texts of Scripture we happen to like, but "by every word that proceeds from the mouth of God" (Matthew 4:4).

I Cannot Tell a Lie

If I were to tell you that I've never told a lie, I would be lying. That is probably the case for you, too, though I only say that because it is likely so for the vast majority of people. I've heard a lot of confessions over the past 15 years, and lying is a very common sin that people confess (at least they do confess!). Why are humans so prone to deny, disguise, or distort the truth?

You'd think we would have learned our lesson from Adam and Eve, who accepted a lie and then reaped its disastrous harvest.

You'd think there would have been a severe admonition handed down to every generation about the terrible things wrought by lies. But no, it has gone on unabated from the fall from Paradise until the present day. "Everyone utters lies to his neighbor; with smooth lips they speak, and a double heart" (Psalm 12:3). Perhaps many are not aware that liars are among those forever banished from the Kingdom of Heaven and tossed into the "lake of fire" (Revelation 21:8,27).

It seems that it is easy to get desensitized to the evil of lying. Everyone does it: the government and the media lie to us; manufacturers lie to wholesalers, wholesalers lie to retailers, and retailers lie to consumers; students and teachers lie to each other, as do parents and children; spouses and neighbors and co-workers lie to each other, and the list goes on. It's convenient, it gets us out of embarrassing jams, it covers up things we'd prefer not be known, it makes us look good in front of those whom we'd like to impress, it may even help advance our careers, though often at the expense of others'. Some even lie deliberately to hurt others. But there comes a day in which lies will no longer stand, and the pure, clear, unvarnished truth will be manifest to all: "Nothing is covered up that will not be revealed, or hidden that will not be known. Whatever you have said in the dark shall be heard in the light, and what you have whispered in private rooms shall be proclaimed upon the housetops" (Luke 12:2-3).

C.S. Lewis gives us a good description of the real sinfulness of lying by showing what it is like to lie in a world that has not yet fallen into sin. In his novel *Perelandra*, the protagonist is on a new world that is still in its paradisal purity, but in talking with the first inhabitant of the place, he told a "little white lie." Lewis describes what happened: "It was a small lie; but there it would not do. It tore him as he uttered it, like a vomit. It became of infinite importance. The silver meadow and the golden sky seemed to fling it back at him. As if stunned by some measureless anger in the very air, he stammered an emendation..." Does that happen to us if we tell even a small lie? It ought to, if we are in the Holy Spirit.

People have all kinds of excuses for the lies they tell, but their self-justification is merely another form of falsehood called self-deception. They lie to others and then excuse themselves by lying to themselves! We have to decide to break the cycle, the pattern, the habit, of taking the easy way out by not telling the truth. Jesus said, "I am the Truth," so we sin directly against Him by lying. The devil He called "the father of lies" (John 8:44), and we don't want to be children of the beast. The only time that we ought not to tell the truth is when it would become a sin of detraction to do so. To say something bad about another, even if it is true, to people who have no right to know such things, is the sin of detraction. But even then we are not to lie, but rather to keep silent. Unfortunately, when it comes to digging up the dirt about others, many people are suddenly all too willing to tell the truth!

It will cost us something to be always truthful; it may bruise the ego, cause a bit of embarrassment, and may even be the occasion of a setback in one's career or relations with others. But think of your angel standing by you listening and recording what you say; think of Him who was crucified after the false testimony of lying witnesses. It is not a small matter, and there's nothing "white" (pure, clean, innocent) about a white lie. Who is the one who will at length enter the eternal sanctuary of God? It is the one "who walks blamelessly, and does what is right, and speaks truth from his heart, who does not slander with his tongue..." (Psalm 15:2).

Wisdom! Let us be Attentive!

You'll hear that exclamation from time to time during Byzantine liturgical services. It usually precedes the reading of Holy Scripture, which is the wisdom of God in human words, and hence deserves our undivided attention. (It can also serve as a sort of wake-up call if you happen to be daydreaming during the service.) I think it was introduced rather early in the history of the Byzantine Churches, evidently because they really did have to call to order the sometimes unruly and boisterous congregations!

I wonder if we have sufficient regard for the wisdom that God has granted us in his word. We hear it so often in church, and we even read it on our own (you *do*, don't you?), so the stories and sayings may end up as the "white noise" of our spiritual life: always there somewhere in the background, but not something to which we pay a whole lot of attention. Our liturgy tries to get us to see how precious and holy is the word of the Lord. When the deacon says that we're about to hear a reading of the holy Gospel, everyone sings: "Glory be to You, O Lord, glory be to You!" And we sing the same after the Gospel has been proclaimed. At Matins (when there happens to be a Gospel reading) there is actually a petition that precedes it, asking that we may be made *worthy* to hear the holy

Gospel. Did you ever stop and think that you might be unworthy to hear the word of the Lord?

The wisdom that is the actual word of God is always available, even if it's not given sufficient attention—but what seems to be a rarer gift these days is that which is an application of the word to daily life. Wisdom, after all, is not merely knowledge or understanding or even revelation, but it is the way to put what is known into practice, in a manner that bears fruit for the kingdom of God. Here we do not speak of the wisdom that is mere philosophy, but the higher wisdom of which St. Paul speaks, the wisdom of the Cross, the wisdom of the Spirit of God.

In today's high-tech, instant-access-to-everything society, it seems that people are less interested in acquiring wisdom than they are in amassing information. There's more "cash value" to the latter. Schools turn out fewer educated persons and more trained technicians. Information and technology can fuel a civilization, but only wisdom can keep culture alive.

Sometimes people ask me how I'd like them to pray for me (isn't that nice?), or what it is I need. My answer is almost always the same: wisdom. If you have that, you have all you really need, because then you know how to live, how to see things, how to behave and to make decisions. You know how to deal with people and how to remain peaceful in tumultuous times and trying circumstances. You know yourself and you are disposed to hear the word of the Lord. You gain the prudence to avoid harmful excesses, and you acquire a taste for what is good, true, and beautiful.

Let us be attentive, for wisdom is still available to those who seek it. There are many hymns to the surpassing value of wisdom in some of the books of the Old Testament. Seek and you shall find. In this chaotic and unquiet age, it is most helpful—and even imperative—to acquire wisdom, the foundation of a life well-lived.

Fear and Fear Not

The fear of the Lord is the beginning of wisdom, says the Bible in several places. It is also a gift of the Holy Spirit and is even said to "delight the heart and give gladness and joy and long life" (Sirach 1:12). So what are we afraid of? These days "fear of the Lord" is seen as just a bit too theologically "retro" for 21st-century well-adjusted integrated Christians. Back in the 1990s, when I was talking to a young man who had confidently jettisoned most of the teachings of the Church, I heard his justification for that: "Hey, I'm a man of the nineties!" I suppose that today he is a man of the new millennium, which would mean he's not a "God-fearing" man.

There is a good kind of fear as well as a bad kind of fear. The good one is the "fear and trembling" that overtakes any human soul to whom God would reveal his blinding and terrifying majesty, with the inevitable experience on the human's part of his own utter insignificance and wretchedness in the face of that absolute holiness and ineffable glory. The good fear is also the healthy respect and reverence we ought to have for the commandments of the Lord, for every word that proceeds from his mouth, and for the Holy Mysteries of the Church. Even on a purely human level, fear is quite beneficial when it prods us to flee or to protect ourselves from life-threatening dangers. Our salutary fear of committing sin and thus offending God is likewise beneficial. It is perhaps unfortunate (because of our sinful weakness), but all the same quite helpful for our salvation, that meditation on the eternal consequences for unrepented sin should "put the fear of God" in us. The good kind of fear isn't opposed to peace, either. We pray in the Divine Liturgy: "Let us stand in fear, that we may offer in peace the Holy Oblation."

The bad fear is the cowardice and anxiety, the psychologically debilitating agitation, dread, or apprehension that is an enemy not only of ordinary inner peace but also of the spiritual life. "Fear of the Lord" is not the same as being *afraid* of the Lord, in the sense I just described. We are often full of all kinds of fears, and we fear fear itself and the very possibility of approaching fearful circumstances or events. To this the Bible says repeatedly: "Fear not!" I read somewhere that this call to abandon inappropriate fear is found 366 times in the Bible: that's one for each day of the year, leap years included!

We learn from St. John that God is love and that perfect love casts out fear—it doesn't cast out "fear of the Lord" properly understood, for a fruit of the Spirit (love) cannot cast out a gift of the Spirit (fear of the Lord). It is rather, as the Apostle says, the fear that fears punishment that is cast out by perfect love. Let us note, however, that until our love is perfected we may still need to be reminded of the consequences of lack of love, and if that motivates us to get back on track, then it is salutary fear indeed! I can't help but accept C.S. Lewis' comments on perfect love and fear: "I am, indeed, far from agreeing with those who think all religious fear is barbarous and degrading and demand that it should be banished from the spiritual life. Perfect love, we know, casts out fear. But so do several other things—ignorance, alcohol, passion, presumption, and stupidity. It is very desirable that we should all advance to that perfection of love in which we shall fear no longer; but it is very undesirable, until we have reached that stage, that we should allow any inferior agent to cast out our fear" (*The World's Last Night*).

Love is the goal; love is what lasts to eternity. There will be love in heaven but no fear (though there will always be reverent and awestruck wonder before the glory of the Lord). Let us begin to understand how to fear and fear not, for each in its own way is enjoined by the word of God. Fear nothing but grieving your God, and you will be advancing in wisdom. May the "evolved" people of the new millennium receive the gift of the fear of the Lord—and rejoice!

Do You Believe This?

Martha was put on the spot. Her beloved brother Lazarus had died four days earlier and was buried in a tomb. Her dear friend Jesus came to see her, and she received an initial word of consolation from Him: "Your brother will rise again." This seemed to her like standard comfort for the bereaved, an appropriate passage from the catechism, as it were, but it wasn't going to change anything in the here and now. So she just responded with a similar one, perhaps with a touch of resignation: "I know that he will rise again—in the resurrection on the last day."

Here's where Jesus puts her on the spot, as He sets aside the catechism: "*I AM* the resurrection and the life! He who believes in Me, though he die, yet shall he live, and whoever lives and believes in Me shall never die [literally, "shall not die forever"]. *Do you believe this?*" (John 11:25-26). The teaching came alive in his own Person; the resurrection was no longer in some indeterminate future. The Resurrection was standing before her.

Martha was taken aback. What did his words mean? What did He think He was going to do? So she dodged his question slightly, not restating it in her answer as in the previous one, but at the same time making a powerful profession of faith: "Yes, Lord; I believe that you are the Christ, the Son of God, he who is coming into the world." In effect she was saying that she believed that since He was the Son of God, the awaited Messiah, whatever He said was true, and whatever He wished to do, He was able. But she may not have been all that sure He was actually going to raise her dead brother. It was too good to be true, too much to ask, even from the Messiah.

This doubt of hers was manifest when Jesus commanded that the stone be taken away from the tomb. She protested, making it clear that her brother was not only dead but already decaying. We have to wait till the last day for resurrection, she may have thought. But Jesus turned to her with fire in his eyes and cried out, "*Did I not tell you that if you would believe you would see the glory of God?*" (11:40). So He called out: "Lazarus, come forth!" The divine voice of Christ echoed through the halls of Hades, and the dead man returned from the netherworld alive, to the utter astonishment of all who witnessed it.

As we read the Scriptures, the Holy Spirit is going to be checking with us: "Do you believe this?" We need to make a profession of faith. We are faced with many questions, many difficult circumstances, many apparently insoluble problems in our lives, and it takes a lot of faith just to keep going on. We hardly know the way to turn, what is true anymore, how to live rightly. Wait a minute, says Jesus: *I AM* the Way, the Truth, and the Life! I AM the Light of the world; whoever follows Me will not walk in darkness. Do you believe this?

The Holy Eucharist may bring up another demand for faith. In the Byzantine Liturgy, before receiving Holy Communion, we offer a prayer that begins with a profession of faith very much like Martha's: "O Lord, I believe and profess that You are truly the Christ, the Son of the living God, who came into the world to save sinners..."

Cling to the word of the Lord. As Jesus often said, your faith is your salvation. He is resurrection; He is life. Do you believe this? If you do, you will see the glory of God.

With Him, Against Him

We are to live by every word that proceeds from the mouth of God, and that means, of course, from the mouth of the Son of God as well. Many of his words are clear and unquestionable as to their meaning and intent, others somewhat obscure. And sometimes He says one thing at one time and another thing at another time that seems contrary to it. Seems.

One of these pairs of sayings is "He who is not with me is against me" (Mt. 12:30) and "He who is not against us is for us" (Mk. 9:40). The former is quite categorical, uncompromising, and unyielding, while the latter seems rather mild and inclusive. So which is it? The contexts will show us that both are true and apply in the context in which they were spoken.

When the first saying was uttered, Jesus was in a dispute with the Pharisees over the source of his power to cast out demons. Here Jesus was quite stern with them, because they accused Him of using the power of the devil to work miracles. In the battle between good and evil, there must be clear lines drawn, everyone must take a side—no fence-sitters allowed. Either you are on the side of Christ or on that of the devil; there's no middle ground. Therefore, if you do not choose to side with Christ, you are on the devil's side by default. Not with Christ? The only alternative is to be against Him, for in the final reckoning there will be only two groups, the "sheep" and the "goats," the former eternally with Him, the latter irreversibly against Him. Jesus forgives every sin if there is repentance, but what He doesn't tolerate is calling good evil and evil good, for that is of the devil and it leads the little ones astray.

This saying has many applications today, perhaps most notably in the hotly-contested moral issues of the day. For example, if you are not *with* Christ and his Church in serious matters involving life (like abortion and euthanasia) or sexual morality (promiscuity, adultery, homosexual activity), then you are by that very fact *against* Him. Many people do make an obvious show of being against Him, but the more insidious cases are those who *say* they are with Him, but whose actions, words, and preferences indicate precisely the opposite.

Now what about being for Him and his Church ("us" in the text above) by simply not being against Him? We have a completely different context here, in which the saying is appropriate. The disciples notice someone who was not of their number casting out a demon in Jesus' name, and they forbade him, "because he was not following us." Here is Jesus' reply: "Do not forbid him; for no one who does a mighty work in my name will be able soon after to speak evil of me. For he who is not against us is for us."

The Pharisees were the ones who "spoke evil" of Jesus, hence placing themselves squarely in the camp of those against Him. Obviously, the man who was casting out demons in Jesus' name was *already* for Him, for he recognized his divine authority and placed himself under it, availing himself to be an instrument thereof, even though at that moment he was not among the group of disciples that Jesus originally had chosen. Doing good in Jesus' name is a safeguard against speaking evil of Him, Jesus explained. Such a saying can have its application in, say, ecumenical concerns. Not all who do good in Jesus' name are "following us," that is, belong to the Catholic Church. But for that reason Jesus would not forbid them to do good in his name. For if they manifest no hostility and do not give other clear evidence that they are in fact against us, we ought to give them the benefit of the doubt that in the divine "economy" they are for us. All genuine Christians are trying to do good in Jesus' name, and we ought to try to recognize that, even when we have also to recognize painful and long-standing divisions. We ought also to strive to be for, and not against, *each other*.

So let us be uncompromising and rock-firm in our commitment to Christ and his Church, in all that pertains to faith and morals, especially in the battle against evil in all its forms. For in this battle if one is not with Him one is surely against Him. But let us also be charitable and accommodating toward those who may be "on the way" but not quite fully integrated in the fold. For if they are not against us, the Holy Spirit will see to it that they are for us.

Eating God's Will

"I have food to eat of which you do not know." Now this isn't a Lenten *mea culpa* of a monk to his Abbot or confessor (though it could be, I suppose), but rather the introduction to an important saying of Jesus.

The Lord was weary from a journey and sat down to rest while his disciples went off to buy food. (Meanwhile He enlightened and converted the Samaritan woman, since He misses no opportunity to save souls!) So when the disciples returned, they urged Him to eat, and his reply was the opening quote of this section. Being the profound mystics they were at that point, the disciples asked among themselves: "Has anyone brought him food?" Jesus always has to take them deeper than surface meanings. He spoke in simple words, but since they were the words of the eternal Word of God, they were always capable of being mined for pure gold.

"My food is to do the will of him who sent me," He replied, "and to accomplish his work" (John 4:34). That's why He engaged the Samaritan woman in conversation instead of taking a nap, even though He needed one. Jesus didn't give that answer as if He never needed to eat, but He wanted to make a point: as food is necessary to sustain the human body, doing the will of God is necessary to sustain the human soul. Jesus had a mission, and He would not rest until it was fulfilled. He lived from his Father's word and will and love, preferring them even to saving Himself from the torturous agony of the Cross. The will of the Father was food and life to Him.

As I quoted above, the prophet Jeremiah experienced something similar: "I found your words and I ate them, and your words became to me a joy and the delight of my heart; for I am called by your name, O Lord, God of hosts" (15:16). Word of God, will of God, these should be our food. We ought to seek them out as a starving man searches for food. It seems that for many, the will of God is not something to be sought and cherished and savored, but something merely to be endured, or even to be postponed or avoided altogether, if possible. That is because it is thought (sometimes correctly) that doing the will of God will cost us something in the way of personal sacrifice, or will even be the harbinger of hardship or suffering.

But we can't afford to live life on such a superficial level. Life will *always* bring a certain amount of suffering and setbacks, and any genuine life will require some personal sacrifice. Rather than flee these, we ought to seek the ways in which God wills to make them meaningful and fruitful unto spiritual growth and salvation. We have a mission, too, and the very first part of it is to recognize that doing God's will is the *sine qua non* of our success in that mission, and of our abundant life, here and hereafter. This life is the time to focus our attention and effort on doing the will of God. In Heaven it's easy to do his will, and one does it joyfully without a second thought, for it is all life and refreshment and bliss. Here we have to *work* at it, for there are many distractions, many contrary and seductive voices. Pray for the hunger for his will, so it will not seem like something that is peripheral or inessential, but something that is a matter of life or death, for in fact it is.

So, take your fill of the divine will (you are encouraged to take seconds, too) and sing with the psalmist, from Psalm 119: "How sweet are your words to my taste, sweeter than honey in my mouth... Your commandments are my delight."

Cutting a Covenant

In the Book of Genesis, you will notice a series of covenants that God has made, most notably with Noah and Abraham (another major one will be coming in Exodus with Moses). A covenant is something like a contract, but not exactly. It's true that an agreement is made, promises are made, but it is not an impersonal transaction. It is a free and loving agreement between persons: "I will establish My covenant between Me and you..." (Gen. 17:7).

But there are conditions to the fulfillment of the covenant. A promise of God that is part of a covenant requires our fidelity to the covenant for its fulfillment. "I have chosen him...to keep the way of the Lord by doing righteousness and justice, *so that* the Lord may bring to Abraham what He has promised him" (18:19). God made a promise, but Abraham must "do righteousness and justice" if that promise is to be fulfilled.

The sign of the covenant God made with Abraham was circumcision. This is a profound act. It requires much more on Abraham's part than on, say, Noah's, in the sign of the covenant God made with him. Noah just had to view the rainbow and relax in God's promise not to deluge the world again. Abraham and his descendants had to pay a very personal price: "My covenant shall be in your flesh" (17:13). And not just anywhere in the flesh, like a little tattoo on the hand or something similar. The covenant of the Giver of Life, the Creator of man who breathed a soul into him, was to be inscribed in the place from which life is transmitted to succeeding generations, for this covenant in the flesh was intended to be "an everlasting covenant." Such respect was paid to this mystery of the transmission of human life that when a particularly solemn oath was made, it was sworn at that very place: "Put your hand under my thigh, and I will make you swear by the Lord..." (24:2-3). The penalty for failure to inscribe this sign of the covenant in one's flesh is expressed in a play on words: whoever isn't circumcised "shall be cut off from his people" (17:14).

There is a new covenant between the Lord and you (let's keep it personal), one that Jesus inscribed in his own flesh. He was circumcised on the eighth day, but that was only the beginning of his shedding of blood for us. As the New Adam, He represents us all. Since we had forsaken the first covenant because of infidelity, idolatry, and iniquities and rebellions of all sorts, we were bound to pay an everlasting penalty, to be forever cut off from God and the happiness of life with Him. The only way to save us was through a new covenant, but the penalty still had to be paid, the broken covenant atoned for. We were utterly unable to do it. So the Son of Man established the new one with his Father on our behalf. This new covenant, however, had more severe signs inscribed in the flesh: thorns in the head, nails in the hands and feet, and a lance in the side. Jesus Christ is the only one in whose flesh this covenant could be cut. But this at last is truly the everlasting covenant.

If we break this one, as the Letter to the Hebrews reminds us, there's no hope for another. But it is a feature of this new covenant that our sins can still be forgiven by constant reference to it, by appropriating its gift through the sacraments. By clinging to Christ we can be sure of remaining in the steadfast love and fidelity of God. We may have a lot to learn about keeping our part of the covenant, but in the meantime the Father still looks at the signs of the covenant cut into the flesh of his Son—and so, while there is still time for repentance, He continues to withhold his just judgment...

Under the Fields

"Short is man's careless enjoyment of earthly goods; match him with the brute beasts, and he is no better than they" (Psalm 49:21). We live in a time and a nation in which material abundance is regarded as one of the chief goods and goals of life. To be prosperous is to be happy, and even if you have to step on somebody on the way up the ladder, so be it—every man for himself.

The message of the Gospel is quite the opposite, for in the eyes of Christ it is the poor and the powerless who are blessed, while the rich and mighty go the way of the man whose gluttonous opulence led him to the place of torment (Luke 16:19-31). Even though there was higher regard for wealth in the Old Testament—it was considered a divine blessing, since there was no reward, so they thought, awaiting them after death—they still had a healthy awareness that it was foolish to pursue it for its own sake or at the expense of others. They were wise enough to acknowledge the brevity of life and the inescapability of death, which wrests all possessions from the hands of men: "No man can deliver himself from his human lot, paying a ransom-price to God... never will the means be his to prolong his days eternally and escape death" (vv 8-10).

A trenchant commentary on this point occurs in verse 12 of the psalm, but it is most clearly expressed in the Knox translation: "Their riches will go to others, and the grave will be their everlasting home. Age after age they will live on there, *under* the fields they once called their own." Under the fields they once called their own! A single line speaks volumes about the irony of human striving for self-aggrandizement. That is why the verse quoted at the beginning is a kind of refrain in this psalm. A wealthy landowner might be enjoying the vista of his extensive acreage, wholly unaware that, sooner than he thinks, his decaying body will be providing fertilizer for the meadow flowers.

Nobody wants to think about such things these days, though the Scriptures and the writings of the saints, especially the monastic fathers, are full of them. It is a common teaching that we ought not cling to anything that will not survive death. That means that the only thing we can take with us when we die is our relationship to God. And if someone does not have that, then he has nothing for all eternity. You can't take it with you; you can't call the fields your own. Even if one could take all his money and possessions with him, where he's going it will do him no good, bring him no happiness anyway.

The wisdom of the saints is to seek the joy that cannot be taken away from us. All temporal joys that come from wealth or possessions or power or pleasure can and will be taken away, but the joy that comes from living in a communion of love with God will not only *not* be taken away, it will continually increase for all eternity. It's the only thing that will survive death.

So, while we're still walking on top of the fields, let us be free from all greed and attachment to things that quickly pass away. Soon our bodies will be under the fields, but may our souls rise to Him whom our hearts have loved during this ephemeral life. We'll be all too glad to rid ourselves of the heavy burdens of earthly attachments—"God will rescue my life from the power of that lower darkness" (v 16)—as we enter into our Master's joy, a joy that no one will ever take from us.

Matthew 25: Wise Maidens

I'd like to focus the next few reflections upon the 25th chapter of the Gospel of Matthew, which is neatly divided into three distinct sections, though the whole chapter is part of what is often called the "eschatological discourse," which is about how we need to prepare for the coming Kingdom.

The first section is the parable of the ten maidens (or virgins). This, and the parable that follows, are comparisons with the Kingdom, as the Lord said, and the final one is more of a description of what we can expect at the Last Judgment.

So, "the Kingdom of Heaven can be compared to ten maidens who took their lamps and went to meet the bridegroom" (v. 1). So far so good, but we immediately learn that five were wise and five were foolish, the former having brought extra oil to keep their lamps burning, and that latter failing to do so. Now this parable, unlike some others, is not precisely about vigilance (since even the wise maidens fell asleep along with the foolish), but more about preparation—though it does conclude with the admonition, "Watch!"

It is sometimes said, based on some difficult or obscure sayings in the Gospels, that not only the early Church but even Jesus Himself thought that his return would be shortly after his ascension. But if we look at a number of the parables in which He speaks of the coming of the Kingdom, we see (as in the next parable, v. 19), that the master only returns after "a long time." In the present parable, this corresponds to the time that the maidens were asleep. The precise length of time is not what's important, however, but rather the suddenness of his arrival. It was midnight, and they were still asleep when the cry arose: "Behold the Bridegroom! Come out to meet him!"

Now we're getting to the point. All of their lamps were going out by this time, but the wise maidens added their extra oil to keep theirs lit, while the foolish ones had run out of oil, due to lack of foresight and preparation. They asked the wise ones for some of their oil, but they said there wasn't enough to go around, so they had better go and get their own. While they were gone the Bridegroom arrived, the wise maidens were welcomed in, and the door to the wedding feast was shut. Now if this were simply a narrative and not a parable, we might be tempted to fault the wise maidens for lack of charity. But it *is* a parable, and its focus and meaning lie elsewhere.

As the fathers of the Church say, the oil in their lamps is virtue, good works, faith and love, etc. We have to spend our lives keeping the lamps of our souls fueled with them, and storing up more in spiritual flasks (like treasure in Heaven), for that time when the Lord will take inventory, as it were, at his return. Since this oil is virtue and good works, etc., it is by nature incommunicable to those without them. We can and should try to help others, by prayer and deed, word and example, but a holy person cannot say to an evildoer, "here, quickly add some of my holiness to your soul." It just doesn't work that way, because of our free will and the demands of cultivating a life of faith, love, and obedience to Christ. Therefore they have to "go and get their own." But the point of the parable is: get your own *now*, before it is too late! Then you'll be prepared, even if the Master delays his coming. You won't be able to produce it on the spot when He suddenly arrives.

There will come a time when the doors of the Kingdom are irrevocably shut, and the Lord will say to those who did not prepare for his coming, as He did to the foolish maidens: "I do not know you." Those are the most terrible words that anyone could ever hear. So the parable concludes: "Watch, therefore, for you know neither the day nor the hour."

It doesn't matter if the Lord might not return for another 500 years. He might return for *you* tonight! What if you were startled at midnight, discovered your soul rising out of your body, and heard the cry: "Behold the Bridegroom!" What panic if you had not prepared! We have a text in one of our services that says at such a moment the soul turns to the angels, but in vain. This is like the foolish maidens turning to the wise ones for some of their oil. The angels would have to reply to us like the wise maidens: "you had better get your own," but by then it would be too late, and we would see the massive door closing before we could reach it.

I'm discovering more and more a simple, obvious truth which, however, many ignore to their peril: we have to take the words of Jesus *seriously*. He speaks the truth for He *is* the Truth. These are not mere imaginative stories with a moral; they're not just sagacious sayings that we can admire and then forget—they're about life and death, yours and mine, now and forever.

Time to get busy filling our flasks with the oil of faith, love, and virtue. Everyone nods off from time to time, but it is our task to be prepared for that unique moment when we are suddenly awakened in the middle of the night of this passing life...

Matthew 25: Talent-ed Servants

The evangelist connects this parable to the previous one, for they are each in their own way about being prepared for the return of the Master. "...you know neither the day nor the hour. *For* it will be as when a man going on a journey called his servants..."

Christ went on a journey back to Heaven at the time of his Ascension, and a long time would elapse (v. 19) before his return. In the meantime, He entrusted his servants with various tasks as well as with the means to carry them out. In the parable the image used is "talents." This term meant a weight used to calculate value, especially of precious metals. We read in the Old Testament of gifts consisting of so many talents of silver or gold. So it is as if the master were giving his servants sums of money with which they were to trade and bring forth a profit for him at his return.

For us, it might be better to use the word "talent" in modern usage, as an ability to do something, which is sometimes called a gift. A talented person, if he or she is *really* talented, is often referred to as "gifted." So the Lord grants us various gifts or talents, and he wants us to use them in such a way as to have something additional to show when He returns. Note that the master in the parable did not give equal amounts to his servants: to one five, another two, and another one—"to each according to his ability." So he did not expect equal returns on his "investments." Therefore he was just as pleased with two extra talents from the one given two as he was with the five extra talents from the one given five. They both doubled what was given them, and so they were found worthy to enter the joy of their master.

If the one with the lesser abilities, who was only given one talent, would have produced just one more, he too would have entered the joy of his master. But no, he was like so many that have a grudge against God, don't like the way He arranged the universe, are lazy in serving but clever in coming up with self-justifying excuses. Probably the master would have had pity on him if he had just made an honest confession: "I didn't do what you asked; I'm sorry; I'm unworthy of you; please forgive me." But the little nogoodnik actually responded by accusing his own master! "I knew you to be a hard man, reaping where you did not sow, and gathering where you did not winnow... Here, you have what is yours."

The master was merciful, but he knew a hard heart when he saw one, so he showed him how easy it would have been at least to gain some interest for him, but the servant evidently didn't *want* to produce any benefit for the master—so he had to be cast into the "outer darkness," that is, outside the Kingdom of Heaven, separated from the joy of his Lord. That is why it is described as a place where there is "weeping and gnashing of teeth."

All of us have been given talents, gifts from God, which He expects us to use for the maximum benefit of others and for enhancing the glory of the Kingdom. They may be physical, intellectual, social, spiritual, or any sort of combination of gifts, to some more and to some less. Not all are expected to produce the same results (in another place He said, "From those to whom more is given, more is required"), but all are expected to do their utmost to return to Him more than they were given. The Master is coming "to settle accounts" with his servants to whom he entrusted his gifts and talents.

How blessed we shall be if we hear these words: "Well done, good and faithful servant; you have been faithful over a little, I will set you over much; enter into the joy of your Lord!" This is what our lives are about: working for the Lord, for the Kingdom, storing up treasure in Heaven, living to please Him who has given us life and offers us eternal happiness. The wicked and lazy servant lived only for himself and therefore was not concerned with his master or the things of his master—he hid the talent in the ground and left it there till the master returned and demanded an account.

We have to be aware that there *is* going to be a settling of accounts. Our choices in this life will follow us right up to the judgment seat of God. Let us realize that our talents and gifts are not merely for our own enjoyment but for the service of God and of his people. The Lord has warned us repeatedly in the Scriptures what we are to expect, how things are going to be On That Day. The final outcome is entering either the Joy of the Lord or the Outer Darkness. Invest wisely now, as a good and faithful servant.

Matthew 25: The End

This third section of Matthew 25 is less a parable than a prophecy or a description of the Day of Judgment. Gone are the images of oil flasks and talents, and the Lord gets right to the point. It is no longer a story about a hypothetical master and his hypothetical servants used as an analogy for the Kingdom. Here it *is* the Kingdom. He's telling it like it is and will be: "When the Son of Man comes in his glory, and all the angels with him, then he will sit on his glorious throne. Before him will be gathered all the nations, and he will separate them one from another...”

All of the sayings in this chapter of Matthew (and in others as well, especially ch. 13) have to do with a final separation: wise maidens from foolish, good and faithful servants from lazy and wicked ones, and now—those who loved and served others from those who didn’t.

This Gospel passage is quite striking, and not only because of the awesome grandeur of the description of the Judgment. It’s striking because of the *criteria* of judgment, and hence of salvation. Those who say that salvation is by faith alone are flatly contradicted here by the Son of God, the Judge of the living and the dead. One could easily get the impression from this passage that salvation is by *works* alone! But taking divine revelation as a whole—as we must if we are to live in the truth—we come to the inescapable conclusion that salvation is a matter of both faith and works. Some would say that we are saved by faith and that our works will serve only to increase our reward. But again this is contradicted by Jesus. Those without works are not merely granted a lesser reward, they are eternally damned!

It behooves us, then, to look closely at these saving works. At first glance, one might be tempted to say that there’s nothing uniquely Christian about feeding the hungry, clothing the naked, welcoming strangers, visiting the sick and the imprisoned, etc. People of other faiths or of no faith can and do perform these works of mercy and charity. But Jesus *makes* them Christian by saying, *I* was the hungry one you fed, *I* was the stranger you welcomed, *I* was the sick one you visited. Those who ministered to the needy ministered to Christ (He loves us so much He identifies with us—to Saul He said, “Why do you persecute *Me*?”). To them He says: “Come, O blessed of my Father, inherit the kingdom prepared for you from the foundation of the world... as you did it for the least of these my brethren, you did it for me.”

But here is the separation: those who *refused* to serve the hungry, sick, and needy refused Christ, and He has no choice now but to refuse them. Like the maidens devoid of virtue and good works, and like the wicked servant who thought only of himself and not of his master, those who looked the other way or even despised the needy are suddenly faced with the gut-wrenching realization that they had been scorning the Son of God all their lives. He says to them: “Depart from me, you cursed, into the eternal fire prepared for the devil and his angels... as you did it not for one of the least of these, you did it not for me."

Note something important here: Hell was never meant to be the abode of human beings created in the image of God. The righteous were told to inherit "the kingdom prepared for you from the foundation of the world." This Kingdom was prepared for *all* of humanity. The other kingdom wasn't prepared for us; it was "prepared for the devil and his angels." We are not fallen angels, and this is just one more reason that Hell is so horrible—it is not meant for humans at all, but for demons, yet if we do not behave according to our humanity created in the image of God, we cannot inherit the kingdom prepared for such. All that's left is what was prepared for the devil and the demons—and there we shall be consigned, if we do not recognize and serve Christ in other human beings, especially when they are manifestly in need of our help. If we act like devils, or in accord with their urgings, then we also have to live with them forever.

This is one of the most sobering and challenging passages in all of Scripture, and we do well to reflect on it seriously and pray to the Holy Spirit to open our eyes—that we may see Christ in others and realize that what we do to others we do to Him. Our examination of conscience may be quite lengthy on this point. But the price of looking away is far too high.

Jesus is saying that his heavenly Kingdom is already prepared for us. The righteous will inherit eternal life. Let us be aware, He has told us beforehand; we have plenty of advance notice. So that He doesn't have to remind us of that on the Last Day, let us love and serve *now* the least of his brethren.

Not Unto Death

We don't usually have a very good understanding of the meaning of the events of our lives, why things happen to us, or in general what the heck is going on. We misinterpret, jump to conclusions, and perhaps think the worst in any given situation. Jesus tries to tell us that there is often a divine plan or mystery underlying the experiences of our lives, and if there is, then all is ultimately well, for God works things for the good for those who love Him.

A classic example is that of Lazarus. He had fallen seriously ill, and his sisters sent an urgent message to Jesus. His response:

"This sickness is not unto death; it is for the glory of God, so that the Son of God may be glorified by means of it" (John 11:4). It is not usually our first thought when we or our loved ones get sick, that this is for the glory of God. But Jesus knew what He was going to do for Lazarus, and He knows what He is going to do for us. A similar example is that of the man born blind. The disciples thought that sin was the direct cause of his affliction, but Christ said: "It was not that this man sinned, or his parents, but that the works of God might be manifest in him" (9:3).

Now there are some physical illnesses that *are* unto death—bodily death, anyway. This must be accepted as an immutable law. We are all going to die one way or another (unless we happen to be still alive at the Second Coming), and often death is preceded by sickness. But even this can be turned into glory for God—who then shares his own glory with those who choose to give Him glory—by simply accepting it in faith and trust. We share the Cross of Christ; we accept that earthly life must come to an end, and we confidently hope to receive everlasting life after bodily death.

It may be that mental, moral, or spiritual sicknesses may be not only harder to endure than physical ones, but also harder to understand as means of glorifying God. Clearly, a sinful habit gives no glory to God, yet even here we are not without hope, if we are at least struggling sincerely to overcome it. The Lord says to us: "This sickness is not unto death," that is, the second death, the everlasting one. He means to heal us, to help us overcome our weakness or defect, to deliver us from evil and to make all things new. In this God will be glorified and we will be overjoyed, for his truth will have set us free. He will cry out to his hidden, disfigured image within us, as He cried out to Lazarus in the tomb: "Come out!" Then, "Unbind him, and let him go free." We also have to be aware that our personal struggles are not unique (and hence without a known cure) but in some way are part of the universal burden of mankind. "No temptation has overtaken you that is not common to man" (1Cor. 10:13). So we ought to be aware of our solidarity with all sinners and saints throughout history. We don't need to despair, for our sickness does not have to be unto death. If Christ could raise the malodorous corpse of Lazarus, He can heal the sin-sick soul.

I just came across a touching passage from John Donne's "Hymne to God the Father," which expresses poignantly both our relentless sinfulness and our awareness that through divine mercy this sickness need not be unto death. (I've modernized some of the old English spellings for ease of reading.)

Wilt thou forgive that sin where I've begun,
Which is my sin, though it were done before?
Wilt thou forgive those sins through which I run,
And do them still: though still I do deplore?
When thou hast done, thou hast not done,
For, I have more.

Wilt thou forgive that sin by which I won
Others to sin? and, made my sin their door?
Wilt thou forgive that sin which I did shun
A year or two: but wallowed in, a score?
When thou hast done, thou hast not done,
For, I have more.

I have a sin of fear, that when I have spun
My last thread, I shall perish on the shore.
Swear by thy self that at my death thy Sun
Shall shine as it shines now, and heretofore;
And, having done that, thou hast done,
I have no more.

∿ Chapter Twelve:
Mother's Day ∾

A book on life in Christ would hardly be complete without a loving acknowledgement of the role played by his Mother Mary—a unique and indispensable one. For if there is no Incarnation, there is no salvation. We honor her not only in theology and liturgy, but also in our hearts, for her motherly intercession and protection are cherished gifts to us. So, as Pope John Paul II wrote in Mother of the Redeemer, *we ought to "take her into all that makes up our inner life," as the Beloved Disciple received her at the Cross.*

Let It Be

I'm not referring here to a Beatles song, but to the exclamation of Mary of Nazareth at the angelic visitation which announced the most decisive event in all of human history: the incarnation of the Son of God.

Our Lady's "let it be" could only be uttered because of her "I am." What she does follows from who she is. "I am the handmaid of the Lord"; *therefore* "let it be unto me according to your word." If she is God's servant, then of course, God's will is to be done in, through, and by her. Simple, not easy. While Mary most likely did not comprehend the full import and consequences of what was about to happen, she was surely aware that it would turn her life upside down and that henceforth her life was not her own.

"Let it be" can also be translated "let it happen," and this latter version seems more dynamic (it also can't be construed to mean "leave it alone" as "let it be" can). Let God act, let God do the work of salvation. She had to let God enter her life in a way He hadn't before, even though her spiritual communion with Him was already profound. She had to let God enter her body as well as her soul; she had to let something happen that had never happened before and that would never happen again—something that was utterly necessary to keep the human race out of Hell. Quite a burden to lay on a teenage girl! But she was chosen from all eternity to rise to the occasion of this very moment. And she was fully aware that she was the handmaid of the Lord. So, while all creation breathlessly awaited her answer, she said yes.

By the grace of the same Spirit who was about to bring about the unprecedented miracle, she exclaimed: "Behold, I am the handmaid of the Lord. Let it be unto me according to your word." Her words have echoed down the centuries as the quintessential expression of surrender to God's will. And her surrender ushered in nothing less than the salvation of mankind. For with God nothing is impossible, proclaimed the Archangel. By his grace it is not impossible even for us to "do whatever He tells you," as Our Lady would later counsel. For she experienced herself the abundance of blessings that came from doing his will, even at great personal cost.

The Lord is asking us *not* to count the cost, but to look to the ultimate and eternal reward for trust, obedience, and fidelity. Sometimes we eventually say yes, after grumbling, resisting, questioning, or simply trying to run away. The message of the Mother to us is: *start* by saying yes. Realize that you are servants of the Lord, and so his will is your daily bread. If you have any questions, ask them *after* you have already agreed to do what He tells you. Thus divine grace will bear its precious fruit in your life, and you will fulfill your divinely-ordained role in the great gathering of souls for the celestial Wedding Feast of the Lamb.

The Lord says to you as Gabriel said to Mary: "Do not be afraid." The Lord loves you. The Almighty, whose name is holy, wants to do great things for you and through you. Say yes; don't first consider your own ideas, feelings, or agenda. *Just say yes*, immediately, irrevocably, and the gates of Heaven will open, sending down light and grace and strength that you may fulfill the Lord's commands and reap the everlasting harvest of joy. We must, through faith, prayer, and humility, "let happen" what God wants to happen, in our own lives and in the world. To do this we must be at his disposal; his will must take priority over our own. Let us ask Our Lady to be our teacher and guide in saying this yes, a yes that must be repeated daily, hourly. Then the Holy Spirit will overshadow us, too, and our own spirits will rejoice in God our Savior.

More on the Annunciation

One little point (though really not so little) that ought to be cleared up is a common mistranslation of Mary's response to the Archangel's greeting. Most bibles have her say: "How can this be?" But this response is little better than Zachariah's a half-chapter earlier, when he asked how he would know that the same Archangel's message would come to pass. (If Gabriel had his way, he might have said: "Because I just told you, that's how!" But He was there only to deliver God's message, and angels are very good at doing just that.) Mary, however, didn't ask: "How *can* this be?" as if she were doubting the Archangel's words. Her response is *Pos estai touto*. There, that clears it up, doesn't it? It means: "How *shall* this be?" That makes all the difference in the world (certainly it did to God, since He struck ol' Zack mute and He blessed Mary beyond all measure). For it means that she already believed and accepted the word of the Archangel, and was awaiting further guidance to its practical working-out.

But why would she have to ask a question at all, if her relationship with St. Joseph was that of an ordinary engaged couple? (Engagement means much more to them that it does to us; as is clear in Matthew's account, an engagement, or betrothal, had the force of marriage and could only be broken by a formal divorce.) There has been speculation on whether or not Mary and Joseph had agreed, even before the great Annunciation, to live married life celibately. There's no way to prove that, but the evidence of the Gospel strongly suggests it.

If they were planning to get married and live as married couples do, and have children as all good Jewish couples did, then the announcement of a child—while certainly being joyful and marvelous (this whole experience was marvelous, what with the angel from Heaven and all)—did not, at that point, have anything particularly miraculous or incomprehensible about it. She was soon to marry, and if she were planning to consummate the marriage, then at Gabriel's announcement, however extraordinary it might be—you will have a child, and He will be the Messiah—she could still see it fitting into the general plan of married life.

Perhaps Mary, as would any pious Jewish young woman, felt like fainting with awe and gratitude at the prospect of giving birth to the Messiah. But she said, "How shall this be, since I do not know man?" That is, since she does not have sexual intercourse. Now, the Archangel and Mary, both being intelligent creatures, knew that "I do not know man" wasn't a smart-aleck answer, as if to say: I don't know man *at the moment*, but as soon as I'm married I will. It only makes sense for her to be unclear as to how a child was going to be conceived if she wasn't planning to have intercourse or children at all, if she had already decided to remain virginal even after marriage. She knew how children came into the world, so if she was planning an ordinary marriage, her question to Gabriel would have been entirely meaningless and unnecessary. But at that unique, pivotal moment in the history of mankind, meaningless or unnecessary questions were not allowed. Also, she was aware of extraordinary conceptions in the past, like those of Samuel and Samson, but even those required the standard combination of man plus woman before there could be a child.

Therefore the Archangel, knowing that the question wasn't meaningless (knowing her intentions), didn't have to say: "*After* you get married you *will* know man, and *then* you will conceive, silly!" No, the holy Archangel knew full well that she would *never* know man, that she was set apart by God from all eternity for a unique and utterly astounding mission—to bear the eternal and divine Son of the Most High in the flesh, and to bear Him alone. Anything else is unthinkable to anyone with even a shred of pious sensibility about things divine and holy. This mission consumed her entire being (how could it not?), and her whole life was focused on Him alone. For Mary, this moment itself was worth a lifetime of reflection, prayer, and gratitude.

So Gabriel proclaimed the reason Mary didn't need to know man, the awesome, incredible, and wholly unexpected truth—I imagine him doing it in the style of the "mighty angel" in Revelation 10: "he called out in a loud voice, like a lion roaring... lifted up his right hand to heaven and swore by Him who lives forever and ever, who created heaven and what is in it, the earth and what is in it, and the sea and what is in it, that there should be no more delay"—and Gabriel answered Mary's question: "*The Holy Spirit will come upon you, and the power of the Most High will overshadow you; therefore the Child to be born will be called holy, the Son of God.*"

Still More on the Annunciation

There's yet another point I'd like to reflect on, concerning this mystery. It's the opening greeting of the Archangel.

There has been a lot of squabbling over the precise meaning of *Khaire, kekharitomeni...* It is usually translated "Hail, full of grace," or "Hail, highly favored one." Non-Catholics tend not to like "full of grace" (sounds too much like the Hail Mary, though the only reason there *is* a Hail Mary is because the Archangel said "Hail, full of grace"; it also sounds too much like it reflects the doctrine of the Immaculate Conception). They settle for "highly favored," I guess because it's more "generic" and doesn't hint at things they'd rather not believe.

Truth is, either version is acceptable as a translation, though "full of grace" is more Christian, as we'll see in a bit. First, though, let's get rid of that "hail". The word *khaire* was used as a general form a greeting in those days, much as we would use "hello" today. But thankfully, most translators don't write "Hello, full of grace," in their versions of the Gospel. To translate it literally, though, would be to say, "Rejoice, full of grace," which is how many of our liturgical texts are rendered in English. Not only does it sound better, it is more appropriate to the occasion, which is one of everlasting joy (potentially, anyway) for all mankind.

Now the plot thickens. "Rejoice" and "full of grace" are actually two forms of the same word! This word, *khairo*, has many forms and meanings, and hence is notoriously difficult to translate. *Khara* means joy, *kharisma* means gift, and *kharis* means grace or favor. So we can see that "full of grace" and "highly favored" both work, but we still have to get deeper. If the Gospel were not a Christian text but just a piece of ancient secular literature, then we must go with "favored one," because "grace" would have been meaningless to the worldlings of the time. But it was part of the early Christian genius to adopt the term *kharis*, freely-bestowed favor (St. Paul was one of the great architects of this linguistic transformation), as a means of expressing God's freely-bestowed divine activity, presence, and spiritually energizing, transforming, and saving gift—in a word, grace. So it is a movement from a secular to a Christian usage to prefer "full of grace" to "highly favored."

There is more. It's the form of the word *kekharitomeni*. This form does lend credence not only to the Christian usage of "grace" but also to "full" with its connotation of Mary's entirely-graced existence. It is a passive perfect form. Passive, because being full of grace is not her work but God's. It was *done* to her. Perfect in the Greek means this: something was, or has been done, and continues in that state. It's like the expression often found in Scripture: "It is written..." That means that it has been written in the past and stands written today. So to say that Our Lady is "full of grace," according to the meaning and structure of the language of Scripture, means that she had already been graced (from the very beginning, according to Catholic theology), and she stands graced at this moment. That means that it wasn't the Incarnation that made her full of grace (though we can hardly begin to imagine the magnificent blessings with which this divine indwelling enriched her), but she was *already* full of grace when the Archangel arrived, for that is what he called her—and angels, as you recall, don't say anything except what God tells them to say.

(It's a similar case, in thought and theology, though not in linguistic construction, when we speak of the Virgin Mary. When we say the "Virgin Mary" we don't mean the "once-used-to-be-a-virgin" Mary, we mean, like the Greek perfect means: once a virgin and still a virgin. Hence the Church has called her, at least for the last 16 or 17 centuries, the ever-virgin Mary.)

So if you want to be academic and secular, say "favored." If you want to be more Christian, say "graced." But if you want the whole truth, say "full of grace." And don't say "hail"; say "rejoice"!

In a Holy Family Way

I'd like to turn now to Paul Claudel and a little reflection of his, from *La Rose et le Rosaire*, on the relationship of Mary and Joseph and her divine pregnancy. A spiritual writer who also happens to be a poet always makes the reflections richer. Perhaps this testimony of love and grace will help express the Apostle's words: "Love is of God" (1John 4:7).

"The screeching of plane and saw; it is Joseph in his workshop... Mary is there. Morning, noon, and evening they pray together; sometimes they sing; they eat from the same plate at the same table; they divide the chores between them... And one day, suddenly...Mary and Joseph look at each other; he guesses the truth and she sees that he has guessed. She says nothing and he says nothing. 'And her husband Joseph, being a just man...resolved to send her away quietly' (Mt. 1:19).

"...Notice how she ushers God into the world: in secret, as an intruder, under suspicion. And watch this righteous man who must be sacrificed, first victim of

Him who said that He had not come to bring peace, but the sword. What can she do? Her lips are sealed; it is not in her power to breathe the Word that is there within her. "He who becomes the friend of God must be prepared for surprises. It is not Judas; it is my love, my beloved wife, bound to me by a tie stronger than marital love, who has betrayed me. In his pain, he hurriedly devises a plan.

"There is something strange in the atmosphere; some new element has been introduced that works against the carrying out of that decision he reached so sorrowfully. Joseph has now the feeling that if he sent this woman away, it would be he and not she who would be excluded.

"And then occurs the event of which we are told in the Gospel: An angel appears to him in a dream, the angel of the Annunciation, we may be sure... Good God, he has understood!

"A day, two days pass. And on the third day Mary does not rise from the table; she lingers there, looking at her husband. She does not look at his eyes, she looks at his lips. His eyes are closed, and tears are rolling down over his beard. His lips are moving; they begin silently to form that first salutation which passed from the mouth of the angel: *Hail, Mary, full of grace, the Lord is with you...*

"The time passes: an hour, two hours, and each is distinguished by an increased solemnity. Joseph's heart repeats the psalms. He understands; he trembles: a certain verse in Hebrew characters appears to him with sweet authority, and another—look, he begins to weep—takes its place, bearing the irrefutable Word!

"O my God, then is it true? This is to be placed in my heart, in my arms? I, the heir of Abraham and Jacob and Judah and David! I have been chosen to be the witness, and more than the witness, You say—the father! 'Jesus...being the son (as was supposed) of Joseph' (Lk. 3:23)."

Perhaps we take the Incarnation for granted. Perhaps we are not sufficiently aware of the very human drama that accompanied the divine. If only we could look upon the Blessed Virgin as Joseph did, with the dawning realization that in her alone, his beloved,

God was entering the world as man, to save us from our sins. It was happening right before his eyes, in his own house—and his own heart was about to burst from wonder, fear, joy and gratitude. He could scarcely grasp *who she is*, the Mother of the Messiah, of the Son of God. Indeed, O Mary, the Lord is with you.

Love Your Mother

The Mother of God is one of the most beloved figures of all time, even though many have tried (and still try) to denigrate or ignore her, unknowingly depriving themselves of a fruitful relationship with their own spiritual Mother. They ought to be honored, as was St. Elizabeth, that the Mother of our Lord should come to them. But they have made her out to be an enemy, as it were, a supplanter, a stealer of the glory due to God. They are afraid to turn to her, and when they speak *about* her it is only to warn everyone not to speak *to* her! But look at icons of her. Is she pushing Christ aside, robbing Him of his light? Is she not rather receiving his love, and showing unto us the blessed Fruit of her womb? How can anyone disdainfully look the other way in the presence of the one who gave flesh to the Son of God and Savior of the world?

A friend of mine who used to be a Protestant (a Wheaton graduate, no less!), and who is now a devout Catholic, told me of the way that the icon of Our Lady of Vladimir—which depicts the Mother and Child cheek to cheek, and his arm embracing her neck—opened her heart to Our Lady. "You see that little hand around her neck? *That's* what drew me to love the Mother of God. If Jesus could love her so tenderly and intimately, then I wanted to do the same." This style of iconographic representation of the Mother and Child is called the "tenderness icon." Mary looks at us, showing us the Savior, holding Him up for our adoration, calling us to repentance and holiness. Their love is not a closed circle. When she experiences the love of her Son, she invites us to share in it.

Why is it, though, that so many who call themselves Christians reject this feminine, maternal dimension of the Faith? In many non-Catholic (and non-Orthodox) churches, there's something sterile about their approach to God. It is often either hyper-spiritualized and cerebral (i.e., disincarnate, the word without flesh, so to speak, devoid of sacraments and sacramentals), or it is characterized by unbalanced emotion. One of the reasons for this is the exclusion of the Mother, that gentle, profound, sweet, nurturing, guiding, protecting, praying presence offered to the Church by Christ, who experienced it in his own life. To exclude the Mother is to break up the family. To exclude the Mother is to produce a spirituality that is "masculine," individualistic, suspicious of mysticism and of the deeper dimensions of spiritual life as well as those that are most profoundly human.

So the modern response to the absence of the feminine, maternal dimension in these forms of Christianity is to cast women in the roles of men, make them more prominent, put Roman collars on them and send them to officiate at altar or pulpit. This is like wresting a woman from hearth and home and telling her to get out there and act like a man, for she needs to be better represented in a man's world, a patriarchal church. But trying to make women fathers does nothing to restore the gift of femininity in the Church. Rather, it obscures it. And the Mother remains excluded.

It is *men* that need to be told to act like men, for many have been cowed and emasculated by the arrogant brutality of modern radical feminism, and so they in turn act like women and want to marry other men. Men want to be women and women want to be men, but the Mother of God still looks at us with those sad eyes, full of sorrow over our missing the whole point of our calling, our creation.

Mothers, sisters, brides, the Church needs your courage, your grace, your tenacious fidelity, your creativity, femininity, and love! We need to you be icons of the Mother, whose beauty and inner strength is all too often obscured by the noise and smokescreens thrown up by the witches, barracudas, baby-killers, and gender-benders of our bizarre and pathetic culture. We need you to be the contemplative heart of the Church. Mary didn't complain that she wasn't chosen to be one of the Twelve, who would be priests of the New Covenant. She didn't demand it as a right. She was the Handmaiden of the Lord, and therefore his will alone was her sanctification. (And what about that twelve? One betrayed Christ, one publicly denied Him, and they *all* deserted Him in his hour of need in Gethsemane. They were in fearful hiding when the women, who alone dared to brave the enemies of Christ, brought them the news of the Resurrection. The women didn't need to be priests to be heroines of the Faith.)

The Mother of God was not a "liberated" woman in the modern sense, yet the Truth set her free. She was not self-sufficient or independent of her religious tradition, but she rejoiced in God her Savior. She lived the unsung life of a simple disciple, yet all ages have called her blessed. She gave herself to humble service, and now she is the Woman clothed with the sun, a crown of twelve stars on her head. She is the Child-bearer, the God-bearer, the new Eve—Mother of all the living. Her whole life teaches us that whoever humbles himself will be exalted. Her eminent place in the life of the Church is well-justified and is a source of consolation, peace, and strength for all those who rely on her prayer and protection, who know the blessing of the holy Mother's love, who deeply appreciate and welcome her presence in their lives—her quiet, gentle, yet uncompromising encouragement to do whatever Jesus tells us.

So, love your Mother. Go to her. It's OK. Wrap your arms around her neck, just like Jesus did. You'll see the divine compassion shining through her eyes. Just open your heart. You need a mother. The whole Church does. Jesus knows that. He loves you and so He shares with you that which is precious to Him, as he shared it with his beloved disciple at the moment of the consummation of his sacrifice: "Behold your Mother."

The Woman, the Mother

In any reflection on the Mother of God, we ought to be aware that her role in the "mystery hidden for ages in God" (Eph 3:9) far transcends the relatively few details about her life recorded in the Gospels. Also, who she was personally, and her involvement in historical events, are taken up into a broader and deeper context involving salvation history, biblical typology, theology, and mysticism. An essential biblical term for understanding Mary's role in these various dimensions, and in linking them together, is "Woman."

The first female human being was called "woman" by the first man because "she was taken from man" (Gen. 2:23). Eve, along with Adam, spoiled the unmitigated bliss of God's original creation through disobedience. But God was undaunted by this blight on his beautiful plan for the happiness of man, and He immediately promised a Redeemer. Yet this promise was not without a price. The woman and her offspring would be at unrelenting enmity with the serpent and its offspring (Gen. 3:15).

Why does Jesus address Mary as "Woman" in the Gospel of John? It was an unusual, though not disrespectful, address of son to mother. In reality, the New Adam was addressing the New Eve; the Woman and her Offspring were about the crush the head of the serpent.

St. John has invested the first two chapters of his Gospel with a theme of the "new creation." "In the beginning" announced the first creation, as it does the Prologue of John's Gospel. Seven days can be counted as Jesus prepares the first manifestation of his glory. The first creation (and the Old Covenant as well), still bearing the curse of the unredeemed, and hence unable to usher in salvation, is signified by Mary's words: "They have no wine" (Jn. 2:3). As the unique icon of the new creation, the New Eve is called "Woman" by the New Adam. The wine of New Covenant will soon be poured out from his pierced side. Jesus' first manifestation of his glory—making water wine—indicates that his hour had indeed begun, that the promised Redeemer had come to undo the curse. God was beginning to "recapitulate" all things in Christ (Eph. 1:10), through the gentle urging of the Mother of Jesus.

On Golgotha the New Eve, Mary, stands next to the New Adam, Jesus. Suspended between heaven and earth, He "loved the church and gave himself up for her...that she might be holy and without blemish" (Eph. 5:25, 27). Our Lady stands here for the whole Church, the Bride of Christ. She is at the same time Mother of all disciples whom Jesus loves. Her universal motherhood was publicly proclaimed from the Cross with the word which brings the first creation (Eden) and the anticipation of the "new creation" (Cana) to their climax: "Woman, behold your son!"

Mary plays and important role in showing forth the inner unity of Cana and Calvary, a unity derived not only from the use of the term "woman," but also from the term "hour." The use of "hour" is obviously theological in John 2:4, but it may be objected that in 19:27 ("from that hour the disciple took her...") it carries the ordinary temporal meaning. I think it is quite likely that John intended a theological meaning here as well. Since Jesus solemnly gave his Mother to the Beloved Disciple as his Mother at the moment of his "lifting up," it is reasonable to think that John was careful about his use of the term "hour." Before Jesus' hour had come—an "hour" which transcended all time and space—Mary was the mother of Jesus only. But "from that hour," i.e., the hour of his glorification which had now fully arrived, and *because* of that hour, Mary became the spiritual Mother of the whole Church as well.

But the climax is not yet the conclusion. If the woman of Genesis and the woman of Cana find their fulfillment in the woman of Calvary, this is still but the beginning of the life of the Church, signified by the woman of the Apocalypse. In this final book of the Bible (12:1) is given the great sign of the "Woman clothed with the sun," who manifests various signs of cosmic sovereignty as she prepares to give birth to the Messiah-King.

There are several layers of interpretation to this great sign. On a literal and personal level, it is uncontestable that Mary is in fact the Mother of the Messiah, despite the attempts of some interpreters to eliminate all reference to the historical Mother of Jesus in this text. On the salvation-history level, the Woman represents the New Israel (12 stars in her crown = 12 tribes of Israel) giving birth in time to the Timeless One, the Fulfillment of all messianic prophecies. Jesus Christ, in all his mysteries, is the climax point of salvation history, to which all past events looked forward, and to which all future events must refer.

From the perspective of biblical typology and theology, the Woman represents the Church of the New Covenant (now the 12 stars = 12 apostles), both in its present struggle and its ultimate and glorious victory. The Church Militant is at war with the Red Dragon, but is specially protected by God. As Type of the Church, the role of the Woman also is interpreted on a spiritual and mystical level. The offspring of the Woman are "those who keep God's commandments and bear witness to Jesus" (Rev. 12:17). Hence Mary is also personally Mother of the Church. Her heavenly state of the realized perfection of our redemption and salvation enables her to be the Church's intercessor and protectress, as well as the mystical icon of its eschatological fulfillment.

It is important to note that in all the above-mentioned biblical events concerning the "woman," the dimension of motherhood is present and inseparable. The woman of Genesis is the "mother of all the living." At Cana (as well as throughout John's Gospel), Mary is referred to by the evangelist as simply "the mother of Jesus." The Mother of Jesus, present on Golgotha, is again called "Woman" by Jesus, but at the moment of the bestowal of spiritual motherhood/sonship, the evangelist simply calls her "the mother". Finally, the Woman clothed with the sun is not only described as the mother of the Messiah, but as the mother of all the followers of Jesus.

We come now to the basis for Mary's universal motherhood that draws its meaning from mysteries which precede the word of the Cross. In the Greek text of Genesis, it says that the first woman was named Zoe, "Life," because she was the mother of all the living.

"Eve" means the same thing in Hebrew, but here the Greek text translates the term into a proper name, rather than simply transliterating it (Eva) as it does elsewhere, and as is usually done for proper names.

Paradoxically, "Zoe" brought death into the world through disobedience. But the Woman, the Mother, brought the Life Himself into the world through obedience, and hence is the new and definitive "Mother of all the living." Because Mary is the Mother of Jesus Christ the Life, she is the Mother of the living, that is, the Mother of all those who live with the life of Christ. We live because Jesus lives; we live because He is in the Father and we are in Jesus, and Jesus is in us (Jn 14:19-20).

Jesus' word from the Cross made explicit what was implicit: the very fact that we have life because of Christ's power to give life, and from his own life in us, makes us spiritual children of Mary. When we are baptized into Christ, the Holy Spirit takes what is Christ's and communicates it to us (Jn. 16:14). Thus his Father becomes our Father, and his Mother becomes our Mother as well.

Therefore, as Mother of Jesus and hence of those having life in Him, and as type and figure of the Church which gives birth to children of God in Christ—who are begotten not by flesh or carnal desire but by God, that is, by water and the Spirit—Mary is without doubt the spiritual Mother of every Christian, and in a wider sense, of every human being. Since everything that went before the Cross was summed up in it, and everything after the Cross draws life and meaning from it, Jesus took that opportunity to unite prophecy and its fulfillment. He united with it all future centuries of living Tradition concerning the Mother of God with the words: "Woman, behold your son... [Son], behold your Mother."

Heaven Couldn't Wait

At the end of time, at the general resurrection, those who have been faithful to God will rise to heavenly and eternal glory, in both body and soul. But there's someone who has been more faithful to God than anyone else, yet she won't rise at the end of time for the reunification and glorification of soul and body in heaven. Why not? Because she's already there! The Mother of God is the first-fruit of the resurrection of mankind, the fulfillment of the promise of Christ to raise to glory all his disciples and friends.

Heaven couldn't wait for the entrance of Our Lady. It is wholly abhorrent to the Christian mind and spirit that the one who gave flesh to the eternal Son and Word of God would be allowed to corrupt in the grave like a common sinner. Her mission in this world was indisputably unique, and her sinless purity (for how could the absolutely holy God enter this world through a defiled vessel?) caught heaven's fancy, as it were, so she was snatched up from the grave of corruption to share the glory of her Son and God, as a living icon or sign of the destiny of all the faithful.

Christ Himself rose from the dead, making possible the resurrection of other human beings. But, being God and the Redeemer, we don't see in his own person the resurrection of the redeemed. Mary is the first of the redeemed, the first to experience the full truth of Christ's promise, and of the words of St Paul: "He who raised Christ Jesus from the dead will give life to your mortal bodies also..." (Romans 8:11).

Even thinking on a human level, what son who loved his mother would allow her to rot in a grave if he had the power to raise her, body and soul, to glory? *A fortiori*, Jesus Christ, whose love for his mother surpassed that of any other loving son, certainly came swiftly to receive her body and soul into his Kingdom as she departed from this life. Try to imagine, if you can (you can't), what it must have been like for Mary—and what it meant for the whole universe—that God, the Creator and Lord of all things visible and invisible, by whom and for whom all things exist, entered into her body and soul, becoming man in order to save us. The God whom her people had worshiped for centuries, the awesomely magnificent, fiery, thundering God of the mountaintop theophanies, entered her womb, and she carried Him within her as a growing baby. How did she not instantly vaporize as the Almighty God permeated her entire being? The Fathers of the Church use an analogy (one among many): as the bush in which God manifested his presence on Mt. Sinai burned without being consumed, so the Virgin Mary received the Fire of the Divinity without being consumed. She was chosen from all eternity to be the Mother of God, that is, the Mother of the Second Person of the Holy Trinity incarnate as man.

(No one says, by the way, that "Mother of God" means mother of the Holy Trinity, or mother of the Father or of the Spirit or of the divine nature as such. But a woman can only be the mother of a person, not a nature, which is an abstraction if it is not realized in a person. She was not therefore merely the mother of

Jesus' human nature, but the mother of a person. Jesus Christ is a Divine Person, that is, God the Son, who became incarnate of the Virgin Mary, thus uniting human nature to his eternal divine nature. Therefore Mary is the *mother* of a Divine Person, that is, God the Son, who took flesh in her womb and was born as the God-Man Jesus. Thus she is rightly called "Mother of God." At least as early as the 5th century, the undivided Christian Church declared it heresy to speak otherwise.)

Let us rejoice, then, that the Mother of God and our Mother has been lifted up to the fullness of life and glory with her Son in heaven. Heaven couldn't wait for her, and I can't wait to get to Heaven! May the Lord's will be fulfilled to glorious perfection in each of us, as it has already been done in her who said: Let it be done to me according to your word.

❧ Chapter Thirteen:
Give Thanks to the Lord, for He is Good ❧

This chapter title is a repeating refrain in the Scriptures, especially the Psalms (its second half is: "for his love endures forever!"). It ought to be a repeating refrain in our own lives as well. We ought to make thanksgiving the theme song of our souls. Yet part of the Christian mystery is that our joy and gratitude must pass through the purifying power of the Cross, to ensure that they are genuine and lasting. The secret of living joyfully a life marked by limitations and trials is revealed to those who know how to give thanks—and who know why they give thanks: the Lord is good and his merciful love endures forever.

You Shall Laugh

In the beatitudes found in Luke's Gospel, the promise Jesus gives to those who are weeping is: You shall laugh. This doesn't mean He's about to tell them a good joke, nor is He speaking about some ephemeral or superficial happiness, but rather that a deep and lasting joy will be theirs if they continue to carry their crosses with patience and with trust in the Lord. The poor, the hungry, the persecuted and maltreated are all invited to rejoice—for their reward will be great in heaven. That is the only reward that ultimately matters. But that doesn't mean He wants us to be morose or lugubrious until we get to Heaven.

The Lord's promise of laughter to those who weep was once manifested to me in quite a striking and extraordinary way. It was a long time ago, maybe 20 years. I was here in the monastery; I think I may still have been a novice. I was going through a period of a rather tenacious depression. The fact that I had given my life to God and was still depressed was even more depressing! Anyway, a good friend of ours, a priest who lived about 100 miles away, came for a retreat. I had always liked and respected him, and I would eagerly listen to his accounts of how the Lord was working in his life and in those of his parishioners. He almost always had a miracle story when he came to visit.

So I asked him if we could talk, because I was hoping he could help me out of my depression. After a while he said he'd like to pray over me, so I said, "OK, it can't hurt," though I wasn't really expecting much more than a few pious but useless words (when one is depressed, everything looks extremely bleak and hopeless, and one becomes proficient at pessimism). We were sitting outside the main house on a bench. He began to pray a more or less standard healing prayer, and I just sort of slouched and listened. After a minute or two, the strangest thing began to happen. The words of his prayer started sounding funny. Not funny-weird or funny-suspect, but ha-ha funny! I couldn't suppress the grin that was rapidly spreading across my face, though I hadn't the slightest idea what was happening and why his prayer sounded so funny.

Suddenly, I just burst out laughing. Now he had seen a lot in his years as a priest, but I don't think he ever saw that, because he got this startled look on his face. He was quite taken aback (and probably was trying to recall what he'd just said and why I would think it hilarious). But soon enough he realized that the Lord had in fact immediately answered his prayer. As for me, I couldn't stop laughing! I thanked him for his prayer and walked away laughing, powerless to contain it. I went over to the shrine of Our Lady and sat on a bench and laughed—nonstop, for about 20 minutes. After that, my depression was gone. (By the way, it wasn't a "manic" episode. I've never had that counterpart to depression, and I hadn't had any such previous experience, nor have I ever had anything like it since.) The Lord was simply telling me in the midst of my inner darkness and depression: You shall laugh! And his word accomplishes the purpose for which it is sent.

I found this in the Acts of the Apostles: "The disciples were filled with joy and with the Holy Spirit" (13:52). This is an important part of what it means to be a Christian. Now there was nothing slapstick about the disciples' joy: they had just been forcibly thrown out of Antioch for preaching the Gospel there. But they had that joy of the beatitude: "Blessed are you when people...exclude and insult you and denounce your name as evil on account of the Son of Man. Rejoice and leap for joy on that day, for your reward is great in heaven" (Luke 6:22-23). Their joy came from the Holy Spirit. The disciples rejoiced because they expected their reward from God, and even because they were simply happy to serve Him—they loved Him so much and they knew his love for them. Jesus Himself "rejoiced in the Holy Spirit" (Luke 10:21), so we know whence true joy comes.

So if you are sorrowful or depressed now, fear not, for you shall laugh. You shall overcome, by the grace of Christ, all the death-dealing, downward-thrusting forces of the prince of darkness. Embrace the beatitudes, for they are a key to accepting the hardships of life with faith and hope—and even with joy. Believe me, if a depressed monk can burst into joy at the word of the Lord, so can you.

It's Worth It

All our efforts toward fidelity and love are well worth the great reward of the Heavenly Paradise. I'd like to share a story here from Dostoevsky's *The Brothers Karamazov* that highlights the marvelous glory that awaits us. (It was originally given in the form of a dialogue with a number of breaks in it, but here I will just present the story. In the novel, the devil discounts it as the kind of thing believed only by "two-hundred-fifty-pound merchants' wives," but that's the devil for you!)

"There was a certain thinker and philosopher who rejected all—laws, conscience, faith, and, above all, the future life. He died and thought he'd go straight into darkness and death, but no—there was the future life before him. He was amazed and indignant: 'This,' he said, 'goes against my convictions.' So for that he was sentenced to walk in darkness a quadrillion kilometers, and once he finished that quadrillion, the doors of paradise would be open to him and he would be forgiven everything.

"Well, so this man sentenced to the quadrillion stood awhile, looked, and then lay down across the road: 'I don't want to go; I refuse to go on principle!' Take the soul of an enlightened Russian atheist and mix it with the soul of the prophet Jonah, who sulked in the belly of the whale for three days and three nights—you'll get the character of this thinker lying in the road.

"He lay there for nearly a thousand years, and then got up and started walking. [He eventually walked the quadrillion kilometers.] The moment the doors of paradise were opened and he went in, before he had been there two seconds, he exclaimed that for those two seconds, it would be worth walking not just a quadrillion kilometers, but a quadrillion quadrillion, even raised to the quadrillionth power!"

That's the overwhelming, exhilarating, all-inviting wonder of the brilliant glory of the life to come in God. That's how worthy it is of our love and sacrifice and suffering. Truly, it has not yet dawned on us what God has prepared for those who love Him. We sell Heaven short, we don't give God credit for being God, the Creator of the universe and the Lover of Mankind, who is more than willing to give us unimaginable riches, inconceivable glories and undreamed of happiness—just for saying "yes" to what He has revealed, putting it into practice, and enduring the hardships of this swiftly-passing life with undying trust in Him. People throw it all away for the sake of ephemeral pleasures and the cheap satisfactions of human pride, ambition, or greed—but if only they knew that Heaven was worth walking $1,000,000,000,000,000^{1000000000000000000}$ kilometers in hope!

These days fewer people seem to "set their hearts on things above" (Colossians 3:1-2), even those who call themselves Christian. Heaven (if they believe in it at all) is understood as at best a happy postscript to this life—instead of the everlasting love story that follows the prologue which is this present life. Heaven is our destiny, that for which we were created. Who would wish to cast aside that marvelous glory, that supremely desirable bliss in the presence of God, with every precious and delightful blessing that an infinitely loving Mind can come up with? Nothing on earth is worth risking the eternal loss of Heaven. Nothing.

Radiation Therapy

One author wrote, in a book on spiritual remedies for ailments of the soul, that to pray before the Blessed Sacrament is to undergo "radiation therapy." I found that rather interesting, since I actually did undergo the conventional (and considerably less beneficial) form of radiation therapy in 1993. It occurred to me that there are some similarities and differences in the two kinds of radiation therapy.

The Blessed Sacrament, the sacramental Presence of Christ Himself, indeed radiates the Uncreated Energy of his divinity, which can be received by all who come to Him in faith and love. You don't have to get sick to benefit from it, but guess what, you already are! We all have the sickness of sin or inclination to sin of one sort or another, so we are all patients of the Divine Physician. The doses of radiation you receive at the medical clinic are measured in "rads," but there's no measure to the grace of God shining through the Holy Eucharist. If there is, it can only be the measure of love, which has no limits.

One of the downsides of radiation, aside from making you glow in the dark (just kidding!), is that it not only kills the cancer cells, it also kills many other cells with which it comes in contact. That is why they have to map you out very carefully, and even put a few little tattoos on you, so they can correctly line up the template every time and not zap anything they're not supposed to. They even have to take certain measures to avoid accidentally sterilizing you. As soon as the technicians assure you that everything is just fine, they all run out of the room and push the button! (That always made me feel just a tad nervous.) Then they give you some pills to keep you from throwing up in response to the therapy. Maybe modern medicine is not all it's cracked up to be...

But the "radiation therapy" of God's love in the Blessed Sacrament needs no map, makes no mistakes, makes you spiritually fruitful instead of sterile, destroys only evil—and Jesus will never leave you lying alone in your sickness and fear! Nor do you need to take some remedy for the remedy, for there are no negative side effects (you may, however, notice new growths of virtue here and there). So I recommend this form of therapy for all men, women, and children. It's impossible to overdose, and the health benefits, while perhaps only gradually noticed, begin from the first treatment.

Regular doses of Divine Uncreated Energy Eucharistic Radiation Therapy are the beginning of God's making all things new within you. Stop by your church for a free treatment. No appointment necessary. Walk-ins welcome. "Let the light of your face shine on us, O Lord!"

My Peace I Give You

Jesus said that his parting gift would be peace. But He also said He came to bring not peace but a sword. How can we understand this? Can these two statements be reconciled?

The key to understanding these sayings on peace is this: "My peace I give to you; *not as the world gives* do I give to you" (John 14:27). When Jesus said that He came *not* to bring peace, He was talking about peace as understood in a worldly sense, i.e., absence of strife or conflict. He knew that his word would create opposition between those who would receive it and those who wouldn't, but the truth has to be embraced even at the price of the superficial "peace" of religious relativism. So even now, as He says He *does* give peace, it is still "not as the world gives," but it is rather *his* peace. What does this mean?

He gives us a hint at the end of the verse: "Let not your hearts be troubled, neither let them be afraid." So his peace is that which removes inner turmoil and fear. The peace of Christ may not remove all external conflicts or threats, but it communicates confidence and hope even in the midst of them. The peace of Christ is the "I am with you," the "I will never forsake you," of which the Scriptures frequently remind us. It is a rootedness in the transcendent serenity of the age to come, which at the same time enables us to act wisely and decisively in the present age. When this peace is firmly established within us, it doesn't matter much if there is unrest around us. Lack of tranquility is the usual state of a fallen world, so we can't expect to calm all troubled waters (though it is still important to work even for outer peace, especially when we see the horrors of war and hateful aggression). But we can be rooted in the One who gives steadfast assurance that all manner of things shall be well, when we walk in his word and will. There will never be peace in the world if there is not first peace—Jesus' peace—in human hearts.

I have wondered how people who have no faith in God can stand to live in this world. When tragedies or random misfortunes visit them, they desperately search for something or someone to blame for their unredressed afflictions. Rage and grief consume them, and if they do think of God, it is only with reproaches for not having preserved them from misfortune, so that they could have continued their illusory existence, ignoring or rejecting Him. They look for peace as the world gives, but the world gives it not, and the world cares not for them in their distress. They have no Rock, no

Anchor, no Beacon in the night saying, "Courage, beloved, do not fear; I am with you; your reward will be great in Heaven."

Peace often comes at a price. It's not just a relaxing, soothing feeling, an insulation from the demanding struggles of a righteous life. Peace may begin with a call to repentance, with some spiritual surgery on our bad habits or attitudes. But once we have that peace, as Jesus gives it, we will wonder how we ever survived without it. Our souls will be like the depths of a great ocean, which remains ever still, even while a storm disturbs the surface. That is because we are anchored in eternity, connected with the Source of eternal life, and our confidence in Him gives us superior strength in any struggle we are called to endure.

"I will come back for you." His promise is still good. We have his peace while we await Him. Don't look to the world for peace; you will only be disappointed. Remember that clever but true saying: "No Jesus, no peace. Know Jesus, know peace." He will never forsake us, and when at length He returns, we'll rejoice that we held fast our confidence.

I Know My Own

As stupid, clueless, wayward sheep, always befouling ourselves in the mud pits of life, we ought to take comfort in the fact that we have a Good Shepherd. He doesn't have a real strict screening process for admitting sheep to his fold; He just asks them to listen and to follow Him. He has ways of taking care of the rest.

Where does our confidence in Him come from? It doesn't come from our being faithful and righteous sheep; we can't even walk in a straight line, let alone follow Him flawlessly. We get a good clue in the Gospel. It's because *He knows his own.* "I am the Good Shepherd; I know my own..." (John 10:14). Now we might think that fact would discredit and disqualify us immediately. When big people say, "Don't you know who I am?" they are puffing themselves up and making their importance felt. When little people say the same thing, they are saying: you must have made some mistake; don't you know what I've done, how rotten, useless, and unworthy I am? Don't waste your time, I'm not worth it!

But things seem to work a different way with God. He knows us better than anyone else does, even better than we know ourselves. Nothing is hidden from Him, even if we'd rather He didn't see our dark or slimy side. Yet, somehow, this full and penetrating knowledge does not make Him flee his foolish flock, as if He were a mere hireling (or a mere sensible person). Somehow it almost endears us to Him. Not that our sin or inveterate weakness is in any way endearing in itself, but when we are in greater need of his mercy and compassion He has a greater desire to grant it to us—and perhaps grant us a good hosing down as well. He came to seek and save the lost, even though it would cost Him much more than a trek through the hills to rescue us: "I lay down my life for the sheep."

We need to hear that word, and to listen for his voice, for our only hope for lasting joy is in staying close to Him. Once He has chosen us, He will stand by us, defend us—correct and chastise us, too—and keep the wolf from tearing us away from the flock. "My sheep hear my voice; I know them, and they follow me; I give them eternal life, and they shall never perish, and no one will snatch them out of my hand" (10:27-28). That last line has always been consoling to me. Many of Jesus' sheep get into trouble long after they become "his," and we might wonder if He's having second thoughts about us, seeing how we turned out, how we fail to be worthy of his gifts and goodness. We might say to Him: You didn't know what you were in for when you called me! Oh, but He did. He saw all our sins, failures, betrayals, defilements, selfishness—and He called us anyway. He gave us a mission anyway.

See, He knows us: the good, the bad, and the ugly. He doesn't get rid of us, because He wants to work with us, to heal and forgive and transform us. So He holds us securely in his hand; He guides us, hoping we'll have sufficient wits to listen to Him and follow. But He won't give up on us. True, we can freely run away from Him, and *keep* running—but if we just tend to get stuck in the mud, there's always plenty of hope for rescue. For we are his own, even if we think we're not worth the trouble. Let Him be the one to decide that. Just follow. He has laid down his life, remember?

His divine generosity, however, is not to be taken lightly—it is meant to reach deeply enough within us to effect a change of heart. "God's kindness is meant to lead you to repentance" (Romans 2:4). We can't be straying forever, you know! Now is the time to open up to his voice and to renew our efforts to follow, with gratitude and with wonder (that He still puts up with us).

How well did the sheep of the early Church get the message of the Good Shepherd? I know that at least one of his most famous lost-and-found sheep got it quite well: "God's firm foundation

stands, bearing this seal: 'The Lord knows those who are his'..."
(2Timothy 2:19).

Whenever Our Hearts Condemn Us

In Romano Guardini's book *The Living God*, he comments on this passage from the First Letter of John:

> "We...reassure our hearts before Him whenever our hearts condemn us; for God is greater than our hearts, and He knows everything" (3:19-20). He wants to stress both sides of the equation: the full and horrible reality of sin, and the fact that God is greater, and forgives.
>
> "The condemnation of the heart means more than [the reproaches of mind or conscience]... From the condemnation of the mind come the painful insights of reason. From the condemnation of conscience comes the bitter conviction of guilt. But from the condemnation of the heart comes...something that affects us in quite a different way...something that gives rise to quite a different kind of sorrow... Life itself condemns us. Life reproaches us for having wronged life itself...
>
> "The sin that the heart condemns is deep-seated. It implies that we have not merely done wrong in the ethical sense, but that we have sinned against life itself. It has a depth and a grief far greater than any other...
>
> "Excuses avail nothing here... In the condemnation of the heart, it is God Himself who condemns. Wrong has been done to Him. Wrong has been done to the gentle and holy life that He has awakened in the heart, to the holy trust that binds Him to his child. How can man's self-defense reach these depths? What possible help is there? John says, 'If our heart condemns us, God is greater than our heart.'
>
> "Observe that this answer comes from the same depth as the condemnation itself... [God] is greater than everything. The holiness to which wrong has

been done partakes of the dignity of God. His trust
has been infringed. That is terrible. But He Himself,
his magnanimity, His creative love, is greater than all
this wrong. [God] does not say, 'Cheer up, it isn't so
bad after all.' God says, 'Give these things their full
weight. Then I will come to you. I am God.'"

For philosophers like Immanuel Kant, the moral law was
absolute. There was nothing beyond that immutable law and
human responsibility toward it. If you break the law you must bear
the consequences, period. No divine forgiveness, no compassion,
just the imperatives of the moral law and the consequences of
human responsibility.

That's part of the picture, but by no means all of it.
God is the author of the moral law but not the servant of it.
God can grant forgiveness to the one who sincerely repents
of breaking the law, for He is the Lord. But the fact that
forgiveness is available does not reduce the severity of the
"Thou shalts" and "Thou shalt nots" of the moral law.
When God forgives, He is not saying, 'Don't worry. I'm not
going to take it seriously.' That would be merely
overlooking a sin, not taking it away. But forgiveness *takes
away* sin, and this can only be done in truth and
repentance. When God does find true repentance, He
delights in granting mercy. Guardini says in the same
book:

"God draws man into the mystery of his
power...to call the guilty to new innocence. A new
creation takes place... man comes forth again
renewed and guiltless. There is no need for God to
avert his eyes from the sin: it no longer exists... He
is not merely the supreme guardian of the moral
law...He is the living God, who is able to forgive... to
Him there corresponds the man of living faith, who
is able to repent. Both constitute a single mystery of
holy life."

One of the great ascetics in the Eastern Church is St. Mary of
Egypt, the penitent harlot who became a great saint and mystic. If
she were only under the moral law of the philosophers, she would
have had no hope, could not have borne responsibility for her
countless grievous sins. But she met the living God, who is able to

forgive, and by his grace she was able to repent wholeheartedly and change her life and even become holy. In the words of St. John, her heart condemned her for her evildoing, but she discovered that God was greater than her heart.

From this we learn something important about the mystery of repentance, something that most people today evidently do not want to accept—that sin is utter darkness, defilement, corruption, and tragic self-destruction, and that grace is boundless light, love, compassion and power to heal the most foul and corrupt soul. True Christian vision, which includes true repentance, sees both the deepest vile darkness of sin and the most brilliant and glorious light of mercy and love. But many people seem to prefer to live in the dull gray of an inadequate understanding of both. They think that sin is no big deal, nothing to be too concerned about (if they acknowledge it at all), and thus mercy becomes relatively meaningless, a way of saying that God good-naturedly looks the other way. When the full sense of sin is lost, so is the full sense of mercy and of holiness. This is tragically wrong.

Going back to what Guardini said, sin is hurting our deepest self, it is doing wrong to life itself, to God Himself. It is only because God is *greater* than all that, that we have any hope at all. We have to realize what this means. It doesn't mean we *deserve* forgiveness because we're basically good people after all. It means that even though we're *not* good, having repeatedly offended God's holiness and wounded his loving heart, He is *so* good as to offer us yet another chance to be faithful. But even though receiving pardon for sins frees us from guilt, it doesn't undo the damage we have inflicted upon our immortal souls. That's why St. Mary of Egypt spent 47 years in the desert. She knew she was forgiven, but she also knew that she had created huge vulnerabilities to evil in her soul, and those vulnerabilities remained for a long time. She fought them for 17 years before the real repairing of the damage took place within her and she progressed along the road to holiness.

Every sin is a setback; every sin harms the soul and must be overcome with labor and prayer and the help of God. If we keep adding to our sins, we delay and hamper our approach to holiness. We have to painfully retrace each step from the places our sin has led us to the place of divine peace, freedom, and joy. With God all things are possible.

So if our hearts condemn us for the deep sin that is beyond minor missteps, we ought to hear it and accept it, and not try to deny or minimize it. But we must remember that God is greater than our hearts, and He knows everything—our sin, our repentance, and above all his love and unceasing willingness to forgive and to save.

Righteous and True

"Great and wonderful are your deeds, O Lord God the Almighty! Righteous and true are your ways, O King of the ages... Righteous are you in these your judgments... Yea, Lord God the Almighty, true and just are your judgments!" (Rev. 15:3; 16:5-7). We might wonder what all this high praise is about. Actually, it is about a series of foul and devastating plagues unleashed on mankind, described as the "wrath of God." Now we might *really* wonder...

In the Book of Revelation, divine justice is seen as something in which we ought to rejoice, since it means the end of the persecutions of God's faithful ones. As the plagues are about to descend on the world, it seems to be quite a glorious thing: "Out of the temple came seven angels...robed in pure bright linen, and their breasts girded with golden sashes. And one of the four living creatures gave the seven angels seven golden bowls—full of the wrath of God." So, upon the earth come painful diseases, and rivers change into blood; the sun scorches men, there are earthquakes and storms of hail the size of basketballs. Rejoice!

The point of all this—for us, anyway—is that whatever God does is good, righteous, true, and just. Whether He is blessing us with peace and prosperity, or raining down blood, fire, or hundred-pound hailstones, his judgments are righteous and true. It may take a little time and effort to get used to this. But if we don't, we're setting ourselves up for a lot of anger and frustration, and if we really decide to rebel against chastisements and purifications, we may end up like the blasphemers who had thrown in their lot with the Beast and the False Prophet. The plagues had a two-fold purpose: to punish evildoers, but at the same time to call them to repentance. For the "wrath of God" is not like human rage—God doesn't lose control of his emotions, get all red in the face, and then impulsively do things He'll regret later. No, God's wrath is simply a righteous, just, and wise response to human wickedness when it has not heeded the repeated call to repentance. God wanted repentance to be the outcome of the plagues, but instead, people "cursed the name of God who had power over these plagues, and they did not repent and give him glory" (16:9). We get a little more detail after some earlier plagues: they "did not repent of the works of their hands nor give up worshiping demons and idols... nor did they repent of their murders or their sorceries or their immorality or their thefts" (9:20-21).

So what must we do? Praise Him for his righteous judgments, of course, and use the opportunities for repentance that are offered by various calamities. Better to endure a few plagues now than the Lake of Fire forever. We really have no idea of the meaning of all the events of our lives, especially the painful ones, so we have to trust Him "who has power over the plagues." Whatever He sends or allows, He does so for reasons righteous and true. It is a hard but indispensable lesson to learn: we have to give Him glory even as the hailstones fall. The vast majority of spiritual writings these days seem intent on creating a portrait of God that is to our liking, that is soothing and consoling to our emotions, and that is not in any way threatening or demanding—in short, "God, as we'd like Him to be."

But the Scriptures reveal to us God as He is, or at least to the extent He has chosen to reveal Himself, and that is the image we ought to keep before us. God is a Lover, a Forgiver, an Embracer, a Savior, a Judge, an Avenger, a Punisher of evil and a Rewarder of good; He blesses his people with peace and He makes fire fall from heaven. There is much more that can be said, but the point is that we have to take God as He is, and not deny his right to judge with justice or even to inflict salutary punishment. For this very judgment of God, as we see in the Book, invites the praise and glory of the saints and angels, who know that everything God does is worthy of praise and honor.

Here are two tiny examples in my own life of the good fruits of praising God for his righteous judgments: one year when it was raining very heavily, and roads were collapsing, and I was digging drainage ditches around the retreat house to prevent flooding, my first inclination was to pray to God like this: *"Stop the rain!"* But then I remembered that I had recently read the above passages from the Book of Revelation, so I decided that I would praise God for his righteous judgments regarding the rain. I did so all day. The rain didn't stop, but the frustration and irritation in my heart did. I was at peace and accepted it all as something God permitted for some good, and felt much better! The change was in me. It is easier for God to change the weather than to change human hearts (because of his great respect for our free will), so He actually worked the greater miracle!

Some time ago they were fixing Tomki Road and traffic would sometimes have to be stopped for a little while. One day I had a doctor's appointment, so I planned to leave early in case I had to wait (even though the wait was usually only 5 minutes or so). As it turned out, I was unable to leave early, and as I approached the roadwork site, I was wondering if I would be able to get through. When I got there, the flagman told me to pull over to the side and wait, for it was going to be about 20 minutes before I could pass! So what could I do? I just decided to accept the fact that I would be 20 minutes late for my appointment (though I don't like to be late for anything!), and if that pleased the Lord, so be it. I praised Him for his righteous judgments, and began to pray the rosary. After just a few Hail Marys, the flagman came over and said, "You can go through now." What a pleasant surprise! I thanked the Lord and was on my way. When I arrived at the doctor's office, I thought I was still a few minutes late, but as I walked in—and this is the only time this ever happened—the receptionist looked at the clock and said, "Right on time!"

So, whether the Lord decides to change the circumstances or change our hearts (or both), we always do better to praise Him for his righteous judgments than to complain or become angry and frustrated. Our heavenly Father knows best. Let us practice now, in the midst of our minor (even if many) trials, so that when the big plagues come we'll be ready to bless and not to curse. "Great and wonderful are your deeds... righteous and true are your ways!" It will all be proven so in the end, anyway. Now is the time to affirm it in faith and trust, so we will at length be found worthy to join the heavenly choirs in praising the all-wonderful—even if mostly incomprehensible—righteous and true God!

You Stood By Me

The following is a poem by Alexander Solzhenitsyn, which describes his sacrifice of faith to atheistic intellectual pursuits, and then his later recovery of faith. Perhaps anyone who has lost and found his precious faith can relate to this.

> When did I so utterly, totally,
> Strew the good grain like chaff to the winds

And shun those same temples where all through my youth
I was lulled by Your radiant hymns?
My dazzling book-garnered wisdom proved more than
This arrogant brain could withstand.
The world with its secrets spread open before me
And Fate was but wax in my hands.

Each new surge of blood as it pounded within me
Lured me on with shimmering hues,
While the faith in my heart, like a building deserted,
Crumbled, soundless, and slipped into ruin.

But picking my way between life and extinction,
Now falling, now scrambling back,
I gaze through new eyes at the life I once followed
And gazing, I shudder with thanks.

It was not my own intellect, not my desiring
That illumined each twist in my path
But the still, even light of a Higher design,
That only with time I could grasp.

And now, as I sip with new-found moderation
From the life-giving waters—I see
That my faith is restored, O Lord of Creation!
I renounced You, but You stood by me.

The whole story could be summed up in the last line—
perhaps the story of each of our lives, in one way or another. There
is something beautiful expressed here about the nature of God.
First of all, He does not deal with us in strict justice, making every
punishment fit every crime. But He also doesn't deal with us in a
kind of condescending generosity, either: "You have done evil, but
now that you have at last decided to amend your ways, I, in my
great magnanimity, deign to grant you pardon." Instead, He is right
there with us the whole time, *standing by us even as we renounce
Him.*

God is the Father of prodigal children. No one has to notify
Him of our return, because He has been watching for us with love
and longing the whole time. He sent his Son to stand by us as one
of us, even as we renounced, condemned and crucified Him
through our sin and rejection of his love. But He doesn't go away;

He doesn't give up. He stands by us, offering us his Spirit of Truth and Love to open our eyes and touch our hearts. He waits as long as He has to. And when our faith is at length restored, his joy is even greater than ours! He doesn't read us the list of our sins and demand an explanation for each, or force upon us the awareness of what it cost Him to forgive us—though all of this will be clear to us anyway, just by standing in the pure light of divine truth. He can speak only the truth to us, but He does so with infinite tenderness: "You renounced Me, but I stood by you." Our response determines our eternal destiny. If we remain hardened in sin (if it is possible once we become aware of this divine compassion), then those words will be our sentence, and will burn in our ears for all eternity. But if we have even a shred of humanity left in us, our tears will burn our cheeks long before hellfire can ever come near us, and those words will be the inspiration for endless hymns of thanksgiving and worship.

No matter what, He stands by us. Let us resolve never to renounce Him again, but let us drink from the life-giving waters of restored faith and renewed love as we commit ourselves to follow the ways of his "Higher design." And let us remember that there are those in our lives who in one way or another renounce us: let us stand by them, waiting in prayer for the grace of Him who has stood by us.

His Inexpressible Gift

"Thanks be to God for his inexpressible gift!" exclaimed St. Paul (2Cor. 9:15). There are many contexts in which we can repeat his sentiment, but today I'd just like to reflect a bit on the Feast of Pentecost, 2006.

For a while I had been having a bit of a rough time, and I grumbled to a couple friends of mine, who responded variously with encouragement, prayer, serious straight talk, and even poetry (and sometimes a sort of combination of them all). Well, thus encouraged and graciously chastened, I entered the celebration of Pentecost.

It would take too long to detail all that happened that Sunday and Monday (the latter happened to be the anniversary of the founding of our monastery, and we held the Divine Liturgy outdoors at our shrine to the Mother of God). But the general blessing and fruit of those days has been for me a greater appreciation and awareness of God's inexpressible gift—the gift of his Son, of his Spirit, of the Holy Mysteries of the Altar.

At my ordination to the priesthood I was struck by the Gospel passage about the eyewitness to Jesus' passion and death, whose "testimony we know is true." This has always been important to me. If I'm going to give my life for something, it must be *true.* Actually, I'm giving my life for some *One.* Sometimes one can get "desensitized" even to holy things and lose the awareness of the greatness of God's gift. So He showed me in several ways—speaking through the prophet Ezekiel in the Scriptures, speaking through *me* as I preached the word of God, allowing me to become aware of his divine glory flowing out of the Eucharistic chalice and filling the sanctuary, telling me that He was indeed present as I elevated the sacramental Lamb before Holy Communion. And when I sang the words, "Blessed are You, O Christ our God…" it was just so *right.* It was as if I had just discovered the key to unlock the meaning and mystery of life, as if I found at last my reason of being, as if the whole universe had been created simply to echo these words from galaxy to galaxy.

Yet all too often I think that the veils are too opaque, too securely drawn over the divine mysteries, and all seems blank or dark, and so I tend towards despondency, and a kind of numb drudgery seems to fill the day. So every now and then the Lord "adapts Himself to my weakness" (as Pope Benedict says) and finds some way to remind me: "It's all true, you know. Really."

Then I begin to thank God for his inexpressible gift. I listen to myself saying the prayers as I distribute Holy Communion, for example: "The servant of God _____ receives the precious, holy, and most pure Body and Blood of our Lord, God, and Savior Jesus Christ, for the forgiveness of sins and for life everlasting." *The forgiveness of sins and life everlasting!* How can these words roll off my lips without my falling to the ground in adoration and thanksgiving? Who am I that I can receive such a gift and be instrumental in giving it to others? Yet such is the mercy and loving-kindness of God, who not only gives the gift, but at such a price—the suffering and death of our Lord Jesus Christ. I'm standing on holy ground, yet I'm too seldom aware of it. But when my awareness finally opens even a little, I realize that "it's all true," and I am encouraged to renew and deepen my faith and love for Christ, and my commitment to serve Him until He comes to bring me home.

So I must persevere, and you must, too. Even when we seem to be walking in darkness, we are guided by a mysterious hand that we may not be able to perceive. But the Lord has arranged everything, worked out all the details, and He's putting together the pieces of our broken lives in ways that can only cause us to marvel when we finally see all He has done for us in his everlasting love. If we can bear our crosses for Him out of love, He will find ways to show us that He is with us always, and He will gently encourage us: "If only you knew the gift of God..." How generous and self-sacrificing, how uncompromising in faith and morality would we be if we could see what the citizens of Heaven see!

The Lord will not take away our freedom to believe or to doubt, to love or to withhold love, to persevere or give up, to hope or despair—but his grace will not be lacking, and when we need Him He will be there. This is the message that the Spirit of Truth brought at Pentecost: the glory, the holiness, the presence, the love of the Lord is all around us and within us. Believe now, see later. But at all times, give thanks to Him for his inexpressible gift!

❧ Chapter Fourteen:
Small and Great Doxologies ❧

Most of our liturgical prayers end with a doxology of some sort, a brief but bright glorification of God. As this book comes to a close, I'd like it to go out in a blaze of glory, with doxologies everywhere, brightly popping up like poppies in a California meadow. The doxologies of daily life come in all shapes and sizes, and come at times from unexpected sources. Let us, then, reap a great harvest of glory—and praise and exalt the Lord above all forever!

Stones Cry Out

Creation tends to worship God in its own way and finds it quite easy, because its sheer existence is a song of praise to the Lord. Aside from the birds, and similar creatures that might rightly be said literally to *sing* unto the Lord, creation needs a mouthpiece. Even the singing creatures need the assistance of rational souls to send the song explicitly to the Creator. That would be us. For all their grandeur, the mountains, the oceans, the stars, the flowers and trees, still need a human voice to direct their homage heavenward. That's one reason God created us. We are the cantors of creation; we direct the cosmic worship: "Praise Him, sun and moon, praise Him, all you shining stars... you mountains and all you hills, you fruit trees and all you cedars... Praise the name of the Lord, for He alone is exalted..." (Psalm 148:3,9,13). The three young men in the Babylonian furnace knew their job well: "Every shower and dew, bless the Lord... all you winds, bless the Lord... ice and snow, bless the Lord... lightnings and clouds, bless the Lord... everything growing from the earth, bless the Lord; praise and exalt Him above all forever" (see Daniel 3:52-90).

I wonder, though, if we know our task as well. All creation seems to be impatiently waiting for us to give it voice, to send its joy to God in canticles of thanksgiving and praise. The Lord hinted at this in a brief exchange during his triumphal entry into Jerusalem. The disciples of Christ were singing and dancing like David before the Ark. When the envious and indignant Pharisees could stomach it no more, they said to Jesus: "Teacher, rebuke your disciples!" Jesus' response, so simple and genuine, reverberates like holy thunder down through the ages: "I tell you, if these were silent, the very stones would cry out" (Luke 19:39-40). Perhaps there are such pregnant moments in human history, that if we fail in our vocation as the mouthpiece of the cosmos, creation itself will be empowered to utter explicit hosannas to the King. But woe to us if the stones must cry out because we have kept silent!

We have to realize that we do not live only for ourselves, and that we are a part of something much greater than ourselves. We are made of the same stuff as the stars and the mountains, yet we have been ennobled with immortal souls; we are created in the image of God. So we are the priests of creation; we stand at the forefront of the cosmos, offering worship and thanksgiving to God in the name of all that is and was and will be. This is one reason that we gather together in church, why we pray and meditate, why we have been given bodily and spiritual senses to perceive the presence of God in all He has made. And Christ's incredible gift to us is that He takes a bit of his creation that we offer Him (bread and wine), transforms and gives it back to us as Himself, as his body and blood. We give Him creation's praise, and He deifies creation and makes it our spiritual food, so that we creatures can experience an ineffable and undreamed-of union with the Creator, in a leap of faith that crosses the cosmos and secures us in the Heart of the Most Holy Trinity, source of all creative power, wisdom, and love.

So don't wait for the stones to cry out. Bless the Lord, praise and exalt Him above all forever! All creation will thank you for it.

Glory Be!

Those who believe in God tend to worship Him. To know Him is to adore Him. Indeed, the word of the Lord commands it. I usually like to know what I'm doing and why I'm doing it, so the other day I asked myself just what it is I'm doing when I worship God.

First of all, we should look at the terms. I was always taught by the good nuns at school that God alone is to be adored. But how times have changed our usage! Nowadays, not only is God adorable, but so are babies and puppies and anything that is really, really cute. So I don't use that word much any more. "Worship" is better, but many people use even that term for praise of (or lust for) things that are not God. We need to recover our sacred terms and keep them in the realm of the sacred. "Awesome" used to be a magnificent word, too, but nowadays it's as cheap as "cool."

Anyway, it seems to me that what we do when we worship God is, fundamentally, to acknowledge that God is the Creator and we the created, He the Infinite and we the finite, etc. We do this in many ways, with words and rituals and obedience to the divine will. To bow down, kneel, or prostrate before God expresses our acceptance of the truth of this essential relationship. This acknowledgement of who God is and who we are ought to be made (or rather, celebrated) in awe and gratitude, in faith, hope, and love.

To worship God is to glorify Him. Not that we can add anything to his eternal, uncreated, all-holy, magnificent splendor. But when we use, for example, our liturgical doxologies (like "Glory be to the Father and to the Son and to the Holy Spirit...") we are situating ourselves in the divine milieu of truth and love and goodness, we are preparing for our ultimate fulfillment in his heavenly kingdom. We connect with the Source of eternal life and joy as we make our way toward Him, day by day.

Job understood, after a dramatic encounter with God, what it means to worship. Oh, before that he did perform the prescribed sacrifices, but it wasn't until a severe crisis brought him to ask the hardest questions of his life that he became truly aware of God the Creator and Job the creature—and he worshiped Him.

After Job shook his little fist at God in his frustration and pain and confusion, God gave an answer that put things in perspective (He often gives me this kind of answer when I question his ways, too): "Where were you when I laid the foundation of the earth?...Who determined its measurements—surely you know!... Have you commanded the morning and caused the dawn to know its place?" God goes on for a long time with similar answers (Job 38-41). Finally Job gets it, realizes who God is and who he is, realizes the foolishness of his small-minded complaints, repents and worships the Lord—who then rewarded him beyond his wildest dreams.

There's much that can be said about worship, but it starts here: God is God and we are not. Accepting that and living accordingly is the beginning of all wisdom. We ought to be grateful that this mighty Creator God loves us so much that He invites us into his presence, and wants to share with us all his infinite goodness.

Well, let the language change as it will. Come, let us worship Him. Glory be to You, our God, glory be to You!

The Call of the Gospel: Joy

I've written quite a bit in the first few chapters of this book about the demands of the Gospel, its disciplines and uncompromising exhortations. You may now wish to hear more about the joy that the Gospel communicates and promises. For joy is very much a part of the call of the Gospel. Words for joy and rejoicing occur nearly 500 times in the Bible, so who says it's all struggle and penance and hardship?

The good news of our salvation begins with an invitation to rejoice. That is how the Archangel Gabriel greeted Mary with the news of the Incarnation. At the birth of Jesus, another angel said to the shepherds: "Be not afraid; for behold, I bring you good news of a great joy which will come to all the people" (Luke 2:10).

Notice that the angel begins his announcement of joy by dispelling fear. This happens many times in the Scriptures. Fear is an impediment to joy. Often God tries to give his people some glad tidings, but his very messenger terrifies them with even a mere reflection of divine glory. But if we were a little more attuned to his presence and willingness to bless us, we would more likely respond with joy than with fear—though we'll never be able to stand before Him without a deep awe and wonder at his divine splendor, and we should rejoice in that, too!

Joy is something that is promised, something that awaits us in the Kingdom of Heaven, but it is also something that Christians ought to experience now. That joy comes to us from the Holy Spirit. Joy is a fruit of the Spirit (Galatians 5:22), and when Jesus rejoiced it was in the Holy Spirit (Luke 10:21). At that time He rejoiced in the Father's love and wisdom for opening the minds and hearts of the "little ones" to the truth of the Gospel.

But the joy to which the Gospel calls us is not mere revelry or superficial fun. Jesus would not have become man to give us something cheap or ephemeral. He wants to give us the very joy of God. It is also true that the Cross is never far from the Christian, so we have to learn how to find a deep and abiding joy even when under the shadow of the Cross. In a sense, the Cross reveals the most profound joy as it teaches us how to send our roots deeper into the soil of faith and hope, to find the nourishing underground stream of life-giving grace, which strengthens and revitalizes us, lightening our hearts and turning them Heavenward. Then we produce the spiritual fruit of joy—a joy that can weather the storms and still keep smiling, a joy that perseveres patiently and prayerfully while the fullness of divine joy is being prepared for us in the Father's house.

Why did Jesus reveal his Father to us, and all the truths and mysteries and counsels of the Gospel? Of course, it was for our salvation, but is there any other reason? "These things I have spoken to you, that my joy may be in you, and that your joy may be full" (John 15:11). The most profound joy we can experience in this life is Jesus' joy in us—and He gave that as the very reason for the things He has revealed through the Scriptures. *His* joy in us! That is what makes our joy full. People who seek happiness elsewhere, especially in forbidden pursuits, will only find a counterfeit, a temporary and ultimately ineffective palliative for the pain and loneliness of this life. But the Lord offers so much more.

So pray for joy. We pray for so many needs, for ourselves and others, but perhaps we need a capacity for joy before we can appreciate God's other gifts. No one can avoid passing through the "valley of tears" while still on this side of Paradise, but the Holy Spirit is waiting to give birth to joy in you and to carry you to that place, that time, when "no one will take your joy from you" (John 16:22). So do not fear, for the Gospel is glad tidings of joy to come, and of joy even in the present moment. We may not always feel "happy," but there can be a place in our hearts that is always rejoicing.

A Symphony of Joy

One bright spring day I found myself sitting on a little cliff overlooking the Pacific Ocean. It was a shining, clear morning, and the sky and sea were all dressed in blue. I put on a bit of music to enhance the experience, and it seemed to blend in with all the other players in this marvelous symphonic burst of glory. I realized partway through that God Himself was the conductor, and He was having a grand time bringing the music out of all He had made.

As the cymbals crashed, the waves did too, as if on cue, against the rugged rocks off shore, sending up glorious sprays of white. As the melodies wove their way through the music, the Lord would point here to a soaring sea bird, there to a dancing butterfly, there again to waving sea oats, then out to the vast expanse of the foaming, sparkling deep. All was on key, all kept perfect time. I leaned back and looked into the sky and noticed with satisfaction that He even placed a crescent moon at twelve o'clock high. As I later began to listen solely to the music of nature—the distinctive gull-cries, the soothing susurrations of the breeze in the tall grasses, and the rhythmic washing of waves on soft sand, finally I got it: all creation is meant to sing!

There's something important that I think many of us miss, caught up as we often are in daily responsibilities and anxieties. God has created the world and filled it with irrepressible life; He has built into it a profound undercurrent of joy—*his* joy—"a torrent of beautiful vigor flowing from a deep source and irrigating all that moves or feels" (R.H. Benson). And He expects us to discover it. There are moments when that reality opens up to us, when it all fits together, when we become part of the cosmic dance, the joy of being, and we delight in the wonderful works of God's hands. His joy becomes ours.

It is true that we still have to work and struggle with the issues of war and peace, wealth and poverty, truth and falsehood, sin and virtue. But we have to step back sometimes and ask ourselves: *why* are we doing this? Is it simply because we feel compelled to right all the wrongs in the world? Or is it rather because we have to remove the scales from human eyes, drain out the poisons of body and soul, so that God's symphony of joy can be heard—and *felt* in the depths of the soul—and we can all start being what He has created us to be?

Once we have learned to preserve a sense of joy (which flows in and out of gratitude, hope, and inner stillness), then we will also learn how to labor and even suffer fruitfully for the Kingdom of God. But if we can't hear the music of sea and sky, of flowered hillsides and rugged cliffs, of starry nights and summer rains—and recognize Who it is that made them all, in and for joy—then we will at best be those "sour-faced saints" from whom St. Teresa prayed for deliverance, and at worst either burnt-out activists or depressed disciples who have lost all courage to live.

The music doesn't cease even for a moment. It's like the angelic worship we read about in Revelation. Take some time to listen, to connect with the underground River of Life and Joy that flows through all creation—and through your own inner depths as well, for the great Conductor wants to create a symphony of joy in your soul as well as in the external creation. Discover it, immerse yourself in it, and experience a fresh renewal of your relationship with the Lord who loves you. Realize that all creation is singing his glory—and that you've got the music in you.

Walking and Leaping and Praising God

One of my favorite stories in the Acts of the Apostles is that of the healing of the lame man at the temple gate. It is the first miracle recounted in Acts after the coming of the Holy Spirit at Pentecost. The man was a crippled beggar who had lost all hope for healing, so when St. Peter and St. John stopped before him, he looked only for a handout. Peter's response is dramatic: "Gold and silver I have not, but what I have I give you: In the name of Jesus Christ of Nazareth, walk!" Immediately the strength returned to his feet and ankles, and he was able to walk.

The man's response is so genuinely childlike and uninhibited. He didn't merely lift pious eyes to heaven, giving silent thanks. Rather, he "entered the temple with them, walking and leaping and praising God" (Acts 3:8). It must have been quite a sight! Not only could he walk, but he could *leap*, and he exercised his newfound vitality to the full, joining it to unrestrained praise of God. (The man was over 40 years old, so he proves to all of us over-40-ers that it's still possible to leap in jubilant exultation in the Lord, the Giver of all good things.) I'm sure he became a believer in Christ at that very moment, and he was so grateful to the two apostles for being ministers of God's healing power to him that "he *clung* to Peter and John" in the temple area.

I wonder if sometimes we lose the spark of joyful praise as we get older, more weary of life's burdens, our spiritual eyes growing dim and less able to see the wonderful works of God in and around us. Perhaps we should take a look at young children, who bubble over with glee at trifles, who do not focus on the "hard facts of life" or use them as a counterbalance to upsurging joy. Not that we should try to avoid the demands and hardships of life by escaping into some infantile la-la land. But I think that for many of us the balance needs to be adjusted: less anxiety, fear, doubt and discouragement, and more walking, leaping, and praising God.

When the people saw that man who was miraculously healed, "they were filled with wonder and amazement." I think people today would also be filled with wonder and amazement if we suddenly manifested our joyful gratitude to God for all He has done for us, if we started showing a brighter face and a more cheerful acceptance of whatever life brings. The Gospel is Good News, after all, and it promises us an eternity of jumping for joy in our Savior. If that sounds a little silly, so be it. Sometimes we take ourselves too seriously and need to lighten up—in the Lord, that is.

There's plenty of time for dealing with serious issues (and we must), and there's also time for deep and silent prayer and meditation. But at least once in a while take a leap of faith and leap for joy in the God who loves you and rejoices over your childlike trust in Him. "The Lord your God...will rejoice over you with gladness; He will renew you in his love; He will exult over you with loud singing as on a day of festival" (Zephaniah 3:17-18).

Beauty is of God

I'm not sure why I'm writing about beauty, since I know very little about it (let alone theological aesthetics), but I just read a book on the subject, so I thought I'd offer a few inchoate mumblings, perhaps just to help me get my own bearings.

My conclusion, which should be obvious to all believers (and which should help lead unbelievers to faith), is that beauty is of God, that beauty in any form is somehow a reflection of God (however pale or inadequate), an expression of his will and wisdom and delight in creating the universe, and even in creating you and me.

The book I read, which I recommend, is *The Evidential Power of Beauty*, by Thomas Dubay, S.M. The subtitle, *Science and Theology Meet*, may be slightly misleading, though he does spill considerable ink in showing how the discoveries of science ought to lead any normal person to discover God behind the marvels of the universe. He relies quite a bit on the works of Hans Urs von Balthasar for the theology of beauty—anyone who can make von Balthasar intelligible to the masses has done a great service—and offers a brief but thought-provoking passage on the cover: "Every experience of beauty points to infinity."

To some extent, the recognition and appreciation of beauty presupposes a minimum of cultural formation and education. On the other hand, being the creations of God that we are, if we have not experienced a definite *de*-formation in all the vulgarities of modern life (as so many lamentably have), we will innately and spontaneously be drawn to the beautiful and at least begin to appreciate its worth. I must confess that I am mostly illiterate in the knowledge of great art and classical music (though I know what I like when I see or hear it), but I recently had an experience that dovetailed rather nicely with what I had been learning in Fr. Dubay's book.

We are fortunate to have as a friend an internationally-acclaimed harpist, Anna Maria Mendieta. We don't get to see her very often because of the demands of her profession, but during her last visit she performed a marvelous little impromptu concert of Christmas and classical music. It became clear to us why the harp has been chosen as the symbol of the music of Heaven. Beauty engages the soul and the spirit in ways that are beyond conscious thought or explanation. An encounter with beauty is a kind of transport to a higher level of life and experience. As Anna Maria played, it was not for me a particularly *emotional* moment, but tears began spontaneously to come to my eyes, simply because it was *so beautiful*. For a few moments I seemed not to be in the monastery refectory any more, but rather at the gates of Heaven. Such an experience can only be of God.

Now there are times when tears have come while listening to other types of music, but that is usually because of the emotional impact of the lyrics, which may or may not be particularly beautiful, but which speak to my emotional state at the time. I finally came to the conclusion that even though some kinds of music are enjoyable, energizing, cleverly crafted, or simply "cool," they are not all *beautiful*. True beauty, something more than a superficially attractive quality, will reach the depths of the soul, and will speak to you there of God, who is in Himself infinitely more than the sum total of all created beauty. (I love that little saying: "I said to the almond tree, 'Speak to me of God,' and it immediately burst into flower." All creation knows Him; why are we lagging so far behind?)

I've just given this one example of music here, but the possibilities of experiencing beauty are practically endless. The world is essentially a beautiful world, intricately and lovingly designed by God for our delight and as a means of discovering his infinitely wonderful Mind and Heart. The ugliness and horrors of this world are largely the product of man, in his ignorance or rejection of God's plan for our happiness and salvation. But God will still intervene to refresh us with beauty, calling us to wake up, to look at the stars, to hear the angels sing. None of this is beyond our reach. If I can experience it, so can you. I would not pass as a "cultured" man, by the standards of cultured people (I was even called a "hillbilly" a few years ago when attempting to navigate my way through standard etiquette during a brief foray into a non-monastic environment). So you don't need to have college degrees in art or music to be able to let the beautiful touch you—it may even help if you don't, because then you won't be tempted to analyze or criticize, but only be enraptured.

Beauty is one of God's precious gifts to us, as is our ability to perceive and appreciate it and allow it to lead us back to the Giver. Beauty is not merely in the eye of the beholder. It is objectively in what God has made, in the radiance and perfection of form, sound, light, color, etc. I have not mentioned it here, but the author rightly concludes his book with a section on the beauty of sanctity, the transformation of the human spirit, of the whole person, into the likeness of Christ, in whom beauty is also love, truth, and goodness. To delight in the beauty of creation is to begin to move toward the glory of God, the ultimate Beauty that eye has not yet seen, nor ear heard, but which God has prepared for those who love Him.

Seaside Musings

On one of our little "bright week" outings (that is, during Easter week) I escaped for the better part of one day to the coast, to sit at the seaside and drink in the wonders of God's creation, in a silent solitude that was nevertheless rich with angels. I think that the ocean is one of God's most marvelous achievements on our unique planet.

A flat rock just slightly above the incoming tide was my vantage point. The sky was clear, eternal, and the water green-blue—rough waves looming large, just as I like them—and the air was slightly cool and very fresh, full of salt and joy. The sound of the surf, rhythmic in its advancing and receding, filled not only my ears but my very flesh and bones, till I resonated like a crystal wineglass to a tone it recognizes as its own.

I watched the waves with delight, as they rolled and rollicked, slipped and somersaulted over themselves in their reckless haste to reach the shore, finally stretching foamy fingers across the dark sand—sometimes depositing cargoes of strange flora that would soon dry in the midday sun and become labyrinthine playgrounds for myriad sand-flies.

Reflecting on the waves, at once ferocious and soothing, I thought that in this they were an image of our Ferocious and Soothing God—ferocious in his uncontainable ardor and passionate pursuit of our perfection (and oh, what this often costs us!), but soothing in his gentle and healing compassion that washes clean the sullied shoreline of our souls.

As the magnificent sun of springtime advanced across the sky, he liberally scattered sparkles across the incoming waves, and they rode the curls to shore with joyful abandon (and I thought I heard them crying out, mysteriously: "He is risen!"). The living, shimmering lights immediately hastened to attach themselves anew to fresh formations of the ceaseless surges of the deep. "Wave after wave, crest after crest," wrote the psalmist. So the restless sea rises and falls with its irrepressible energy of worship, giving its blue and white glory to God, inviting all observers to join the chorus of praise.

"Let there be life!" cried the Lord God as He created the ocean, and soon it was pullulating with every kind of fantastic form of life. Just in my little corner of the sea there are barnacles, mussels, and sand-dollars, crabs, starfish, and seals, several varieties of wailing sea-birds, and a curious array of shiny, rubbery ocean plants that could have been conceived only by the Divine Imagination.

Time passed unnoticed, as I gazed out upon what appeared to be a living, blue eternity, stretching to untold reaches and endless ages—yet held in that same divine hand that set the stars in their places and is greater still than the majesty of his works.
Soon my little rock was becoming gradually engulfed by the advancing embrace of the inexorable sea. I thought that perhaps it was *my* turn to recede, lest the creamy brine begin to give me love-taps on the face in its playful mischief. So I reluctantly made my way back to artificial things like automobiles which had to carry me home—when I would have much preferred to be transported on the wings of the wind. I was refreshed but not satiated; it's always good

to leave the table just a little hungry, for then it is easier to hear the call to return, and to drink a bit more profoundly the next time.

For deeper than the ocean is the treasury of God's grace and glory, which we descry as we approach the shores of his heavenly sanctuary.

Holy, Holy, Holy

"Lo, in heaven an open door!" (Rev. 4:1). Would that we could all see through this door, if only for a while. After St. John received the messages for the churches, he was granted a vision of the glory of God and the heavenly worship. To me, this section (chs. 4-5) and the closing two chapters are really the essence of the book, for they are, as the first words of this chapter indicate, an open door to Heaven. Chapters 2-3 let us know the spiritual and moral requirements for walking through that door, and chapters 6-20 indicate what we'll have to endure before the end, but here let us gaze Heavenward for a moment as the door opens to us.

If you're hoping for a precise description of Heaven, you'll not find it here, for everything is written in symbolic language. Does God the Father *really* look like jasper and carnelian (these are only green and red chalcedony—not even precious stones!), and is there an emerald rainbow around his throne? The point is, everything is shining and sparkling and colorful and beautiful— when the door of Heaven opens for *you*, you can describe it in your own way!

There are 24 elders around the throne of God, symbolizing the 12 tribes of Israel plus the 12 apostles. Then there are those four "living ones" who seem to be seraphs, since they have six wings. But they are "full of eyes" and have faces like animals or birds. This is similar to what Ezekiel saw in his vision. The many eyes symbolize knowledge and vigilance. But the most important thing is not what they look like, but what they do: "Day and night, they never cease to sing: 'Holy, holy, holy, is the Lord God Almighty, who was and is and is to come!'" When they do this, all the "living ones" and angels and saints and elders fall down and worship God.

The awesome holiness of God is a major theme in this Book, but the awareness and respect for it is often missing in our daily lives, our prayer, and even our worship. Sure, people say "holy, holy, holy" during the Mass, but the way it is celebrated in the post-Vatican II liturgical wasteland often falls far short of the glory that must be given to God, and it does not create the atmosphere of deep reverence and awe in which one would naturally be inclined to fall prostrate in adoration. The Byzantine Divine Liturgy, while it still can be celebrated poorly, at least is *designed* to foster reverence and a sense of the transcendent, holy God. This awareness needs to be recovered in all Christian worship.

"Holiness" is difficult to describe well, and I won't attempt it here, except for one aspect that is repeated in these chapters of Revelation: worthiness. God's holiness means He is worthy of adoration and everlasting praise. "Worthy are You, our Lord and God, to receive glory and honor and power..." (4:11). Then the Lamb enters the vision, and He alone is found worthy to open the scroll of the mystery of God and of salvation history. (Don't take this vision literally, either: He has seven horns and seven eyes; these symbolize fullness—the perfect number 7—of power and knowledge.) "Worthy are You, to take the scroll and open its seals..." And finally, "myriads and myriads and thousands and thousands" of angels sang out: "Worthy is the Lamb who was slain, to receive power and wealth and wisdom and might and honor and glory and blessing!" (5:9-12). We express our awareness of God's holiness by exalting his worthiness to receive our worship.

Finally, in the climax of this vision through the open door of Heaven, the whole cosmos enters into ecstatic worship of God. "And I heard every creature in heaven and on earth and under the earth and in the sea, and all therein, saying: 'To Him who sits upon the throne and to the Lamb be blessing and honor and glory and might forever and ever!' And the four living ones said, 'Amen!' and the elders fell down and worshiped" (5:13-14). Not your average Sunday at church, but it *should* be! The point is, *everything* is inexorably moving toward this cosmic climax; this is the goal of all visible and invisible creation. How devastating it would be if we were to realize—all too late—that through our sins we had cut ourselves off from this endless, joyous, triumphal celebration! We'll see later in the book that indeed all those who did not give glory to God on earth, who did not exalt the worthiness of the Lamb, will be plunged into the everlasting sulfurous torment of the dragon and his foul minions—wholly and forever excluded from the boundless rejoicing on the other side of Heaven's door.

So give glory to God, fall down before the throne with incense and prayer, and join the myriads of heavenly powers in their unceasing cry: Holy, holy, holy! Do not settle for less, and do not be seduced into the idolatry of whatever does not give glory to God and to the Lamb. This passing life is moving toward its climax. Make sure you are found worthy to walk through the door to Heaven!

The Solitude of the Sea

I return now to the sea, a favored place of reflection. I like to go to the ocean by myself, to enter into an enriching solitude. For me, the ocean isn't a place to party but to pray, and to enter into a deep peace and spiritual refreshment.

As soon I found a strategic position on an outcropping of rock, I settled in to enjoy the view, as incoming waves slapped against the side of the rock, sending up playful white geysers that splattered all around me. I hope you aren't one of those unfortunate people who have never been to an ocean (I'm partial to the Pacific, but the others have their glories, too). It's not something you can readily imagine, and even the best of videos cannot adequately communicate its awe-inspiring grandeur, perpetual motion, and soothing song. For me it is like finding the fountain of youth, flushing my radiator, charging my batteries, defragmenting my disk, cleaning my closet, airing out my attic— whatever image works, it's a rejuvenating immersion!

As I gazed out to the seeming infinity of its sparkling sapphire expanse, I also looked up into the boundless blue canopy of the sky and detected a slim decrescent moon—struggling to be noticed within the brighter shine of its elder brother—inching toward the slightly hazy horizon. I read in the psalms early that morning: "this is a holiday of the Lord's own choosing," so I knew it would be a blessed day.

To be in solitude at the sea is not, however, to be alone. Aside from the divine omnipresence, which seems almost tangible in this amphitheater of joy, I have a few other friends, like starfish and pelicans. We briefly acknowledge each other's presence and then return to our respective reveries. I was not entirely without the company of my own species as well. From the sand a short drop below my rocky outpost arose the squeals of a few little girls who derived endless delight from fleeing each round of the advancing tide. After a while, however, they compelled me to conclude that the hour had indeed arrived for me to seek a more silent stretch of shore.

I turned my gaze from the western infinity to the southern coastline to observe the white-crested waves gliding effortlessly but with great speed, as if they had some urgent business waiting on the shore. Row after row, they spent themselves in tumbling crashes on the sand. They've been doing this day and night for millions of years, but it's always like seeing it for the first time, so enthralling is their majesty and power.

To speak of majesty and power is to refer, of course, to their Maker. But this time I thought more of mercy than majesty. We sometimes say in our penitential liturgies that our sins are more than the sands of the seashore. Yet behold, wave after wave of the Ocean of Mercy washes them clean! For every sin a new wave hurries to the shore, ready to scour the oft-trodden sand till it shines. It's his nature, after all, to forgive. He delights to forgive; He *must* forgive. Do not disappoint his desire by your indifference toward repentance. Give the Lord the joy of forgiving your sins! Someday we will see clearly this torrent of everlasting love, and it will be our delight to plunge in it forever!

I prayed a modified "Jesus Prayer" by using the first and last lines of one of our Pentecost hymns: "Blessed are You, O Christ our God... O Lover of Man, glory to you!" It was so apropos to the moment, as were a few little verses from a hymn to the God-bearer Mary that I interspersed with the rest, like, "you are higher than the heavens, more radiant than the sun..." There were the heavens, there was the sun!

As a rather anti-climactic moment, when I was clambering down the rock, someone asked me (and this wasn't the first time this happened): "See any whales?" So, that's what my ecstatic contemplation looked like to the casual observer. So be it. I didn't see any whales, but I saw the glory of God!

I seem not to be able to get enough. Each time I leave the shore, I feel like I haven't stayed long enough, haven't drunk in the whole ocean. I dream of someday having a little hermitage on the coast, though I don't yet know if that is God's will. Perhaps He wants me only to get a few glimpses of glory, lest I become surfeited and lose my thirst. Would I regard the ocean as the frustrated rural woman regarded the great mountain under whose shadow she lived, in the song, *Penny to My Name*: "It's just a dumb ol' mountain, I see it every day"? I've seen Mt. Shasta, one of California's mighty boasts, but if I lived right there, would its majesty eventually fade? I can't imagine ever calling the Pacific a "dumb ol' ocean," but who knows? I leave it up to God, who has prepared infinitely greater gifts, and meanwhile I embrace my precious moments of glorious solitude by the sea.

Bless the Lord!

"Bless the Lord, O my soul!" cries the psalmist numerous times in his songs of praise. But what does it mean to "bless" the Lord? Scripture tells us that "it is beyond dispute that the inferior is blessed by the superior" (Hebrews 7:7). Wait a minute! How then can we, the infinitely inferior, bless the Lord, the Supremely Superior?

It should be obvious that the term "bless" is used equivocally. It cannot mean the same thing when we say the Lord blesses us as it does when we say we bless the Lord. The Lord blesses us by bestowing his grace and bounty upon us, granting us what we could in no way provide for ourselves, since He is the divine Benefactor, as our liturgy often calls Him. Only God can bless as Superior to inferiors (when a priest blesses, it is not with his own blessing, but with the blessing of God).

There are two main things that we do when we bless the Lord. The first is synonymous with giving thanks and praise. Some translations actually say, "Give thanks to the Lord," where others say, "Bless the Lord." So, blessing the Lord is praising Him and giving thanks to Him—for blessing us! The other thing we do when we bless the Lord is to proclaim Him blessed. Here I think I'll have to make a distinction between "blessed" and "blessed." For clarity's sake, this distinction is between "blessed" and "blest"—though I don't really like that form of the word—the former in two syllables and the latter in one. The former is a state of being, the latter a consequence of something having been done or given to someone.

When we call God blessed, we are saying something about who God is. He is blessed, which is a synonym for "holy." Blessed is God, the Father of our Lord Jesus Christ! The Byzantine Divine Liturgy always opens with the glorious and magnificent "Blessed is the Kingdom of the Father and of the Son and of the Holy Spirit, both now and forever and unto ages of ages!" When we speak of God as the recipient of our blessings (praises and thanksgivings), then He is blest. May the Lord be forever blest! Sometimes both meanings can apply simultaneously. When Our Lady said, "All generations shall call me blessed," it means both that all generations acknowledge her holiness and that all generations acknowledge that she has been uniquely blest by God.

I have another reason for saying all this, however, besides explaining the difference between "blessed" and "blest," and besides saying that it is fitting and right to bless the Lord. The reason is this: it is *imperative* that we bless the Lord, because too few people do it, and He deserves better that that from us!

I mentioned in the previous section that when I was at the ocean I would pray by repeating a couple lines from one of our liturgical hymns: "Blessed are You, O Christ our God... O Lover of Mankind, glory to You!" I have continued to do this, and it is now a significant part of my daily prayer. I'm beginning to see that blessing the Lord is a *vocation*, and not merely an occasional prayer formula for times when one is feeling happy.

Let's face it, for most people, the two main forms of prayer are Asking and Complaining. We come to God with a list of petitions, and if we don't get what we want, we complain and grumble, or else we merely manifest our ongoing discontent with The Way Things Are. Many remain perpetually in that asking and complaining cycle—with occasional forays into the uncharted areas of repentance or thanksgiving—but the Lord would have us come up higher.

Blessing the Lord covers just about everything, and I find it to be a real "lift" in my prayer life. The Byzantine Liturgy, along with glorifying God, has a very strong emphasis on penitence and asking for mercy. We ask for mercy dozens of times a day in liturgical offices (hundreds of times if you include the Jesus Prayer). But asking for mercy, while indispensable, is still not the whole of prayer. What are we doing, anyway, when we seek mercy? We are imploring the Lord to enter into the sinful and suffering condition of the world, to heal and forgive and save. But blessing God can do the same thing, and it's less depressing than focusing on the world's miseries—or our own! To bless the Lord is to ascend to a higher and more noble level of awareness, to gratefully recognize God's universal providence, to honor his wisdom and his plan for the spiritual growth and salvation of all. It is a resounding "Yes!" to all God is and does. This does not mean that we are oblivious to the evil in the world; we simply acknowledge that God's wisdom, compassion, and timing are better than ours, and we bless Him in trust. To bless the Lord makes us "transparent" to God's grace, an opening for his light to come in to the world, while we simply lose ourselves in Him. I like the image used by St. Teresa

Benedicta of the Cross (Edith Stein): "...like a windowpane, which lets through all the light but itself remains unseen."

We may very well do more good for ourselves and for the world by blessing the Lord than by asking for what we need. "For your Father knows what you need before you ask him... Seek first his kingdom and his righteousness, and all these things shall be yours as well" (Matthew 6:8, 33). That doesn't mean we *shouldn't* ever ask, for Jesus also said, "Ask, and you shall receive," but I think that our asking ought to be balanced by (at least) equal amounts of blessing.

So, bless the Lord, O my soul, and you, soul, who are reading this, bless the Lord! Proclaim his blessedness, his holiness and infinite goodness, and make sure that He is forever blest by your gratitude and praise. Gather all your prayers—petition, penitence, praise, worship, and thanksgiving (and even your complaints, if you must!)—and send them to Him in a package labeled: "Blessed are You, O God!" It'll get there faster than any other.

God, Crickets, and Birds of Dawn

The older I get, the more things I notice—the more important things anyway. I tend to forget or be oblivious to many daily details, much to my chagrin, but I think I'd still prefer to notice the finer things, if the choice came down to that.

Some things can only be noticed at certain times of year. During the summer, and only during a certain few weeks of the summer, our monastic schedule enables me to notice something. It has to do with the coming of dawn. (At all other times of year the dawn comes too late.)

There's a certain moment when the birds wake up to greet the dawn. I don't know how they do it. They don't need alarm clocks, but they never oversleep—must be that healthy lifestyle! Now the crickets, they are the lords of the night. Their rhythmic and relaxing nightsong is quite compatible with silence, and even at their fullest chorus one would not be tempted to call the night anything but still.

If I am the celebrant of the week, I go down to church 20-25 minutes earlier than usual, to perform in silence the preparatory rites for the Divine Liturgy. That would be around 4:50 AM. At this time I know, because of chirping crickets and silent birds, that it is still night. But if I go down just those 20 minutes later, the hills are alive with the polyphonic joy of the dawn-welcomers. (No clever studio-mixing could reproduce this experience of immersion in a singing forest.) The birds know the precise moment of the dawn and are singing their greeting as if on cue. These are very special birds, it seems. I hear their calls only at dawn; other birds bear the burden and heat of the day. There's one dawn-bird with a delicate little voice that sings outside my window for about a half-hour each morning—unceasingly—but is not heard again until the next dawn breaks.

So there's a moment of passage between night and day, and all creation knows it. While most people are snoring (or perhaps grumbling as they smack their snooze button once again), the crickets and the dawn-birds are singing the praises of Him who made us all, who tells the sun the time of its rising and setting, who made the moon to mark the months, who tells the seas they can go thus far and no farther. You may say—if you can't see beyond your textbooks—that all these things are governed by physical or biological laws. Well, I say that laws presuppose a Lawgiver, and that random associations of molecules don't just blindly happen to commence singing precisely at dawn.

We live in a world of wonders, though it seems that many people are too busy to notice, or worse, are *not interested* in noticing the delicate displays of divine artistry, intricate design, and delightful harmonies abounding among the works of God's hands. Life has its inescapable stresses and demands, but they are not the *whole* of life. Life is full of God, and because of Him it is also full of crickets and dawn-birds, morning glories and honeysuckle, sea-foam and mountain peaks, shooting stars and crescent moons, autumn leaves and jackrabbits and blue herons and mighty clouds of joy!

Don't let life pass you by without your noticing all these things, and so much more. As I walk along our paths during springtime and see the wildflowers joyfully popping up on this side and that, I say to my soul: "See, He even strews your path with flowers!" One of our brothers used to say: "Lord, I'm not worthy, but I'll take it!" God doesn't immerse us in blessings because we're worthy, but because He loves us. He wants us to open our eyes to the abundance of his gifts and simply give thanks, simply sing to Him at dawn. We tend to forget why we are here, why God made us in the first place. He made us to sing for joy, to be fountains of praise, to marvel at his glory and to imbibe his living love. Lord knows, we still have to carry the cross, but that's why He provides resurrection. He knows that the seed must fall to the earth and die, but that's why He gave it power to produce flowers and fruit. When we're fully aware that we're wading in wonders, we'll know how to deal with the challenges our lives bring. We will be much less inclined to turn away from our God when we know that walking with Him opens such a panorama of goodness and beauty.

All that the Lord gives us now is a preparation, a little foretaste of the glories of a new and ever-fresh Morning. In comparison with that, our life on this earth is a mere cricket chirp in the night. But if He abides in us and we in Him, we will acquire a kind of connaturality with Heaven, a "sympathetic resonance" with the voice of the Holy Spirit. Our whole being will be turned toward the Light, and we will be attuned to the still far-off sound of the angelic trumpet. The irrepressible gift of grace will well up within us, and joy will become the very air we breathe as we realize the hour has come at last. We will recognize the precise moment of the Dawn of the everlasting Day—and we will *sing*!

↝ Chapter Fifteen:
Consummatum Est ↞

That means "It is finished." Those words may signify the end of this book, but much more importantly, they are Jesus' own dying words. So I end with a poem on dying. You may wonder why, after traveling from darkness to dawn, I end with death. Well, death is both darkness and dawn, an end and a beginning. It may be seen, from the perspective of those who are losing a loved one, to be the night of tears. But for the one who is making this journey, it is arrival at the joy-bringing dawn, a new and eternal adventure in the life that never grows old, never dies. We're all going to pass this way, but if we have heeded the word of the Lord there is nothing to fear. Death is the necessary prelude to resurrection. On that day, the Risen Lord Jesus will grant us a joy that no one can take from us.

Good Day, Good Night

A long day, all too short;
the fading sun
completes its homeward arc
and sinks into the sea.
Night comes,
when no one can work.

Sunrise unremembered;
the events of the day
a jumble of joys and sorrows.
At day's end, the will,
that mighty, stubborn flame,
flickers softly, subdued.

Eyes closing,
at last beginning to see.
Darkness approaching,
cold encroaching,
yet whence the faint chorus
of alleluias?

Hands falling open,
nothing left to hold.
Nothing left to give?
Relinquish, return
the dust you are.
Prepare the Great Exchange.

Your regrets, if-onlys,
sins and shame,
drowned now in the Blood,
constrained now—somehow—
to serve the Mercy.
Take the lowest place,
come up higher.

It is your hour
to commend your spirit—
to the Great Void?
Or to Abba?
The void has no hands,
but Abba does. There!

Give birth, O dying body,
to your immortal child.
Exhale, part the veil
of the eternal Temple,
and enter.
Consummatum est.
Yes. Amen.